A History of the Musical Theatre

From the diverse proto-musicals of the mid-1800s, through the revues of the 1920s, the "true musicals" of the 1940s, the politicization of the 1960s and the "mega-musicals" of the 1980s, every era in American musical theatre reflected a unique set of socio-cultural factors.

Nathan Hurwitz uses these factors to explain the output of each decade in turn, showing how the most popular productions spoke directly to the audiences of the time. He explores the function of musical theatre as commerce, tying each big success to the social and economic realities in which it flourished.

This study spans from the earliest spectacles and minstrel shows to contemporary musicals such as *Avenue Q* and *Spider-Man*. It traces the trends of this most commercial of art forms from the perspective of its audiences, explaining how writers and producers strove to stay in touch with these changing moods. Each chapter deals with a specific decade, introducing the main players, the key productions and the major developments in musical theatre during that period.

Nathan Hurwitz is Assistant Professor of Musical Theatre at Rider University, USA.

A History of the American Musical Theatre

Musical Theatre

No Business Like It

Nathan Hurwitz

Routledge
Taylor & Francis Group

LONDON AND NEW YORK

First published 2014
by Routledge
2 Park Square, Milton Park, Abingdon, Oxon OX14 4RN

and by Routledge
711 Third Avenue, New York, NY 10017

Routledge is an imprint of the Taylor & Francis Group, an informa business

British Library Cataloguing in Publication Data
A catalogue record for this book is available from the British Library

Library of Congress Cataloguing in Publication Data
Hurwitz, Nathaniel, author.
A history of the American musical theatre / by Nathan Hurwitz.
pages cm
1. Musicals–United States–History and criticism. I. Title.
ML1711.H87 2014
782.1'40973–dc23
2013035068

ISBN: 978-0-415-71507-2 (hbk)
ISBN: 978-0-415-71508-9 (pbk)
ISBN: 978-1-315-85022-1 (ebk)

Typeset in Sabon
by Taylor & Francis Books

Contents

List of figures

Acknowledgements

This book, appropriately titled *A History of the American Musical Theatre*, is just one approach, one prism through which to view this history. My greatest debt is to my colleagues and predecessors, the scholars and historians who have written before me. Any history book can only reflect the author's perspective; but the body of histories of the American musical theatre, taken together, yields a rich and fully dimensional understanding of this history. This book is my contribution to that body of study.

I owe my parents a great debt for instilling in me a love of the arts, an insatiable curiosity and a love of books. Most importantly, I need to thank them for encouraging me to spend my life working at something I love. In addition, I have been blessed with some of the great theatre teachers of the twentieth century who have inspired in me not only a passion for the craft of the theatre, but a deep and abiding love of its history. To Stella Adler, Jack Garfien, Lehman Engel, Mel Gordon, Joseph Roach, James Coakley, Atillio "Buck" Favorini, Dennis Kennedy and my other teachers I offer my profound thanks for preparing me to write this book. I offer the same to my teaching colleagues at Northwestern University of Louisiana, Syracuse University and Rider University.

The rigors of academic work enhance the creativity of artistic endeavors and vice versa. For that reason I must also thank the artistic colleagues and collaborators I have engaged with over a thirty-plus year career as a musical director and director.

I can only begin to thank my wife, Dana, for her help keeping me relatively sane during the writing of this book. She balances me, and helps me find new ways of viewing things every day. For this book I must also thank Buddy for his companionship and my three step-children, Jordyn, Max and Alex for ever-broadening my perspective.

Setting the stage

1   A very good place to start
The beginning, up to the eighteenth century

In the beginning

We gather together in darkened places to share the stories of our shared humanity; to spin tales of gods and men, goodness and evil, monsters, murderers, lovers, lunatics and dreamers. We always have; it is a part of human genetic makeup.

Storytelling traces back to the cavemen around the evening fire. As they chanted, grunted, gesticulated and acted out the events of the hunt, they accompanied themselves on drums of taut animal hides and early flutes. There is comfort in gathering together to share a story of a hero (the hunter) and a villain (the prey), with thrills and adventure, fear and with pathos. Plot, characters, imitation, recognition, reversal, thought, music, lighting (spectacle) – many of the elements Aristotle would later identify as the essence of the drama in these early musical enactments, these musical entertainments.

Greek theatre

Formalized Western theatre started with the Greek theatre, which flourished from 525 BC (Aeschylus' birth) to 386 BC (Aristophanes' death). This was the first great age of drama; it was a period of astounding dramatists writing plays that continue to resonate with audiences today. Looking back at ancient Greek theatre, it is not the actors we think of, it's the three great tragic dramatists, Aeschylus, Euripides and Sophocles, and the great comic dramatist Aristophanes. Their plays are still produced and inspire new generations to study and adapt them even 2,500 years later.

The term "musical theatre" would have made no sense to ancient Greeks or Romans. To qualify theatre as musical would have made as much sense as qualifying fire as hot or water as wet. Theatre in ancient Greece was musical in every way that we think of the musical theatre today. Sung music, chanted and intoned passages (recitative) instrumental music, dance and other choreographed movement, spectacle, all were part of the Greek plays.

Greek dramatists used speaking, chanting and singing to evoke varying levels of dramatic and emotional intensity – this range from speaking to singing was one of the tools in the dramatists' palette. Greek choruses spoke, chanted or sang in unison; the power of passages spoken, chanted or sung as one voice cannot be overstated. Characters and the chorus, which would comment on the action or advise the characters, moved between speech, chanting and song. Just as today we transition from speech to song because the emotional stakes are heightened, so the Greeks shifted between speech, chanting and song. None of the music of the Greek plays has survived, nor is there an indication of who wrote the music, although it is supposed that the music was written by the playwrights, who would also frequently stage their own plays. Scholars believe that sung music was accompanied by flute, lyre and lute.

Acting in an outdoor amphitheater seating from 17,000 to 30,000 viewers dictated an acting style of large, clear physical gestures. Each gesture had to speak clearly about character relationships; choruses were choreographed in unison movements. Larger than life masks with megaphone-like insets in them helped give physical and vocal size to the actors, as did tall platform shoes, *cothornous*. The large gestural acting style and the unison movements and choreography of the chorus define the physical life of the Greek dramas.

It was the duty of every free male citizen to attend the theatre; it was a social, civic and religious obligation. Plays were presented in drama competitions that were festivals to Dionysus, God of grapes, winemaking, ritual madness and ecstasy.

Tragedies dealt with the topics of religion and man's place in the world and in society, like Oedipus' excessive pride or Agamemnon's lack of humility. The comedies were satirical, political and extremely scatological. Long passages about genitalia, flatulence, and so on were always popular. The word "comedy" comes from the Greek *komos*, which means revel, and *odé*, which means song. Greek comedies were accompanied by flute and lyre. They included fast comic songs, sometimes based on rapid patter and clever rhymes displaying verbal bravura, ribald double entendre – as were many of the more popular and successful songs of Gilbert and Sullivan, Noël Coward, Cole Porter, Stephen Sondheim and Jason Robert Brown.

In *The Poetics*, Aristotle identifies six elements of tragedy: plot, character, diction (or language), thought, spectacle and song. These same elements define *Show Boat, Pal Joey, Oklahoma!, West Side Story, Hello, Dolly!, A Chorus Line, Sweeney Todd, Miss Saigon* and *Wicked* – the American musical theatre of the twentieth/twenty-first century. So, while ancient Greek theatre differed from ours in some substantial ways – it played outdoors during the day, it grappled with the "big" questions that one associates with religion today, audience and players were male, and attendance of the theatre was a social, civic and religious obligation – it was a distinctly musical theatre, in many ways not different from the American musical theatre of the twentieth century.

Roman theatre

The Roman theatre flourished from 375 BC to AD 197. The Greek theatre had been a great period of dramatic literature; the Roman theatre saw the development of many performance and production traditions. While the Romans lacked the great dramatists of the Greeks, they took all the Greeks had developed and adapted the Greek plays to their needs.

In the hands of the Romans, the later comedies of the Greeks – which were romantic and situational rather than political and satiric – developed into bawdy, rowdy formulaic comedies. We still see the Roman characters, situations and structures in our comedies today. Every successful sitcom is based on these characters and situations, played out again and again. Roman comedy was as musical as Greek comedy, judging from Plautus and Terence, the two Roman comedy playwrights whose works survive. Most of the characters in *A Funny Thing Happened on the Way to the Forum* are stock characters taken directly from Roman comedy, many plot points are taken directly from those plays and the style of the writing is based on Roman comedy informed by the traditions of vaudeville and burlesque.

The stock characters of Roman comedy, recognizable in the contemporary musical include:

- the *adulescens* – the hero who is young, rich, love-struck, not terribly brave (Cornelius or Ambrose in *Hello, Dolly!*);
- the *senex* – the *adulescens'* father who is either too strict or too lenient, loves his son, is madly in love with the same woman as his son but never gets the girl, often he is cheap (the fathers in *The Fantasticks*);
- the *leno* – runs the brothel, only interested in money (the Engineer in *Miss Saigon*);
- the *Miles Gloriosus* – the braggart soldier, very much in love with himself (Gaston in *Beauty and the Beast*);
- the *servus callidus* – the *adulescens'* clever, loyal slave, he usually drives the plot and resolves all at the end (Luther Billis in *South Pacific*);
- the *ancilla* – maid or nurse, a good source of exposition (Mrs. Potts in *Beauty and the Beast*);
- the *matrona* (mother) – a shrew who loves her children but browbeats her husband (Golde in *Fiddler on the Roof*);
- the *meretrix* (prostitute) – an older woman who has been around the block (Reno Sweeney in *Anything Goes*);
- the *virgo* (young maiden) – the love interest of the *adulescens*, beautiful and virtuous with very little personality (Johanna in *Sweeney Todd*).

The musical theatre is filled with examples. These characters exist in musicals, plays, movies, television and literature, and throughout popular culture.

In addition to codifying these types, the Romans added elements of design and architecture. Whereas Greek amphitheaters were built into the sides of hills, Roman theaters were freestanding structures designed and built specifically for their function. The theater was still outdoors, but awnings could be pulled over the audience. A roof covered the stage and there was a stage house behind the stage. The stage façade usually offered three to five doors. In Roman theatre, the chorus becomes less prominent.

Oscar Brockett says, "although the Romans did not value music highly, it was used more extensively in Roman than in Greek plays. Up to two thirds of the lines of Plautus' plays were accompanied by music, and it figured only slightly less prominently in the works of other authors."[1] We know little about the music of the Roman plays, but we do know that each troupe's own flute player probably acted as composer. Evidence suggests the use of conventional motifs used to identify characters. The flute player would have the two pipes bound to his head in order to free his hands, and was thought to have been onstage throughout the performance, able to move about throughout the characters.

Liturgical drama – mystery, morality and miracle plays

In AD 197 the rapidly growing "cult" of Christianity demanded their followers not attend theatre and excommunicated actors; as the church grew, theatre entered the Dark Ages. Ironically, the church itself is inherently theatrical in the way it employs plot (the Bible), character, diction (Latin), thought, spectacle and song in telling its story. The church needed to squelch the "competition" – the secular theatre. Ultimately the church realized the power of theatre as a tool to indoctrinate and began producing their own theatre. These liturgical dramas take three forms: mystery plays, morality plays and miracle plays.

The mystery plays retold stories of the Bible, particularly stories about Jesus and his disciples. Starting in the thirteenth century, the production of mystery plays was taken over by civic organizations, as each professional guild in a town would assume a story from the Bible to dramatize. As towns presented a series of these plays sequentially, these events evolved into the Mystery Cycles. The most well known of these today are the Wakefield and Chester Cycles. Retellings of these stories changed from town to town and from year to year, but prompt books and other primary documents make clear that these productions included both spoken and sung music as well as choreographed dance.

The morality plays were allegorical. The central character encounters the personification of a moral attribute, with names like "Virtue" or "Avarice." The most well-known morality play *Everyman* is still produced today. Morality plays also included sung music, choral passages and instrumental accompaniment.

The third type of liturgical dramas, the miracle plays, celebrated the life of a religious person or saint. The Virgin Mary and Saint Nicholas were popular subjects as they had active cults at the time. Miracle plays included choreography, the use of tableaux and call and response songs as would be appropriate in a church.

The Renaissance and the Elizabethan theatre

The fifteenth- and sixteenth-century renaissance brought a rebirth of intellectual and artistic pursuits throughout Europe. Although the Renaissance's greatest impact was on the visual arts, this period of "rebirth" triggered a renewed interest in the classic Roman and Greek plays. In England, re-workings of Roman plays were more favored during periods when the Catholic Church held sway, and Greek plays when the Protestant Church did. English playwrights began creating secular works to place themselves outside the religious wrangling.

By the late sixteenth century, English theatre companies, licensed and sponsored by the throne, created a need for original works, which led to a flowering of English language playwrights. Christopher Marlowe (1564–93), Ben Jonson (1572–1637) and William Shakespeare (1564–1616) were the three greatest dramatists. The Elizabethan Era, named for Queen Elizabeth I (1558–1603), was the greatest age of playwriting since the Greeks.

The Elizabethan plays spoke to their audiences as they continue to speak to us today; however, they had to speak a lot louder then than they do today. Elizabethan theatre was performed in the sunlight where no spotlight could focus an audience's attention, the actors had to hold attention while vendors were selling oranges, people played games of chance in the pit and pickpockets roamed the crowd. Because Shakespeare and his contemporaries needed to hold the attention of their audiences, they used any theatrical devices that would keep their audience focused on the stage: music, dance, swordplay, brawling, verbal jokes, slapstick and more. Today we differentiate between musical theatre and plays; this was not so in the Elizabethan theatre of Shakespeare, Jonson and Marlowe.

Elizabethan plays included songs, underscoring, incidental music, social, court and theatrical dances in comedies and dramas alike. Many composers throughout the years have set Shakespeare's lyrics as well as his sonnets and other poetry. Galt MacDermot set Hamlet's "what a piece of work is man" speech for the tribal rock musical *Hair*. Stephen Sondheim set Shakespeare's "Fear No More the Heat o' the Sun" from *Cymbeline* for his adaptation of Aristophanes' *The Frogs*.

Shakespeare has also provided great source material for adaptation into contemporary musicals. Obviously, *Romeo and Juliet* is the source for *West Side Story*, but *Hamlet*, *A Comedy of Errors*, *The Taming of the Shrew*, *Twelfth Night*, *The Tempest*, *Two Gentlemen of Verona* and *A Midsummer Night's Dream* have all been adapted to the American musical.[2] Shakespeare's plays lend themselves to adaptation to contemporary musical theatre, because they are inherently musical.

Court masques

The great flourish of dramatists did not last forever. In 1593 the playhouses were closed because of the bubonic plague. They were closed for a year again in 1596 and again in 1603. By 1642 Parliament issued an ordinance suppressing all stage plays, followed by an even stricter law in 1647. The theatres were reopened in 1660 when King Charles II was restored to the throne of England.

Beginning in the early sixteenth through the seventeenth century another form of music theatre came into vogue, the court masque. A masque was a court entertainment of tremendous spectacle, paying homage to one central figure, usually the host, frequently the king. Masques included declamatory speech, a story usually using well-known mythological characters making an allegorical allusion to the real-life central figure of the occasion, tableaux, ballets, music, opulent costumes and scenery and strikingly advanced scenic effects and mechanics. The guests all wore masks and would participate to varying degrees, usually joining in the final dance of exaltation. Great importance was placed on the architect, the scenic painting, the decoration, the ballet as well as the writing and performers.

Ben Jonson wrote as many masques as he did plays, many in collaboration with architect and scenic designer Inigo Jones. Jones was one of the great early innovators of scenic design for musical entertainments. Jones and Jonson argued over which was more powerful, words or visual design. Here is Jonson's description of Jones' design for Jonson's *The Hue and Cry After Cupid*:

> The scene to this masque was a high, steep, red cliff, advancing itself into the clouds, figuring the place from whence ... the honourable family of Radcliffes first took their name ... before which, on the two sides, were erected two pilasters, charged [decorated] with spoils and trophies of Love [Cupid] and his mother, consecrate to marriage, amongst which were old and young persons figured, bound with roses, the wedding garments, rocks [simple devices for spinning] and spindles, hearts transfixed with arrows, others flaming, virgin's girdles, garlands, and worlds of such like ... and overhead two personages, Triumph and Victory, in flying postures, and twice so big as the life, in place of the arch ...[3]

Seventeenth- and eighteenth-century opera

In the seventeenth century, power in Italian cities shifted from the church to merchants and business families; the greatest of these were the Medicis. These families had lavish masques created to celebrate themselves. These became opera, originally staged for private audiences of invited guests, to celebrate events such as weddings. Eventually operas moved to opera houses, built by the rich of Florence, Rome, Venice and so on. The first opera house opened in Venice in 1637, the Teatro San Cassiano, followed by the Teatro Santi Giovanni e Paolo in 1641. Great and powerful men erected these structures in homage to their own wealth and power. Just like Trump Towers today, no one ever wondered who had built the Teatro Santi Giovanni e Paolo; it was the Grimani family. The Grimani family and the Vendramin family were the primary builders and owners of opera houses throughout Italy.

Opera spread throughout Europe and in short order became one of the most popular theatrical forms among the upper classes. By the early eighteenth century, opera had split into opéra-seria (serious opera) and opéra-comique (comic opera or operetta, which sometimes included spoken dialog).

In opera the dramatic text is completely sung or played by musicians. In opera the emphasis is placed on revealing the characters' emotion through the musical tone and line. As the Greek and Elizabethan theatres represented golden ages of dramatic literature, operatic literature flowered in the eighteenth century. Going to the theater or the opera was different in the 1700s than it is today. It was an occasion to be social, to see and be seen, rather than to submit oneself to gaze upon the artistry on the stage. Opera's popularity reflected the growing wealth and free time of the upper middle classes.

> Theatres were noisy, chaotic places and the aim was to see and be seen. The stage and the auditorium were lit from great chandeliers that hung from the ceiling and the audience was as visible as the performers. Audiences would chat, walk around and play games. It wasn't unknown for ladies to have a card table in the box for a game of cards during the performance.
>
> The aisles in the pit were known as "Fops Alley" and young men would cruise up and down flirting with the ladies. In addition there was standing room on stage for audience members which provided another distraction from the focus of the performance.
>
> Audiences stopped talking to listen to the aria which was the great show piece that everyone recognized. Then they would resume their conversation, card game or perusal of other members of the audience.[4]

The Beggar's Opera

English poet, satirist and dramatist **John Gay (1685–1732)**, created the ballad opera in his satirical *The Beggar's Opera*, which began the tradition of English language music theatre, and established a new business model for music theatre, the long run.

Opera was popular in the English-speaking world, but only among the rich. One reason for opera's lack of broader appeal is that it usually dealt with mythological figures or revolved around characters of royal blood – not characters that the lower classes could empathize with. Also, opera was written and performed in Italian, French or German; those who only spoke English couldn't follow the plots.

John Gay was raised and schooled by his uncle, Reverend John Hammer, and apprenticed to a silk merchant. Displeased with his work, he quickly made his way into the literary and social circles of London. Gay supported himself working as a journalist and was known as a wit and a satirist. His circle of friends included writers and wits, including Jonathan Swift, author of the satiric novel, *Gulliver's Travels*. Swift gave Gay the idea for Gay's greatest success, the musical *The Beggar's Opera*, when Swift suggested that the morals of the criminals incarcerated in Newgate Prison were no different from those of the upper classes. *The Beggar's Opera* premiered in 1728, when Gay was forty-three.

The Beggar's Opera is the first ballad opera, which became a tremendously popular musical theatre form. It was a satirical response to the incredible success and popularity of Italian opera. Ballad opera contains satirical and racy spoken dialog in English in between short songs, usually just a stanza or two, also in English. The story usually involves the lower classes – criminals, prostitutes and other disreputable types – satirizing the high moral tone of aristocrats and of Italian opera. They contained references to contemporary political figures and events.

Satirizing Sir Robert Walpole and his government, Gay put the thoughts and spoutings of Walpole's government into the mouths of pimps, thieves and whores, and he put Walpole's sentiments into the mouth of his character Mr. Peachum, a fence of stolen goods. The melodies of the songs were familiar to the audience and included drinking songs, folk songs, popular songs and even children's songs. Gay took suggestive and inappropriate lyrics and set them to the sweetest and most docile music. Gay even satirized a famous fight between the two reigning divas of the Italian opera stage in the fight between Jenny and Polly. *The Beggar's Opera* lampooned Italian opera in the same way that the burlesques of the nineteenth century lampooned a wide range of cultural and political events and trends – and they all made an awful lot of money doing it.

The Beggar's Opera revolves around Peachum, the fence and bounty hunter, who begins the play by justifying his life. The Peachums, learning that their daughter, Polly, has secretly married the highwayman, Macheath, worry about how Polly will be able to support her husband, until they decide to kill him for his money. Macheath, surrounded by the lowest of women in the tavern, discovers too late that Peachum has hired two of the "ladies" and Macheath is taken off to Newgate Prison. The jailor's daughter Lucy Lockit and Polly both lay claim to Macheath, who tells Lucy that Polly is crazy and Lucy helps him to escape. Lockit learns of Macheath's promise to wed his daughter and fears that if he is recaptured and hanged, Peachum may have claim on his (Lockit's) money. Lockit and Peachum find Macheath and decide to split his fortune. Polly tries to reach an agreement with Lucy, but Lucy tries to poison Polly. Macheath recaptured, the two ladies plead for his life. But Macheath discovers four more pregnant women, each claiming that he is the father. Macheath declares that he is ready to be hanged. The narrator interrupts, claiming that although the moral ending would be for Macheath to be hanged, theatrical decorum demands a happy ending, and Macheath is reprieved. All are invited to a dance of celebration to celebrate his wedding to Polly.

Ballad operas:

- are highly satiric, with a particular target on the government in power
- satirize the conventions of grand opera
- use familiar music with new English language lyrics written to fit pre-existing music
- use spoken English dialogue between songs
- feature the lowest class of character and equates them with the highest.

Gay originally approached Colley Cibber, manager of the Drury Lane Theatre, about mounting the show, but Cibber turned him down. John Rich, who managed the Lincoln's Inn Fields, took a chance on T*he Beggar's Opera*. Despite, or perhaps because of, its original nature, the show was a smashing success. *The Craftsman*, a London weekly paper, said:

> This Week a Dramatick Entertainment has been exhibited at the Theatre in Lincoln's-Inn-Fields, entitled The Beggar's Opera, which has met with a general Applause, insomuch that the Waggs say it has made Rich very Gay, and probably will make Gay very Rich.[5]

The Beggar's Opera made so much money that it enabled Rich to build the Royal Opera House in Covent Garden in London. The original production of *The Beggar's Opera* ran for sixty-two consecutive performances; at the time a successful show ran for three or four performances and then joined a repertoire schedule. Those sixty-two consecutive performances held the record for the longest run of a play or musical for almost 100 years.

The Beggar's Opera indicated that there was an audience for English language music theatre, for satire, both political and cultural, for the use of pre-existing and familiar music. But, more important, *The Beggar's Opera* was the beginning of an entirely new business model, based on long and extended runs. Although it took almost 100 years for its record to be matched, the financial model of how musical theatre is created changed with those sixty-two performances. Not only could the production of music theatre yield a profit, but suddenly, within this new model, putting more substantial monies behind the production made sense. Under the old repertoire model it made no sense to invest in specific sets or expensive costumes – the technical end of the production had to be kept minimal in order to hope for a meager profit. Under this new model it made sense to invest money into the production elements of new musical entertainments.

The Beggar's Opera is the grandfather of the contemporary musical theatre; suddenly commerce and art exist side by side. With the birth of a viable business model that allows for a popular art form that appeals to a broad and diverse audience, everything aligns for the creation of what will eventually become the modern American musical theatre. The evolution of the American musical theatre is market-driven. No matter how world events shift, or the demands of the marketplace change, the musical theatre always adapts to provide something relevant, something salable.

Chapter summary

- Pre-Greek musical theatre.
- Greek drama and comedy.
- Roman theatre.
- Liturgical drama: mystery, morality and miracle plays.
- Renaissance and Elizabethan theatre.
- Court masques.
- Seventeenth- and eighteenth-century opera.
- John Gay's *The Beggar's Opera*, the beginnings of an English-language musical theatre.

Notes

1 Brockett, Oscar. *History of the Theatre*. Boston: Allyn & Vacon, 1968.
2 *Hamlet* became both *Rockabye Hamlet* and *The Lion King*. *A Comedy of Errors* became *The Boys From Syracuse*. *The Taming of the Shrew* became *Kiss Me Kate*. *Twelfth Night* became *Your Own Thing*. *The Tempest* became *Journey to the Forbidden Planet*. *Two Gentlemen of Verona* became *Two Gentlemen of Verona*. *A Midsummer Night's Dream* became *Swinging The Dream*. And there are many more examples.
3 "More Stage Designs by Inigo Jones," Internet Shakespeare Editions, 9/1/10, Best.
4 "Eighteenth Century Opera," Victoria and Albert Museum, June 1, 2011. Web, http://www.vam.ac.uk/content/articles/0–9/18th-century-opera/
5 "The Craftsman," London, February 3, 1728. Unknown.

Further reading

Greek and Roman theatre

MacDonald, Marianne and Michael Walton. *The Cambridge Companion to Greek and Roman Theatre*. Cambridge: Cambridge University Press, 2007.

Liturgical drama

Harris, John. *Medieval Theatre in Context: An Introduction*. London: Routledge, 1992.

Renaissance and Elizabethan theatre

Brissenden, Alan. *Shakespeare and the Dance*. Princeton, NJ: Princeton Book Club, 2001.
Lindley, David. *Shakespeare and Music: Arden Critical Companions*. London: Arden, 2005.

Court masques

Ravelhofer, Barbara. *The Early Stuart Masque: Dance, Costume, and Music*. New York, NY: Oxford University Press, 2006.

Seventeenth- and eighteenth-century opera

Glixon, Beth and Jonathan Glixon. *Inventing the Business of Opera: The Impresario and His World in Seventeenth-Century Venice (AMS Studies in Music)*. New York, NY: Oxford University Press, 2007.

Rosand, Ellen. *Opera in Seventeenth-Century Venice: The Creation of a Genre*. Berkeley, CA: University of California Press, 2007.

The Beggar's Opera

Winton, Calhoun. *John Gay and the London Theatre*. Lexington, KY: The University Press of Kentucky, 1993.

A comprehensive website on *The Beggar's Opera*, created by University of Michigan students: http://www.umich.edu/~ece/student_projects/beggars_opera/

2 Early musical theatre in America, 1735–1865

Ballad opera in America

The first documented musical theatre performance in the American colonies was *The Opera of Flora, or Hob in the Well*, a ballad opera by Colley Cibber, the theater manager who had originally rejected *The Beggar's Opera*.

Ballad operas, the rage in London since *The Beggar's Opera* in 1728, had become the reigning paradigm in musical theatre. Great shifts in paradigm do not occur often in the development of an art form, but when they do, their effect is profound. Gilbert and Sullivan shift the paradigm 143 years later; Jerome Kern, Guy Bolton and P.G. Wodehouse shift it again with the Princess musicals 43 years after that; Richard Rodgers and Oscar Hammerstein II shift it again with *Oklahoma!* 28 years later; and Stephen Sondheim and Harold Prince 27 years after that with *Company*.

Ballad opera satirized bombastic Italian opera, politics, politicians, the class system and social conditions. The central characters were rogues, scoundrels, thieves, whores and whoremongers – the presentation of lower classes on the musical stage was new and titillating to contemporary audiences. Characters in ballad operas spoke in racy and rude spoken dialog rather than the traditional recitative, and sang lyrics that were set to the tunes of popular songs (known as broadsheet ballads), folk tunes, drinking songs and familiar church hymns. Ballad operas were accessible; being performed in English, rather than the traditional French or Italian. By performing in English, singing to the tunes of well-known songs, and using characters that were of the lowest class, ballad opera was accessible to English-speakers of all classes. Ballad opera opened up a whole new potential audience.

On February 18, 1735, *Flora* made its American première at the courthouse in Charleston, South Carolina, presented alongside "the dance of the two Pierrots, and a new pantomime entertainment in grotesque characters, called *the adventures of Harlequin and Scaramouch, with the Burgomaster trick'd*"[1] as advertised in the *South Carolina Gazette*.

The following year, the first professional theatre in the U.S. opened, the Playhouse on Dock Street in Charleston. The Playhouse housed local amateur players as well as professional troupes from London. Tickets cost 30 shillings for seats on the stage or balcony boxes, 25 shillings for pit seats (orchestra seats) or 5 shillings for the gallery. The Playhouse was destroyed by fire in 1740, but was rebuilt twice on the same location.

By 1753 the first professional company opened in New York. Lewis Hallam had arrived from London with a British company. Each member of Hallam's company received one share, Hallam received a second share for managing the troupe, one share went to each of Hallam's children and the remaining four shares were profit for the financial backers. Upon arrival in New York, Hallam found the only existing theatre (on Nassau Street) too small, tore it down and built the New Theatre, "a very fine, large and commodious new theatre,"[2] which opened in 1753, presenting a series of twenty-one different entertainments. These included comedies, farces, Shakespearean tragedies, and the masterpieces of Cibber, Lillo, Farquhar, Addison, Rowe and Fielding. The company performed on Mondays, Wednesdays and Fridays; and ticket prices ranged from 8 to 3 shillings. Members of the company included Mrs. Becceley, a singing soubrette, Mr. and Mrs. Love, two of the dancers in the company, and Mr. Hulett who "was for many years the only dancing master in New York."[3] The first season included *Flora, or Hob in the Well, Damon and Phillida, The Beggar's Opera, Devil To Pay* and *Virginia Unmasked*; in addition, they presented shorter musical entertainments as afterpieces for the non-musical plays.

As his first season concluded in New York, Hallam announced his move to Philadelphia. Pennsylvania law had allowed plays and operas to be read publicly, but not acted or staged; and music could not be sung by vocalists, only played by instrumentalists. The Quakers considered plays and actors indecent and a threat to morality, and in an effort to suppress such activity the Pennsylvania Blue Laws made it illegal to attend performances – patrons could be fined up to 500 pounds. Hallam fought these laws, and in 1759 The Orpheum Club, an amateur musical society, was founded in Philadelphia, and the following year the Southwark Theatre opened in Society Hill for the presentation of operas, ballets and concerts. Attempts to close these venues met with rebounded efforts by the community, and by 1766, this portion of the Blue Laws was repealed.

On April 20, 1767, the first musical written by an American was scheduled to open at Philadelphia's Southwark Theatre, a ballad opera, *The Disappointment or The Force of Credulity: A New American Comic Opera of Two Acts by Andrew Barton, Esq.* Unfortunately, although the city fathers had lifted the ban on theatre, *The Disappointment* was too low, crude and too direct and personal in its satire – it was shut down before it opened. On April 6, 1767, the Philadelphia newspapers heralded the upcoming performance but on April 16 the newspapers announced that the performance was cancelled.

The Disappointment satirized contemporary political and social figures. The story involved a scam using a phony letter that gives the location of a bogus hidden pirate's chest. Despite the cancelled performance, *The Disappointment* was published within the year. *The Disappointment* finally premiered 200 years later in 1976 in Washington, D.C., produced and recorded by the Library of Congress.[4]

Early American musical spectacles

The tradition of spectacle-driven musicals in America dates back to 1781 and runs through today – early theaters housing these entertainments seated up to three times as many people as today's Broadway theaters. These theaters required production elements on a massive scale in order to fill such large spaces. The spectacle-driven musical continues through the revues of Ziegfeld, in the 1910s and 1920s, known for their scenic opulence and special effects, and through the mega-musical imports of the 1980s and 1990s and today to shows like *Cats*, *Les Misérables*, *Phantom of the Opera* and *Spider-Man: Turn Off The Dark*.

There was theatrical activity throughout the American Revolution (1770–81), but very little of it was musical; the next American-written musical appeared in 1781, two months after the decisive Battle of Yorktown. Francis Hopkinson, a signer of the Declaration of Independence and avid amateur musician and poet, wrote *The Temple of Minerva*, a musical spectacle in the style of the European court masques, which was presented in Philadelphia on December 11, 1781 by the French Minister to honor George Washington. The following week, *The Freeman's Journal* wrote:

> On Tuesday evening of the 11th inst. His Excellency the Minister of France, ... entertained his Excellent General Washington, and his lady ... with an elegant Concert, in which ... was introduced, ... The Temple of Minerva, An Oratorical Entertainment.[5]

The Temple of Minerva included an overture, six solos, two trios, a duet and a grand chorus,[6] and was written in two scenes, which depicted the Goddess Minerva and her High Priest uniting the Genius of France with the Genius of America. It is an ancestor of the extravagant tableaux of the Ziegfeld revues of the 1910s and 1920s. *The Temple of Minerva* is the earliest example of American musical spectacle.

Playhouses and performance style

The later eighteenth century saw scant activity and less innovation in the musical theatre. However, a wave of European immigration to the United States and a wave of migration from rural areas to the cities created a need for amusement for the vast northern urban audience. The Park Theatre had been built in 1789 on Chatham Street in New York; originally a 300-seat theater, tickets cost an off-putting $2.00, $1.50 and $1.00. But the theater was rebuilt in 1821 with a seating capacity of 2,500, more than eight times its former capacity. With so many more seats, the ticket prices were reduced to roughly a third of their previous expense, 75¢, 50¢ and 37½¢ – still allowing for substantially greater profits. Shortly after, the Bowery Theatre opened with a seating capacity of 4,000 and had "a price range that made the Park seem expensive."[7]

With so many more tickets at lower prices, the Park and Bowery were popular, and the growing population turned out in droves. They came to see the shows, to see each other, to converse with each other, to respond vocally to the stage, and, of course, to be seen. Commonly, audiences yelled out their approval or disapproval regarding the choice of material or the performance. Audiences routinely shouted down the contemporary European arias in favor of patriotic American songs. Throughout the nineteenth century during performances audience members shouted to each other, fights broke out, picnics took place, all manner of refreshments were sold, and reportedly prostitutes plied their trade in the upper balconies.

All of this activity in the theatre necessitated a style of performance that was big enough to hold focus. Actors needed to be big enough in their vocal performance to keep the attention of patrons, and the pace of their performances could not allow for deep feeling or introspection. The tempo and vocal energy required to hold an audience in this environment depended on a highly energized performance style. In addition, gas lighting was still relatively new and offered general illumination without much ability to focus light. In such large theaters, with so many distractions going on, without controlled lighting helping to focus the audience's attention, actors needed to employ a large gestural style of acting to keep the audience focused on the actors. Arising out of the desire to keep the focus on the stage, there was constant activity onstage – songs, dances, animal acts, comedians, circus acts or the display of freaks between acts or as shorter pieces between longer dramatic pieces was common.

Tom and Jerry – and their imitators

In 1823 the Park Theatre presented a British import by William Moncrieff, based on Pierce Egan's book, *Tom and Jerry; or, Life in London: An Operatic Extravaganza in Three Acts. Tom and Jerry* had run for two years in London, breaking the record held by *The Beggar's Opera*. In New York, subtitled *An Extravaganza Burletta of Fun, Frolic, Fashion and Flash in Three Acts, 21 Scenes,*[8] *Tom and Jerry* only ran for four months at the Park Theatre; but it inspired so many revivals, sequels and imitators that it represents an important structural model for a successful nineteenth-century musical.

Jerry Hawthorn, from the country, comes to visit his city cousin, Corinthian Tom. In the play's twenty-one scenes Tom and Jerry explore the city, running into all manner of people and situations along the way. It was a "day around town" panorama of city life, seen through the eyes of an innocent country cousin. Scenes included: the Burlingham Arcade, Tattersals, a street fight and the ensuing courtroom scene, a gambling house and more. The scenes, songs and dances could be altered to accommodate available talent. The rambling structure allowed one specialty act to be replaced with practically any other.

Tom and Jerry, and all of its subsequent revivals, sequels and imitators, were not driven by a narrative plot, but rather by a panoply of scenes and acts. From a business perspective, this was very useful; if a particular act's contract was up, or they asked for more money, they could be easily replaced. In fact, changing scenes and songs with regularity was good for encouraging repeat business.

The "day around town" was a model for many successful musicals throughout the 19th and 20th centuries. After its initial run, *Tom and Jerry* held a place in the repertoire and had frequent performances throughout the season. At the end of the season, there was a burlesque of *Tom and Jerry*, produced by a Negro company, called *The Death of Life in London, or Tom and Jerry's Funeral*. In addition, Tom and Jerry shows appeared from season to season in revivals or new variations. Sometimes similar characters would appear in knock-offs, always using the same format – an unsophisticated fellow would visit his sophisticated city friend and together they would encounter a broad range of modern city life. Some of these shows include: *A Glance at New York in 1848*, *A New Glance at New York*, *The World's Fair or London in 1851* and *Apollo in New York*. In 1856, John Broughman finally transported Tom and Jerry themselves to New York in *Life in New York, or, Tom and Jerry on a Visit*, which played the Bowery Theatre.

The *Tom and Jerry* shows became the model for the musicals of Harrigan and Hart at the end of the century. According to Bordman, Harrigan and Hart "provided much of the impetus for both modern musical comedy and revue."[9] Vestiges of this structure can even be seen in some modern musicals; *Open a New Window* from *Mame*, in which the innocent Patrick and his sophisticated Aunt encounter a range of zany city characters or *N.Y.C.* from *Annie*, with the innocent Annie and the sophisticated Warbucks harken directly back to this model.

Niblo's Garden and the theaters of the 1800s

Niblo's Garden was the greatest entertainment complex of the 1800s. Opened originally in 1823 as the Columbia Garden, it was called San Souci in 1828 and took the name of owner, William Niblo, in 1829. Initially a coffeehouse and catering establishment, Niblo started offering entertainment to attract customers and built the first of several theaters on the site in 1834. Located on Broadway near Prince Street, Niblo's Garden was a theater complex encompassing several stages, which presented all sorts of entertainments; it quickly became one of the hot spots of New York nightlife. The original theater included a 3,000-seat primary stage, several smaller stages, an exhibit room for panoramas and an outdoor garden. Niblo's featured variety musical selections in the Grand Saloon and other novelties, such as P.T. Barnum's first exhibition; admission was 50¢. In 1846, the theater burned down and was rebuilt as a 3,200-seat theater, the most up-to-date of its time. It remained immensely popular until its final performance in 1895 when it was demolished to make room

VIEW OF THE INTERIOR OF THE OPERA HOUSE, AT NIBLO'S GARDEN, NEW YORK.

Figure 2.1 Gleason's Pictorial Drawing-Room Companion, Vol. 4 No. 20 (Saturday, May 14, 1853), p. 308, Boston

for an office building. Niblo's Garden was home to all manner of entertainments, operas, plays, and variety entertainments; and is the first in a trend of large entertainment complexes with theaters with very large auditoriums. These came to dictate the style of production as well as the style of musical theatre acting in the latter half of the nineteenth century (see Figure 2.1).

With so much of the audience so far from the stage, these theaters demanded a big physical and vocal acting style and production with massive scenery to fill the large facility. The mid-to-late 1800s were a golden period of scenic painting; sometimes impresarios would advertise the name of a scene painter or the inclusion of a particularly beautiful scenic backdrop, transformation scene or other special effect along with the names of the writers or stars.

The 1800s saw a boom in the construction of theaters and entertainment complexes in New York, and the larger the better. New York had two professional playhouses in 1820, the number had risen to four by 1830, eight by 1840 and fourteen by 1850. By 1870 the number was twenty, and by the end of the century there were twenty-six theaters in Manhattan. Some of the Manhattan theaters from 1732 to 1900 include:

- Nassau Street – 64–66 Nassau Street (1732–65), the first theater in New York.
- John Street Theatre – 15–21 John Street (1767–98).
- Barnum's American Museum – Broadway and Ann Street (1800–65).
- American – at Mercer and Houston Streets. Nicknamed the African, presented the first African-American stage entertainments in New York (1822–23).

- Bowery Theatre – 46 Bowery. First New York theater lit by gaslight. It burned down and was rebuilt four times, in 1828, 1836, 1838 and 1845 (1826–1929).
- Niblo's Garden – Broadway and Prince Street. A complete entertainment complex, the most fashionable theater of the 1800s (1828–95).
- Bowery Amphitheatre – across the street from the Bowery. The birthplace of the minstrel show (1835–unknown).
- Broadway – six theaters had this name: 410 Broadway (1837–38); 326 Broadway, a 4,500-seat theater (1847–59); 728 Broadway, home to George Fox and Harrigan and Hart (1865–84); 485 Broadway, originally called Broughman's Lyceum (1850–69); 1221 Broadway (1879–1920); 1445 Broadway (1888–1929).
- Winter Garden – 667 Broadway (1850–67).
- Barnum's New Museum. Seated 3,000 – 539 Broadway (1851–68).
- Academy of Music – 14th Street and Irving Place. A world-class facility for theatre and opera (1854, demolished in 1926).
- Laura Keene's Varieties (later re-named the Olympic when the first Olympic burned down) – Broadway and Houston Streets (1856–80).
- Fourteenth Street Theatre – 14th Street between 6th and 7th Avenues (1866–1936).
- Daly's – Broadway and 30th Street. Seated 2,265 (1867–1920).
- Casino – Broadway and 39th Street. Theater, café, roof garden, home of many hits (1882–1930).
- Lyceum – 4th Avenue and 24th Street. The first theater entirely lit by electricity. Electric installation by Thomas Edison personally. (1885–1902) (see Figure 2.2).

This surge of theater construction and productions is a result of New York becoming the economic and cultural center of the U.S. in 1822. There are two reasons for this. The industrial revolution, from roughly 1750 to 1850, caused a great migration from the rural Southern states to the cities of the North. Increasing reliance on technology and the need to distribute goods from centers of commerce drove more people to cities of the northern United States. With so many surrounding mills and manufacturing towns, New York was a natural location for the center of commerce. Also, in 1817 ground was broken for the engineering and construction project of the century; in 1825 the Erie Canal opened, connecting New York City to Albany and Buffalo, providing a vital Atlantic Ocean link to the entire Northeastern United States. Becoming the central hub for the transport and shipping of mercantile products changed New York from a moderately sized American coastal city to the major commercial center and seaport in the populated Northern half of the U.S.

The population of the U.S. was growing, and thanks to the Erie Canal, the population of New York was booming (see Figure 2.3). As the transportation of goods throughout the northeastern United States centered in New York City, people flocked to New York for the jobs created by this economic boom,

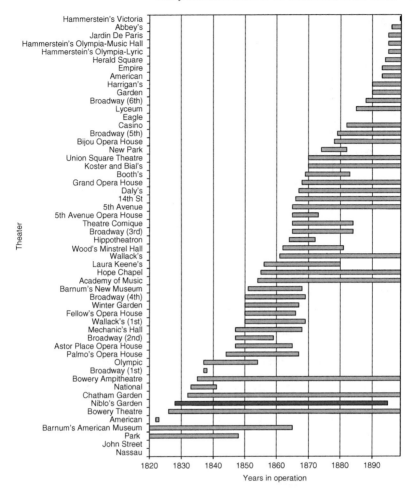

Figure 2.2 Theaters operating in New York (Manhattan only), 1820–99

helping New York become the largest city in the country. As the city grew, so did the need for entertainment – there were always entrepreneurs ready to step in and see that need filled. The musical theatre has always existed at the crossroads of art and commerce.

At the beginning of this period, many of the huge theaters and entertainment complexes housed imported operas, operettas performed in their original languages, mostly Italian and French, and English language plays featuring touring British and European artists. In addition, these theaters housed great European musical and dance artists.

The American Theatre, built in 1822, featured the first African American stage entertainments in New York, but received a hostile reception from journalists, other theater owners and racist mobs and had to be closed down within

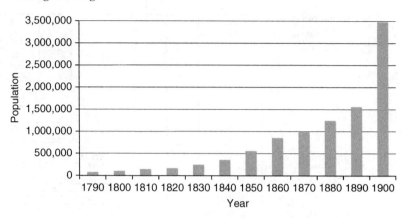

Figure 2.3 The population of New York City (Manhattan), 1790–1900

the first year. Many theaters built later in the century housed the earliest forms of American musical entertainments: minstrel shows, burlesques or variety shows. Slowly but surely American musical entertainments began to appear and gain momentum.

The minstrel show – a uniquely American entertainment

In imitation of the European traditions of masking and carnival, minstrel shows began in the 1830s from a tradition of white men dressing up as plantation slaves and performing black music and dance styles in a grotesque parody of African Americans. This popular art form hit its stride in 1832, when comedian Thomas Dartmouth (T.D.) "Daddy" Rice first performed his "Jump Jim Crow," a song and dance, in blackface. "Daddy" Rice was not the first "deli-neator" or "Ethiopian delineator," which is what white performers who black-ened their faces with burnt cork and put on such displays were called, but he was one of the most popular and started the rage of "Jim Crow" performers. Supposedly one day Rice spied a crippled black man singing and dancing in an awkward manner and realized that this could be incorporated into his act – at that point and with the awkward crippled dance "delineators", "jumping Jim Crow" took off.

Thomas Dartmouth (T.D.) "Daddy" Rice, 1808–60, was one of the most popular blackface entertainers of his day. He created and popularized the character of "Jim Crow."

Theaters at the time presented a number of shorter plays on a single eve-ning's bill and Rice achieved success and popularity performing this number between acts of plays in which he was appearing. Rice's performance, a

T. D. RICE AS THE ORIGINAL "JIM CROW."
From the collection of Thomas J. McKee, Esq.

Figure 2.4 Thomas D. Rice (© Bettmann/CORBIS)

grotesque mockery of African Americans, garnered him tremendous success. He quickly developed a repertoire of songs, jokes and patter, and toured the world with this blackface character (see Figure 2.4). The original "Jump Jim Crow" song wasn't set, but changed from performance to performance; there were many verses; W.T. Lhamon, in "Jump Jim Crow" lists forty-four verses. The most common form of the lyric and two sample verses appear below:

Come listen all you galls and goys,
I's just from Tuckyhoe,
I'm goin' to sing a little song.
My name is Jim Crow.

Weel about and turn about and do jis so,
Eb'ry time I weel about and jump Jim Crow.

Oh I'm a roarer on de Fiddle,
And down in old Virginny,
They say I play de skyentific
Like Massa Pagannini.

> Weel about and turn about and do jis so,
> Eb'ry time I weel about and jump Jim Crow.[10]

Rice's success evolved into the minstrel show. In the early 1840s a troupe of European performers, called *the Tyrolese Minstrel Family*, toured America with a program of European folk songs and dances. In 1843, Dan Emmett, Frank Bower, Frank Pelham and Billy Whitlock – four actors who had made their livelihoods as delineators – came together to satirize the European troupe in an entire evening made up completely of blackface entertainment, titled *Dan Emmett's Virginia Minstrels*. The *Virginia Minstrels* presented an entire evening of songs, dances, jokes and comic banter between the four "black" characters, all white men who had "corked up." The simple staging involved four chairs put in an arc. The *Virginia Minstrels* introduced songs that are still sung today, including "The Blue Tailed Fly" and "Polly Wolly Doodle."

The form was so natural, it seemed improvised – and much of the evening was. "But most of all, there was exuberance and excitement. The minstrels, in their wide-eyed, large-lipped, ragged-costumed absurdity, rolled onto the stage in a thundercloud of energy, which hardly ever dissipated. They insulted each other, they baited each other, they made mincemeat of the language, they took the audience into their fun, and, in one night, they added a new form to show business in America – in fact, the world."[11]

Dan Emmett's Virginia Minstrels played around the world during the year that they were together and inspired an unimaginable number of imitators. By 1856, there were ten resident minstrel companies in New York alone.

The minstrel show was in three acts. The first part was a series of songs, dances and jokes – the characters of Bruder Bones and Bruder Tambo, named for the noisemaking clacker (or bones) and the tambourine they played, sat on the outside of the arc, while Mr. Interlocutor and the balladeer sat on the inside. The balladeer would sing the more serious romantic songs that separated the comic songs and comic patter. The second part of the show contained more of the same kind of material from the first part, but presented in a less structured manner. The third part of the presentation was a skit with songs and dances; the skit could be a depiction of life on a southern plantation or spoofs of current events or popular plays – *Uncle Tom's Cabin* was a favorite. Minstrel companies were comprised exclusively of white actors until the 1870s and exclusively male actors until the 1890s. Minstrel shows' popularity continued into the 1950s.[12]

The long, grotesque history of minstrelsy in America has left a profound mark on race relations and questions of racial identity. Spike Lee's brilliant film *Bamboozled* grapples with this issue. In John Kander and Fred Ebb's final musical, *The Scottsboro Boys*, they told the story of nine black teenagers in Alabama falsely accused of rape and imprisoned in Alabama in 1931; Kander and Ebb told their story using the performance traditions of a minstrel show.

Early American burlesque

The 1840s saw another popular form – burlesque. Burlesque is "the mocking of a serious matter or style by imitating it in an incongruous way,"[13] from the Italian *burlesco* or *burla* meaning to mock or make fun of. This is how burlesque began in the 1840s. The word is also defined as "a variety show of a type that often includes striptease"[14] and that is what burlesque became by its end in the mid-twentieth century.

From its inception, burlesque's success was based on selling sex, in the form of the display of the female limb in a fleshly manner, usually clothed in tights. The most important producers of burlesque in New York in the mid-nineteenth century were William Mitchell, James Robinson Planché, John Brougham and Laura Keene. Nineteenth-century burlesque ranged from short musical entertainments to entire evenings; and while anything was fodder for satirizing or burlesquing, the more serious and self-important the subject, the better. Just like *Forbidden Broadway* has satirized each Broadway season from 1982 forward, the burlesques of the nineteenth century satirized the cultural highpoints of their times.

William Mitchell presented burlesque at the Olympic Theatre from 1839 to 1850. His first season included a parody of Bellini's opera *La Sonnambula* (*The Sleep Walker*) (which had received its New York première in 1835 at the Park Theatre) entitled *The Roof Scrambler*, a satire of the famed ballerina Fanny Elssler (who had made her American debut that same season) called *The Musquitoe*. The advertisement for *The Musquitoe* states "the ballet is founded upon the well-known properties of the Musquitoe, whose bite renders the patient exceedingly impatient, and throws him into a fit of scratching, slapping and swearing delirium."[15] The pieces on Mitchell's bill changed as fads and cultural events came and went. Mitchell offered as many as eighty-six pieces in a single season,[16] replacing pieces as they became out of date.

As prolific as Mitchell, English dramatist James Robinson Planché contributed many short pieces that appeared in various theaters. Some of the more successful burlesques include: *King Charming, The Invisible Prince* and *The Captain of the Watch*.

Laura Keene was America's first great actress-manager. Among other ventures, she leased the Metropolitan Theatre, which she renamed *Laura Keene's Varieties*, and assembled a company, which ran successfully 1856–63. A gifted writer, actress, producer and business woman, her accomplishments were overshadowed by her having starred in *Our American Cousin* at the Ford's Theatre in Washington, DC on the night that President Lincoln was shot. It was Keene who cradled the mortally wounded President's head in her lap.

The self-serious nature of burlesque's targets – from Shakespeare to ballet and opera – made them ripe for satirizing. References and allusions to local figures and current events would be included; and female flesh was on display, often gratuitously, but it was a part of the burlesque. Although burlesque would shift in form, eventually losing its legitimacy and becoming tawdry, it would last well into the 1960s, all told, over 120 years.

Burlesque provided a training ground for writers, designers and actors who would move on into long and successful careers in vaudeville, the "legitimate" theatre, and later movies and television. As burlesque began to compete with vaudeville, burlesque became defined by its nudity and its salacious nature and ultimately shed its satirical nature. By its end, in the 1960s, burlesque was one of the seedier, more disreputable forms of popular entertainment; but that's not how it started out. Among the great artists who started in burlesque were: Fanny Brice, Mae West, Eddie Cantor, Abbott and Costello, W.C. Fields, Al Jolson, Bert Lahr, Sid Caesar, Danny Kaye and Sophie Tucker.

Variety arts and the birth of vaudeville

> A kaleidoscopic stage world of singers, dancers, comics, jugglers, acrobats, magicians, hat spinners, ventriloquists, knife-throwers, trained chimpanzees and what have you, [...]. Almost every sizable town had a Bijou or Gaiety Theatre featuring "Count them – 12 Big Acts – Count Them," and booking offices routed thousands of performers over a network of circuits that covered the country from coast to coast and border to border. It was big entertainment. It was also big business.[17]

Tony Pastor (1837–1908), actor, singer, blackface performer, ringmaster, writer, director and impresario, was the father of vaudeville.

"Gather together some performers if you want to put on a show. But if you want to make show *business* – a paying operation that provides a living for a wide variety of professionals involved – that requires managers."[18] D. Travis Stewart's point is that vaudeville is defined by the organizational structure and the driving force behind this structure is the manager. Vaudeville houses from the Northern Territories of Canada to the southernmost reaches of the United States offered quality entertainment to the continent, and the mechanism for creating this was the development of the vaudeville business model at the hands of the managers. The first of these, the great innovator, was the father of vaudeville, Tony Pastor (see Figure 2.5).

There begins, with Tony Pastor, a long period in which American musical theatre is ruled by a string of theatrical renaissance men, some individuals, some partnerships. Tony Pastor, George Fox, Harrigan and Hart, Weber and Fields, George M. Cohan; all of these men or teams produced, directed, wrote and starred in their own works. Combined, they represent fifty years of being the kings of the American musical.

Born in New York in 1837, Tony Pastor began putting on shows in his parents' basement for the neighborhood by the age of seven. His natural appeal to audiences was apparent to "The Hand in Hand Society," a temperance society,

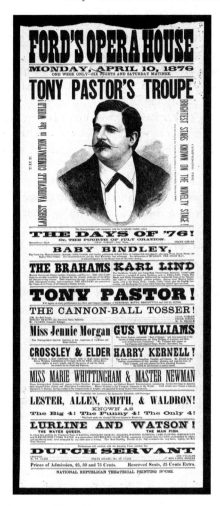

Figure 2.5 Vaudeville showman Tony Pastor

that hired him to sing at temperance meetings. Pastor became enthralled with minstrelsy and would blacken his face with burnt cork and practice in front of the mirror for hours. He offered himself as a volunteer to assist the minstrel troupe at Croton Hall. Tony soon had a job as part of a minstrel troupe performing at P.T. Barnum's museum, followed by a succession of jobs touring the country with circuses and menageries as a minstrel, a clown and, ultimately, a ringmaster.

By the 1860s, the population of Manhattan had reached 814,000; Brooklyn was the country's third largest city, at 267,000. With so many thirsty mouths to service, New York was crammed with pubs and saloons. In order to best their competition, many saloons offered entertainment to attract customers. For these concert saloons, the "concert" was the loss leader that, along with pretty waitresses, brought customers into their establishments to buy drinks.

Shows at the concert saloons were called varieties or variety arts. Tony Pastor entered the world of the variety arts in 1860 and was an instant success. Pastor was a charismatic and versatile performer with a wide range of skills and talents. His most successful skills were performing patriotic oratory and songs and performing songs commenting on the latest current events, some comic and some deeply emotional.

By the age of twenty-eight, Pastor presented his first show as a manager – and *Tony Pastor's Variety Show* was a huge success. Although acts would come and go throughout the run of the show, the opening night of *Tony Pastor's Variety Show* included:

> ... dances and ballads by Ernestine DeFaiber, exotic capers by Mlle. Marie Bertha, a Zouave drill in complete uniform by Carrie Austin, more dances by Ellen Collene, comic songs by Amelia Wells, funny business with the banjo by James Gaynor, Irish jigs and ditties by Doty Duly, and various other musical and comic specialties by the likes of Johnny Wild, Willis Armstrong, and Sheridan and Mack [and] a comic named Robert Butler. Pastor, of course, was on hand with "New Comic Songs, Humorous Ballads, and Admirable Adaptations." There were also several sketches, an afterpiece and possibly a ballet.[19]

Pastor's most important innovation to the variety arts was to make it family friendly, opening his doors to women. Concert saloons were exclusively a man's domain; occasionally a matinée would be opened to women, but the variety arts audience was almost exclusively men. Pastor realized that if he could create a family entertainment, he would be able to sell multiple tickets rather than one. It was this shift that would define vaudeville. The two changes that Pastor had to effect in order to attract families were the behavior in the house and the behavior onstage.

Pastor proclaimed that the auditorium was to be off-limits for both smoking and drinking. In the *New York Clipper* of July 22, 1865, Pastor advertised the opening of his new theater, predicting "that ladies and gentlemen alike would be delighted with the 'versatility of the performances and the high moral excellence of the program.'"[20] However, Pastor wisely located a saloon – "Tracy's Billiard and Refreshment Saloon" – in another part of the same building, very near by the auditorium; the theater and the saloon had different entrances, the theater's clearly marked with big signs, the saloon's practically hidden, but once inside there was easy access from one to the other. In this way, the theater itself was respectable for women and children, while still offering the men the pleasures that they had come to expect in the theater, and continuing to profit from the sales of alcohol and tobacco. Pastor's family-friendly entertainment was an immense success, so much so that the market was almost immediately flooded with imitators.

Pastor had a reputation as a perfectionist, obsessively concerned with the smallest details of his shows, but also as a fair and friendly employer, one who treated his acts well. He hired his ensembles, both singing and dancing, under one-year contracts while the acts (which included singers, dancers, jugglers, mimes, acrobats, athletes of all kinds, freaks and anyone else who he thought might draw a crowd) were contracted for one or two weeks. Acts constantly changed to keep his audience coming back for more. Pastor appeared in most of his shows, usually singing songs commenting on the current events of the day in a big untrained baritone voice – he was always a popular attraction.

By 1881 Lower Manhattan was getting more crowded and expensive; so, like many businesses, Pastor's moved to the outskirts of the city where rents were less expensive. Pastor moved his operation from the Bowery Theatre to 14th Street, where he rented a theater called The Germania and renamed it the 14th Street Theatre. In 1888, Pastor built his own theater, alternately known as "Tony Pastor's" and "Tony Pastor's Opera House" on the same block; there he produced vaudeville and the occasional opera until his death in 1908.

Almost all major musical theatre artists in the late nineteenth and early twentieth century worked for Tony Pastor early in their careers. Harrigan and Hart started as a blackface act at Pastor's and Weber and Fields also got their start from Pastor. The Four Cohans, including the young George M. Cohan, worked for Pastor and learned the audience appeal of rousing patriotic songs watching Pastor open and close each performance with them. As the young Pastor had learned the art of management from P.T. Barnum, so Cohan, Weber and Fields, Harrigan and Hart and so many others learned their craft from Pastor. Every generation of musical theatre innovators has stood on the shoulders of the generation before.

Chapter summary

- Ballad operas.
- The Playhouse in Charleston, South Carolina.
- Lewis Hallam's company.
- Early American spectacles.
- Early American theaters.
- Tom and Jerry musicals.
- Niblo's Garden.
- The growth of New York.
- Minstrel shows.
- Burlesque.
- Tony Pastor.

Notes

1 *South Carolina Gazette*, February 15, 1734/35.
2 *New York Gazette*, September, 1753.
3 Arthur Hornblow, *A History of the Theatre in America From its Beginnings to the Present Time*, Volume 1, Philadelphia: J.B. Lippincott Company, 1919. p. 92.
4 *The Disappointment* is an important piece, as the first American music theatre piece, and there are many great sources and references for further investigation. One very

good place to begin would be *American Opera* by Elise Kuhl Kirk, published by University of Illinois Press, 2001. The Library of Congress recording, out of print and difficult to find, was released by Turnabout Records, Catalog Number PZ-S34650.

5 Oscar George Theodore Sonneck, *A Bibliography of Early Secular American Music*, Washington, D.C.: H. L. McQueen, 1905, p. 150.

6 Gillian B. Anderson, "'The Temple of Minerva' and Francis Hopkinson: A Reappraisal of America's First Poet-Composer," *Proceedings of the American Philosophical Society*, Vol. 120, No. 3 (June 15, 1976), p. 166.

7 Robert C. Toll, *On With The Show: The First Century of Show Business in America*, New York: Oxford University Press, 1976, p. 4.

8 "Tom and Jerry: or Life in London," Internet Broadway Database. Web, accessed November 9, 2012, http://ibdb.com/production.php?id=411833

9 Gerald Bordman, *American Musical Theatre: A Chronicle*, New York: Oxford University Press, 1978, p. 9.

10 W.T. Lhamon, *Jump Jim Crow: Lost Plays, Lyrics and Street Prose of the First Atlantic Popular Culture*, New York: Harvard University Press, 2003, pp. 95–96.

11 Lee Davis, *Scandals and Follies: The Rise and Fall of the Great Broadway Revue*, New York: Limelight Editions, 2000, p. 31.

12 One of the most provocative explorations of blackface and minstrelsy is Spike Lee's movie *Bamboozled* in which Mr. Lee examines the idea of a contemporary (2000) minstrel show.

13 *Microsoft Encarta College Dictionary*, ed. Anne H. Soukhanov, New York. St. Martin's Press, 2001, p. 188.

14 *Microsoft Encarta College Dictionary*, ed. Anne H. Soukhanov, New York. St. Martin's Press, 2001, p. 188.

15 Gerald Bordman, *American Musical Theatre: A Chronicle*, New York: Oxford University Press, 1978, p. 10.

16 Gerald Bordman, *American Musical Theatre: A Chronicle*, New York: Oxford University Press, 1978, p. 9.

17 Parker Zellers, *Tony Pastor: Dean of the Vaudeville Stage*, Ypsilanti, Michigan: Eastern Michigan University Press, 1971, p. xi.

18 D. Travis Stewart, *No Applause, Just Throw Money: The Book That Made Vaudeville Famous*, New York: Faber and Faber, Inc. 2006, p. 82.

19 Parker Zellers, *Tony Pastor: Dean of the Vaudeville Stage*, Ypsilanti, Michigan: Eastern Michigan University Press, 1971, pp. 27–28.

20 Parker Zellers, *Tony Pastor: Dean of the Vaudeville Stage*, Ypsilanti, Michigan: Eastern Michigan University Press, 1971, p. 45.

21 Mary Henderson, *The City and the Theatre: The History of New York Playhouses: A 250 Year Journey from Bowling Green to Times Square*, New York, NY: Back Stage Books, 2003, blurb.

Further reading

Ballad opera

Dizikes, John. *Opera in America: A Cultural History*. New Haven, CT: Yale University Press, 1995. While this book only references ballad opera peripherally, it desribes the history of opera in the U.S.

Early American playhouses

Henderson, Mary. *The City and the Theatre: The History of New York Playhouses: A 250 Year Journey from Bowling Green to Times Square*. New York, NY: Back Stage

Books, 2004. A chronicle of the history of theaters in New York which "relates the development of theatre to the social, political, economic and cultural climate of the time."[21]

Tom and Jerry

Cruikshank, George and Pierce Egan. *Tom and Jerry: Life in London; Or the Day and Night Scenes of Jerry Hawthorn and His Elegant Friend, Corinthian Tom.* Whitefish, MT: Kessinger Publishing, 2010.

Minstrel shows

Lhamon, W.T. *Jump Jim Crow: Lost Plays, Lyrics, and Street Prose of the First Atlantic Popular Culture.* New York: Harvard University Press, 2003.

Toll, Robert C. *Blacking Up: The Minstrel Show in Nineteenth-Century America.* New York, NY: Oxford University Press, 1977. Fastidiously researched and documented.

Burlesque

Allen, Robert C. *Horrible Prettiness: Burlesque and American Culture.* Chapel Hill, NC: The University of North Carolina Press, 1991.

Tony Pastor

Fields, Armond. *Tony Pastor, Father of Vaudeville.* Jefferson, NC: McFarland, 2012.

Prologue

Prologue

3   First stirrings, 1866–1902

The first American musical phenomenon

Many historians cite *The Black Crook* as the first American musical. It is the first that made it clear that the musical theatre could be more than marginally profitable.

The 1866–67 theatre season in New York was full and varied. With the Civil War over for a year and a half, the economy was in excellent shape – there was money for promoters to mount productions and for theatergoers to attend them. Tony Pastor provided and imported musical entertainments – operas, operettas and European artists in concert. The hit of the New York season was *Rip Van Winkle*, starring Joseph Jefferson.

Across the Atlantic on the musical stages of Paris and Vienna, light operas and operettas of Jacques Offenbach and Johann Strauss were all the rage. Still defined by European tastes, New York saw its own productions of Offenbach's and Strauss's operas and operettas; sometimes recreations of their original productions, sometimes bastardized versions of the originals.

Two American impresarios, Henry C. Jarrett and Harry Palmer imported a French ballet troupe to perform the ballet *La Biche au Bois* (*The Hind in the Forest*). The ballet, set deep in the woods, presents scenes of nature, redemption and transformation. The dancers were dressed in pink flesh-colored tights creating the illusion of nudity – extremely risqué in the 1860s. Jarrett and Palmer had a potentially profitable commodity in *La Biche au Bois,* but unfortunately, the Academy of Music, which they had hired to present the ballet, burned down while the company was in transit to New York. When the company arrived in New York, Jarrett and Palmer approached William Wheatley, the manager of Niblo's Garden, in hopes of presenting their ballet there. Unfortunately, Wheatley was already committed to a second-rate romantic German drama by stage-manager-turned-actor-turned-playwright, Charles M. Barras, *The Black Crook.*

The Black Crook tells the story of the evil Count Wolfenstein, who tries to steal the heart of Amina by having her boyfriend, Rodolphe, abducted by Herzog, the evil crook-backed black magician (the black crook). Herzog, who is obliged to give the devil one soul on every New Years, is planning to offer

Rodolphe's soul, until Rodolphe saves a dove, who turns out to be Stalacta, Fairy Queen of the Golden Realm, who in return saves Rodolphe and reunites him with Amina.

As rehearsals of *The Black Crook* progressed, it became clear that Wheatley had a disaster on his hands and, in an effort to hedge his bets, he agreed to combine his play with Jarrett and Palmer's ballet.

Wheatley used the ballet to draw attention from the awful play. Every time the play started to lag, Wheatley had the ballet troupe with the seemingly naked ballet dancers perform an interlude. There were certain similarities in tone between the ballet and the play, their rustic settings and mythic themes, which helped them to appear vaguely integrated. Fortunately, *La Biche au Bois* already included ballet sequences that made sense in *The Black Crook*, "specifically, ballet dances for 'flowers,' for sea creatures set in an underwater grotto, for masked dancers in a fairy-tale ballroom, and for various supernatural beings who alternately threaten and rescue the central romantic couple."[1] Nevertheless, coherence and singularity of artistic vision were never central to the evening's entertainment.

Olive Logan, an actress of the time and later a feminist lecturer, wrote: "When *The Black Crook* first presented its 'nude' woman to the gaze of a crowded auditory, she was met with a gasp of astonishment ... but it passed; and, in view of the fact that these women were French ballet-dancers after all, they were tolerated ... they represented in their nudity imps and demons. In silence they whirled about the stage; in silence the trooped off. Some faint odor of ideality and poetry rested over them."[2] The aesthetic imprimatur of being imported from Europe and the ballet dancers elevated the evening making it acceptable – titillating, but acceptable. All the better ... and all the more marketable.

Not trusting that adding the ballet troupe into the proceedings would keep his audience engaged and entertained, Wheatley interpolated songs by several composers and lyricists. He also offered a high degree of scenic spectacle. Wheatley spent $50,000 mounting the production, including $5,000 to dig out the basement so that entire scenes could appear to sink into the earth and disappear beneath the stage.

In the 1860s, most scenery was painted. With staggeringly low salaries for chorus people, it was more cost-efficient to hire a huge chorus of people to fill up your stage than to fill it up with dimensional or architectural scenery. Painters specialized in particular kinds of scenes and were hired on a scene-by-scene basis – the idea of a single scenic designer was years off. Of *The Black Crook*'s scenery, *The New York Tribune* particularly liked the storm scene (painted by R. Smith) and the second act finale:

> a vast grotto ... extending into an almost measureless perspective, Stalactites depend from the arched roof. A tranquil and lovely lake reflects the golden glories that span it like a vast sky. In every direction one sees the bright sheen or the dull richness of massy gold. ... One by one, curtains of

mist ascend and drift away. Silver couches, on which fairies loll in negligent grace, ascend and descend amid a silver rain. Columns of living splendor whirl, and dazzle as they whirl. From the clouds droop gilded chariots and the white forms of angels.[3]

Reviewers singled out two pieces of scenic painting, D.A. Strong's painted drop of "A Wild Pass in the Hartz Mountains" and James E. Hayes' depiction of "Valley at the Foot of the Hartz Mountains." *The Black Crook* also boasted an extravagant transformation scene, a shift from one lavish and opulent scene into another, transformed in full view of the audience. *The Black Crook's* transformation scene took the audience from a rocky grotto to a fairyland throne room. In addition to the painted spectacle, *The Black Crook* also offered its audience a waterfall, live and onstage.

The original program for *The Black Crook* described:

> This evening the original grand, romantic, magical and spectacular drama in four acts by Charles M. Barras, entitled The Black Crook, introducing the combined Viennoise and Parisienne Ballet Troupes, who will appear in the most costly and magnificent spectacle ever presented in America.

Towards the bottom of the cover page:

> Grand Corps de Ballet and Figurantes of one hundred ladies, the whole under the direction of the celebrated ballet master Signor Davide Costa. In addition to the above, The Wonderful Majiltons, comprising Mons. Charles Majilton, Mons. Henryi Majilton & Mlle. Marie Majilton. Messrs. Moe & Goodrich, the renowned painters. A powerful dramatic company. Gorgeous new scenery, by that Master of the Scenic Arts, William Voegtlin, assisted by M. Reitzky. Wonderful Transformation Scene, entitled "The Palace of Dew Drops." Painted by the Brothers Brew of London and purchased by Messrs. Jarrett & Palmer, expressly for this piece, at a cost of fifteen thousand dollars. The Rizarelli Brothers, the gymnasts of the World. Mons. Seagrit and his two children aged 3 and 4 years in their beautiful salon entertainment.[4]

This mishmash agglomeration of play, ballet, musical and scenic spectacle opened on September 12, 1866. It was long, running for five-and-a-half hours; and it was a massive hit. At a time when a successful play might run for a few weeks, *The Black Crook* ran for 474 consecutive performances, well over a year, and earned over a million dollars in profit from the initial run alone. For his $50,000 investment, Wheatley saw $87,000 in just the first five weeks alone. In addition to the record-breaking original production, and extensive touring, *The Black Crook* saw the first of its eight Broadway revivals less than two years after it first closed and its second revival eight months after the first revival closed. Joining drama, music and dance into a single theatrical piece is what marks *The Black Crook* as the first American musical.

The Black Crook had three things going for it. First, respectable women, who had ventured out of their homes to run businesses during the Civil War, no longer felt tied to the home and attended theatre much more in 1866 than they had in 1860. Second, the railroad system across the country was substantial by 1866, so *The Black Crook*, even with its extraordinary scenic elements, was able to tour the country – which it did for almost seventy years, well into the 1930s, playing for millions of people and netting tens of millions of dollars in profit. Third, *The Black Crook* carried with it the whiff of scandal. Decried by religious leaders and in newspaper editorials, everyone wanted to see what the hoopla was about. Half-clad women? Naked-limbed dancing girls? Who could resist the shocking and profane? The only performers singled out for mention by *The New York Times* critic were the principal dancers, " … the ballet success of the night, the witching *Pas de Demons*, in which the Demonese, who wear no clothes to speak of, so gracefully and prettily disported as to draw forth thunders of applause. No similar exhibition has been made in an American stage that we remember, certainly none where such a combination of youth, grace, beauty and élan was found."[5] Sex sells – and in *The Black Crook*, it sold big. *The Black Crook* established a new business model in which substantially longer runs made the amortization of larger expenses business as usual.

It was clumsy, clunky and cobbled together, but it was a hit. The audience did not go to the theater to see a cohesive musical drama driven by a narrative, it went for an evening's entertainment – and that *The Black Crook* gave them. It established an important principle in the musical theatre, one long practiced in all other areas of popular culture – sex sells. While *The Black Crook* clearly lacked in substance or focus, it gave the audience girls in pink tights and the American musical theatre never looked back.[6]

Early imitative efforts

During the next fifteen years the usual Parisian, Viennese and London imports continued to be offered, as did the variety entertainments, but alongside them American musicals began to appear with some regularity. Many of these American musicals emulated *The Black Crook*; fantastical stage spectacles, musical extravaganzas, were very much the fashion. They tended not to focus much on plot or characters, the songs had little to do with the story, and the stories, such as they were, usually included element of whimsy, fairyland or some other mythic time and place. Wheatley personally attempted a sequel to *The Black Crook*, *The White Fawn*, but it was a major disappointment. *The White Fawn* was a bigger spectacle than *The Black Crook* was and with its large overheads (the show required eighty stagehands between carpenters and gasmen), it lost most of Wheatley's investment despite lasting for 176 performances.

Theatrical dynamos of the nineteenth century

> **George Lafayette Fox** (1825–77) – American pantomime master and great
> comic dancer and performer. Born in Cambridge, Massachusetts, died at
> 52. Most famous role was Humpty Dumpty.

Tony Pastor had been a star, writer, producer and director – the period of
the one-man dynamo (or two person team-dynamo) was in full swing.
Throughout the century, three theatrical forces dominated the Broadway musical theatre; George Fox and the teams of Harrigan and Hart and Weber and
Fields all performed these kinds of multiple functions. This trend continued
into the turn of the twentieth century with George M. Cohan.

In the latter half of the nineteenth century, American pantomimes were
immensely popular. The pre-eminent American pantomime artist was George
Lafayette. Between 1865 and 1877, Fox created pantomimes and burlesques,
acting as writer, director, producer, stage manager and star. Fox's most famous
character, Humpty Dumpty, was named after the Mother Goose character;
Humpty was a low-class clown, a boor and a boob, although, as Bordman
points out, "he drew both sympathy and laughs with a performance that contained as much pathos as humor."[7] Fox's shows included: *Humpty Dumpty*,
Humpty Dumpty Abroad, *Humpty Dumpty at School*, *Humpty Dumpty at
Home*, *Humpty Dumpty in Every Clime*, *Humpty Dumpty's Dream*, *Richelieu
of the Period!*, *Wee Willie Winkie*, *Little Faust!*, *Macbeth*, *Hamlet*, *Medea*, *The
Bronze Donkey*, *Harlequin Jack*, *Hiccory Diccory Dock*, *Little Boy Blue*, *Jack
and Gill Went Up The Hill*, *Sinbad the Sailor* and *Old Dame Trot and Her
Comical Cat*.[8] In each he either played the Humpty Dumpty character or a
thinly veiled variation, a buffoonish clowning lout – even in such burlesques as
Richelieu of the Period!, *Medea*, *Macbeth* and *Hamlet*. The original *Humpty
Dumpty* was the runaway hit of 1867, running for 483 performances, and
grossing $1,406,000 in its New York run and initial tour.[9]

The plot of these shows had Fox's character engage in a series of adventures
and encounters – much like the *Tom and Jerry* shows. Dances and other specialty
talents (roller skating, billiards and so on) were performed by specialty acts
hired for the production between Fox's scenes, giving Fox a chance to make
costume changes. Topical matters were routinely referenced and satirized:

> In an allusion to the growing political graft and to the postwar inflation,
> the[y] pay a call on New York's new $100,000,000 City Hall. At one point
> our "manifest destiny" was acknowledged then nurses carried two babies
> onstage. The babies were called Alaska and St. Thomas [referring to our
> recent acquisition of those territories].[10]

Fox offered the scenic spectacle his audience expected. *Humpty Dumpty*
settings included fairyland locales – the abode of Romance by moonlight, the

Farm of Plenty, the Enchanted Garden, and contemporary New York locales – the Olympic Theatre by night, a candy store, City Hall and a grand transformation to the Retreat of the Silver Sprites.

Fox's performance style arose out of the physical realities of the theaters in which he played. His large, swaggering, intense physicality would seem over the top or too large to be believable to us today. However, in the large New Bowery and Olympic Theatres, where he most often played, that size was necessary to project to the audience. The oratorical and declamatory style of delivering lines was also needed in those huge theaters with no amplification; actors had to deliver every line in a loud, well-supported voice, facing the audience. Just as today, the style of vocal production is defined by the proximity of the microphone to the singer's mouth, in the 1800s the theaters and technology defined the performance style needed to be heard, seen and understood by audiences. Twentieth-century movie and television acting, intimacy for the camera and microphone, was decades away.

Pantomime and burlesque were both highly physical. There was dialog, but the driving mechanism was the actor's physical work – appropriate for the large venues. Describing Fox's physical dexterity onstage, Alan Ackerman writes, "Fox's extremely violent physical humor consolidated and represented the brutal street life of the Bowery, or what the *New York Herald* disparaged as 'the coarseness of the east-side.' Fox's slapstick, claimed one witness, 'was all action – action – action'."[11] Fox was beloved because of his brash, bold, energetic, intense physicality; his persona was a wise guy, a slightly cocky swaggerer who wears his heart on his sleeve – attributes we see increasingly identified as essentially American. These attributes begin to appear in the new American musicals of the nineteenth century.

By 1875, Fox's behavior became erratic; he would interrupt his own performances with emotional breakdowns or incoherent diatribes. On at least one occasion, he attacked several audience members during a performance, throwing props at them from the stage. Fox was replaced on November 15, and less than two weeks later he was hospitalized. He never returned to the stage and died two years later, at the age of fifty-two. Fox was the highest paid actor of his time and the first real star of the American musical theatre.

American musicals of the time were not cohesive musical plays; they included songs, sketches, specialty performances, and so on. Even the imported light operas from Vienna and Paris included these elements. While imports outnumbered American shows, most American musicals fell into five categories:

- Burlesques such as Fox's *Little Faust* or *Hamlet*.
- Pantomimes – frequently structured as a night out in New York and set in various New York locales or in a fairytale land.
- Imitators of *The Black Crook* – romantic spectaculars set in Europe. These include such shows as *The Twelve Temptations* and *The Three Hunchbacks*.

- Plays with music in which a German immigrant comes to New York and goes in search of his sister. Some of these titles include *Fritz, Our German Cousin*; *Carl, The Fiddler*; and *The New Fritz, Our German Cousin*.
- Variety entertainments/vaudeville. Anyone who could recite a speech, whistle a tune, ride a unicycle or pick a lock wanted to get into vaudeville. Today we have reality shows like *America's Got Talent*; the 1870s had vaudeville.

> **W.S. Gilbert** (1836–1911) and **Sir Arthur Sullivan** (1842–1900), the British composer and lyricist/librettist team, created a repertoire of English-language comic operas. They are grandfathers of the American musical theatre.

By 1878, with Fox dead and no new star or style in sight, American musical theatre had to either revive old hits or create new pieces that imitated them. At this time two teams arrived in New York that pointed the way forward for the musical theatre. Those two collaborative teams were Gilbert and Sullivan and Harrigan and Hart.

The light operas of the British lyricist W.S. Gilbert (1836–1911) and composer Sir Arthur Sullivan (1842–1900) represent the most popular and long-lasting musicals of the English-speaking musical theatre. Their comic operas are still produced and adored around the world today, over 140 years later. These comic operas established the paradigm, the basic dramatic form for the musical theatre that would follow. Together with theater manager Richard D'Oyly Carte, they developed a new commercial model. Dealing with issues of copyright law, marketing, merchandising, running a resident company in repertoire in London while maintaining international companies simultaneously, the D'Oyly Carte Opera Company was way ahead of its time.

Richard D'Oyly Carte (1844–1901) was a British composer, agent and promoter. In 1875, as manager of London's Royalty Theatre, he was presenting a short comedy, *Chryptoconchoidsymphonosomatica*, and Jacques Offenbach's short French operetta, *La Pericole*, together. Knowing that Victorian audiences expected a fuller evening, D'Oyly Carte brought together two of his acquaintances to write an afterpiece to be performed on the same bill – librettist W.S. Gilbert and composer Arthur Sullivan. Gilbert and Sullivan had previously collaborated on a short Christmas piece, *Thespis*, for London's Gaiety Theatre in 1871. However, the afterpiece they created for D'Oyly Carte, *Trial by Jury*, marked the beginning of a twenty-five-year collaboration between Gilbert, Sullivan and D'Oyly Carte – the most important collaboration in the musical theatre of the nineteenth century.

Trial by Jury was instantly beloved by British critics and public alike. It continued to play at the Royalty Theatre after its companion pieces had closed and in the next couple of years was put on the bill at the Opera Comique, the theater that D'Oyly Carte built and managed, playing for more than 300 performances in total in its first two years. *Trial by Jury* is a light-hearted satire of the legal system of England at the time; the plot revolves around a breach of promise of marriage lawsuit. The plot of *Trial by Jury* is preposterous, but the characters behave as if the events were perfectly normal. The "topsy-turvy" nature of this world describes all the Gilbert and Sullivan works.[12]

At a time when most light opera in England was French, D'Oyly Carte wanted to develop an English language form of light opera. To this end, based on the success of *Trial by Jury*, he formed the Opera Comique, and commissioned another piece from Gilbert and Sullivan. This next piece, *The Sorcerer*, won critical acclaim and spurred D'Oyly Carte on to commission yet another, which would become the team's first full-fledged international hit.

HMS Pinafore takes place aboard the ship of the same name and satirizes the strict class rules of Victorian society – the captain's daughter is in love with a lower-class sailor. In true Gilbert and Sullivan form, the topsy-turvy plot goes through a series of twists and turns until all is somehow right. Along the way, the good-natured humor takes swipes at patriotism, party politics, the Royal Navy, and unqualified people who rise to positions of authority.

On May 23, 1878, *HMS Pinafore: or The Lass That Loved a Sailor* opened at the Opera Comique. It was at first met with moderate disinterest, but thanks to D'Oyly Carte's marketing the box office quickly picked up. D'Oyly Carte marketed the show aggressively as family fare, and managed to get a symphonic suite from *Pinafore* included on the program of the Promenade Series at Covent Garden Opera House. Quickly the show became so popular that, in a time before recorded music, television or radio, when the sale of sheet music was the means of marketing music, the vocal score to *Pinafore* sold 10,000 copies in one day.

On January 15, 1879, *HMS Pinafore* made its New York debut in a pirated production, opening at the Standard Theatre in New York – other pirated productions had already opened in Boston in September, in San Francisco in December and in Philadelphia earlier in January. The show was such a success at the Standard that a little over a week later the Lyceum Theatre in New York presented its own version. That spring, twelve New York theaters mounted their own productions of the show. Many weeks saw three or more productions running simultaneously, and at one point the same show was playing in eight different theaters within a five-block radius. Among these productions were a Yiddish language production, an all-black production, an all-Catholic production and an all-children's production. International copyright law was in its infancy and all of the American productions failed to pay royalties to Gilbert, Sullivan or D'Oyly Carte. For the U.S. premières of all of their subsequent shows, the trio very quickly opened their own productions of their shows in New York in order to secure the U.S. copyright. By the time Gilbert, Sullivan and D'Oyly Carte arrived in New York to mount their authorized version of *HMS Pinafore* in November 1879, the U.S. had already seen 150 productions, and all of them unauthorized, and from these hugely successful productions Gilbert and Sullivan and D'Oyly Carte saw not one cent.[13]

"Pinafore fever" took hold, and images of characters from the musical were used to sell every imaginable product from photographs of the actors in costume, to dolls made in the characters' likeness, to sheet music, card games, celery glasses and trading cards. *HMS Pinafore* was the first musical to see such a blitz of merchandising and licensing of ancillary products – an entirely new business model.

The structure of Gilbert's libretto became the basic structure in the musical theatre. Boy meets girl, boy loses girl, boy gets girl – this was the basic plot structure for all of their works except for *Utopia Limited* and *Princess Ida* and has been the predominant plot structure in the musical theatre into the 1960s and beyond.

On both sides of the Atlantic, musicals of the 1800s and early 1900s featured specialty performers, popular acts that were placed in the show usually regardless of their relevance to the plot. Specialty dance groups, ukulele players, jugglers, billiard players and so on were written into musicals. *HMS Pinafore* was without these specialty acts – in fact without any distraction from the fun of the convoluted plot. In Gilbert and Sullivan's musicals, book, music and lyrics (as well as scenography, staging and stagecraft) were all at the service of the plot. The forward momentum of the evening was not defined by the pacing of the acts; it was driven forward by the plot, another innovation that would become the norm in the musical theatre to come.

Gilbert and Sullivan offered their audience wit and sophistication in the musical theatre. Denny Martin Flynn calls Gilbert, "the first star lyricist."[14] Before Gilbert and Sullivan if a star writer existed, it was the composer – Johann Strauss, Jacques Offenbach, and so on – people went to the musical theatre to hear glorious melodies. Gilbert and Sullivan initiated a genuinely literate and literary musical theatre. People went to see *HMS Pinafore* for the lyrics, dialog and the story – the music took a back seat. Gilbert's plots pushed the boundaries of absurdity without stepping beyond them – he always stayed true to the internal logic of the "topsy-turvy" worlds he created. As John Gay had satirized the political and social elite of his day, so Gilbert satirized the stiff and stuffy rules and recognizable characters of Victorian society. Gay's satire was based on putting the words and sentiments of the powerful and rich into the mouths of thieves and whores and Gilbert's was based on taking the "rules" of society to extremes. In this, it is easy to see Gilbert and Sullivan's influence on all great musical satires that came afterward, from *Of Thee I Sing* to *Urinetown* and *Bat Boy*.

Plot-driven musicals are direct descendants of the works of Gilbert and Sullivan, and we see their influence on the Princess musicals of Kern, Bolton and Wodehouse, on such shows as *Show Boat*, *Of Thee I Sing*, *Oklahoma!*, *Candide* and so on. Practically every major musical theatre figure of the first half of the twentieth century attributes their passion for musical theatre to early exposure to the works of Gilbert and Sullivan.

The company founded by D'Oyly Carte and Gilbert and Sullivan to produce these works lived on and continued to produce Gilbert and Sullivan's comic operas from the 1870s through 1983, and reopened from 1988 to 2003. In addition to the D'Oyly Carte company, opera companies and Gilbert and Sullivan societies the world over continue to produce their works continually. In addition to *Thespis, Trial By Jury* and *HMS Pinafore*, these works include: *The Sorcerer, The Pirates of Penzance, Patience, Iolanthe, Princess Ida, The Mikado, Ruddigore, The Yeoman of the Guard, The Gondoliers, Utopia Limited* and *The Grand Duke*.

After the death of George Fox, without its greatest practitioner, pantomime was fading and the sprawling opulent spectacles in the style of *The Black Crook* were losing their audience appeal. There were still occasional attempts to revive the epic spectacle, pieces such as *Enchantment* (1878) and *Hiawatha* (1880), but they were few and none were substantially successful. The team of Harrigan and Hart filled the void. Harrigan wrote, produced, directed and co-starred with Hart, who was known for his beautiful voice and the excellence of his female characters.

Actors, writers, directors, producers and theater managers **Edward "Ned" Harrigan** (1844–1911) and **Tony Hart** (1855–91) were the biggest things on Broadway in musical theatre from 1874 to 1888. They played multiple characters of varying ethnicities and genders in each of their shows. They gregariously exploited ethnic stereotypes.

Edward "Ned" Harrigan was born and raised mostly in the Lower East Side of Manhattan, the son of an Irish immigrant. Most of the characters in Harrigan's plays were Irish, Italian or German immigrants, people he would have known from the neighborhood where he grew up. When Harrigan's parents divorced and his father remarried a severe Methodist, Harrigan left home, winding up in San Francisco where he began his career as a song and dance man; starting at an amateur night he quickly became a favorite in the variety houses of San Francisco. Harrigan quickly worked his way through two partners and across the country back to New York. He was "a stocky, serene man who had practically no interests outside of the theatre."[15] Through his life Harrigan created eighty or ninety variety sketches, and at least thirty-five full-length plays, in which Harrigan acted, sang, produced, financed and directed, frequently in theaters under his own management. Harrigan wrote the scripts and lyrics and the music was most often written by his father-in-law, David Braham. Harrigan was so faithful to and so dependent on the company of supporting performers that he surrounded himself with, that many stayed in Harrigan's employ for life. Harrigan's shows were adored and wildly successful in their time; they always involved a high degree of physical comedy, slapstick and rowdy, knockabout behavior.

The Germans, the Italians, the Negroes, and particularly the Irish who inhabited Gotham's Lower East Side were his special subjects, [...]. His characters were grocerymen, butchers, barbers, dock workers, "river rats," undertakers, pawnbrokers, tailors and an assortment of loveable bums and waifs. Their locales were never far removed from the Five Points, a tenement area [...] commonly known as the vilest place in town. [...] The plays [...] dealt with ward politics, the policy racket, body stealing, what would now be called "urban renewal," domestic celebrations and misunderstandings, the battle of the sexes, and, incessantly, clashes among the Irish, Germans, Italians, and Negroes.[16]

Tony Hart (1855–91) was born into a poor Irish family in Worcester, Massachusetts. Being small and slightest of frame he was the butt of much of his large family's teasing and when his retaliations got out of hand he was sent away to reform school. Running away, Hart took to the stage, ultimately joining forces with Harrigan in Chicago. Being a small man with small features, Hart played the female roles – he is reported to have been astoundingly convincing even though he brought a male sensibility to his female characters, imbuing them with the same rough-and-tumble, knockabout quality of all of the characters Harrigan wrote. Hart, who reigned over Broadway with Harrigan from 1878 to 1885, died at age thirty-five of syphilis.

A friend said that Hart "caused more joy and sunshine by his delightful gifts than any other artist of his time. ... To refer to him as talented was an insult. Genius was the only word that could be applied. He sang like a nightingale, danced like a fairy, and acted like a master comedian. ... His magnetism was compelling, his personality charming. He had the face of an Irish Apollo. His eyes were liquid blue, almost feminine in their dovelike expression. His head was large and round and covered with a luxurious growth of brown, curly hair, which clustered in ringlets over a strong brow. His feet and hands were small, his smile almost pathetic. His disposition turned December into May. ... Tony Hart was the friend of all mankind and my especial pal. I have loved three men in my life and he was two of them."[17]

George Fox had Americanized the pantomime. Harrigan and Hart, basing their success on the exploitation of ethnic stereotypes, created the first true American musicals in their reign over Broadway, from 1874 to 1888. By 1874 they had worked their way from Chicago to New York, where they found employment at Tony Pastor's Variety Theatre. They moved from there to New York's Theatre, which Harrigan quickly took over as manager. George Fox's illness and departure from the stage left a void that Harrigan and Hart quickly filled. In their shows, we see recognizable American characters, singing songs in the style of the popular American songs. Gifted comic character actors, Harrigan and Hart played multiple and wildly divergent roles in their shows – in one show Hart played six roles, three male and three female.

In the 1870s, many New York neighborhoods had neighborhood militias, which were little more than excuses for the members (all men) to get together and drink. Harrigan and Hart's first and most enduring success, *The Mulligan's Guard*, satirized these militias. In all, Harrigan and Hart musicals featuring the Mulligan's Guard include: *The Mulligan Guard's Picnic, The Mulligan Guard's*

Ball, The Mulligan Guard's Chowder, The Mulligan Guard's Christmas, The Mulligan Guard's Surprise, The Mulligan Guard's Picnic (revised for 1881), *The Mulligan Guard's Nominee* and *The Mulligan's Silver Wedding*. Harrigan played the politically ambitious saloon owner named Dan Harrigan. Hart played the more diminutive men and most of the leading female characters; one of his more popular characters from this series was the African-American washerwoman Rebecca Allup.

In addition to the Mulligan's Guard shows, they created: *The Lorgaire, The Major, Squatter Sovereignty, The Blackbird, Mordecai Lyons, The Nutty Day, Cordelia's Aspiration, Dan's Tribulations, Investigation, McAllister's Legacy, The Grip, McNooney's Visit*. All twenty of these musicals were produced in the nine years between 1878 and 1887 – an astounding period of productivity.

The comedy was based on exploiting ethnic types, on puns and ethnic dialects. The lyrics were slangy and filled with ethnic slang, dialects and poor grammar – something not heard before in musicals. The tunes were very much in the style of the standard popular songs of the day, and Harrigan's songs became popular. Songs frequently had very little to do with the plot, which did not matter to the audiences of the day. Their musicals were bawdy and brawling and energetic, they were rowdy and physical. Here is the plot of *The Mulligan Guard's Picnic* (1878):

> Not only does the tailor shorten Dan [Mulligan]'s trousers to the point of absurdity, but the picnic he had planned is disrupted by the claims of a Negro society to the picnic grounds and by a wild fight between Gustavus Lochmuller and Tommy Fagan. The Full Moon Union has planned a balloon ascent, singing "Second Degree, Full Moon Union." The fight develops because Lochmuller has mysteriously disappeared, and, assuming him dead, Tommy has announced he will court his "widow." A hasty trial is held at Squire Cohog's Grocery and Court, where sassy black Rebecca Allup proves a hilariously hostile witness.[18]

Harrigan and Hart, as Irish-American artists, came along at the right time. The 1845 Irish potato famine had triggered a wave of immigration. Upwards of two million Irish persons immigrated to America between 1840 and 1860, and many had settled in New York's Lower East Side. By 1877, the large Irish population had established themselves enough to be interested in attending the theater. Many of their first-generation American children were already adults by the late 1870s.[19] They loved seeing themselves represented up on the stage in the form of two of their own.

After Harrigan and Hart

The busy seasons between 1878 and 1892 saw eighteen to twenty shows opening per season, but many of them were revivals or European imports. In addition to Gilbert and Sullivan's British light operas and Harrigan and Hart's American musicals, these seasons were filled with imported French or Viennese operettas or imitations. These light entertainments were about barons and archdukes and masked balls – things foreign to the average New Yorker. The success of the raucous, fast-paced Harrigan and Hart musicals inspired a surge in farce-comedies with music; some of these proved successful.

By 1885, Harrigan and Hart had parted company – neither would find the success alone that they had achieved together. Harrigan and Hart had shifted the emphasis from pantomime to knockabout farce and raucous satire.

In the 1890s, farce-comedies with music took hold; "these shows had loose plots involving 'ordinary people,' offering enough gags and dialog to get from song to song. Any number of composers might contribute to the score."[20] In 1891, just such a show, *A Trip to Chinatown*, established a new record, 657 performances, a record held for almost thirty years. *A Trip to Chinatown* ran for almost two years, boasted several touring productions crossing the country simultaneously, and at one point even had two identical productions running simultaneously in New York to meet public demand. In *A Trip to Chinatown*, two young couples plan to spend the evening at a masquerade ball, but fear that the wealthy guardian of two of them, Uncle Ben, would not approve, so they tell him that they are taking "a trip to Chinatown." They have invited a chaperone, Mrs. Guyer. However, Mrs. Guyer's letter of acceptance is intercepted by Uncle Ben, who mistakes it for an invitation to a romantic rendezvous. The two young couples, Uncle Ben and Mrs. Guyer all find themselves at the same restaurant, where Uncle Ben, who has forgotten his wallet, has gotten drunk while waiting for Mrs. Guyer. After much chaos and confusion, order is restored.

Charles Hoyt's script was essentially a series of vignettes, loosely cobbled together to allow for the various musical numbers and specialties, which changed over the course of the show's life. Hoyt was one of the most successful writers of comic farce, writing eighteen shows between 1883 and 1899. Hoyt's first wife died five years after they were married and his second wife died four years after they were married. After the death of his second wife, he suffered a breakdown and was committed to an asylum; four months after his release he passed away.

Lew Fields (1867–1941) and **Joe Weber** (1867–1942) were the most popular attraction on Broadway from 1892 to 1902. As Harrigan and Hart had exploited their Irish heritage, Weber and Fields' success was based on exploitation of their German heritage.

George Fox reigned over Broadway from 1865 to1875 and Harrigan and Hart had from 1878 to 1885. Joe Weber and Lew Fields were the kings of the New York musical theatre stage from roughly 1892 to 1904.

Short and fat, Weber played the put-upon character of Mike, while tall, skinny Fields played Meyer, the bully. This is a familiar comic trope; the short, fat, put-upon partner and the tall, skinny, acerbic bully recurs in teams like Laurel and Hardy, Abbot and Costello, and even Jerry and George in the *Seinfeld* TV series. While Harrigan and Hart had played on their Irish heritage, Weber and Fields were German. Harrigan and Hart's success followed a wave of Irish emigration, so Weber and Fields' followed a wave of German emigration. In 1870, the Castle Garden entry station in New York cleared 56,000 Irish immigrants, and 118,000 German immigrants.

Weber and Fields worked their way up through variety and vaudeville in the 1880s, and in the 1890s made the transition to the musical theatre stage. Mike and Meyer, the characters they played, were loving exaggerations of recent German immigrants; this allowed the more assimilated German Americans in the audience a chance to laugh at their naiveté and feel superior. Mike and Meyer had heavy German accents and old-world fashion and grooming, like pork pie hats and long beards. Their humor was based on mangling the English language and Fields pummeling Weber. As with Fox and Harrigan and Hart, the act was intensely physical and rough-and-tumble.

> The act usually began with Fields pushing the smaller Weber onstage, with Weber indignantly squealing, "Don't pooosh me, Meyer, don't pooosh me!" [...]
>
> In the course of their banter, one would unintentionally offend the other, with verbal insults turning into all-out battles with punches, kicks, pratfalls, etc.[21]

Weber and Fields worked together for almost thirty years. In their last eight together they opened Weber and Fields' Music Hall, where they were the most successful team in the musical theatre, producing and starring in twelve hit musicals between 1896 and 1904. They parted company in 1904 and never achieved the success apart that they found together.

A *Gaiety Girl*

Weber and Fields were the most successful performers of their time, but the single biggest hit of the 1890s was a British import, *A Gaiety Girl*, which takes its title from the Gaiety Theatre and the line of chorus girls who worked there.

In act one, at a garden party, the officers neglect the society girls in favor of the Gaiety Girls, who have also been invited. Meanwhile, a divorce court judge at the party tells stories about some of the various ladies who have appeared before him. Meanwhile a chaplain dances inappropriately. The society ladies' chaperone is worried that the judge will not remember her divorce case. One of the Gaiety Girls is falsely accused of theft. In act two, the ladies all appear on a beach at the Riviera in their bathing suits and the judge and chaplain flirt with the chaperone and a good marriage is made at the end.

Even though it was slight, it was silly, fun, light and it had a chorus of pretty girls wearing bathing attire and the latest fashions. It was so successful that it ran for 413 performances in New York and inspired producer, George Edwardes, to create a series of musicals that imitated it, which ran in London's Gaiety Theatre. Many of those shows proved successful on Broadway as well: *The Shop Girl*, *The Geisha*, *The Quaker Girl*, *My Girl*, *The Circus Girl*, *The Utah Girl* and *A Runaway Girl*. All these shows were either about a poor girl who loves an aristocrat and wins him against all odds, or a girl who, trying to escape an unwanted marriage, leads a merry chase through interesting places.

A Gaiety Girl presented contemporary recognizable characters instead of far-off Bavarian barons or lords of the underworld. They spoke (and sang) in the language of the day; contemporary slang was embraced and gone was the conflated romantic language of the operas and operettas and the epic "Black-Crook-esque" melodramas. Contemporary opera still maintained the older conventions, but the newly emerging musical theatre only resorted to those conventions when burlesquing them.

But, mostly, it is about the girls. The Gaiety Girls were beautiful, sophisticated, fashionable and trendy – they danced, sang, and looked great. Wealthy gentlemen, called "stage-door johnnies," would wait outside the stage door, hoping to escort the girls to dinner, out for the evening, or even into marriage and a step into "good" society, even the nobility.

A Gaiety Girl, successful in London, New York and on the road, helped open the door for contemporary pieces about contemporary characters who spoke and sang in the vernacular. And, even if the songs were irrelevant, there was a vaguely coherent plot.

Business practices at the century's end

The two most successful musical theatre teams of the nineteenth century had both exploited their ethnic heritage and stereotypes at a time approximately twenty to thirty years after a wave of immigration from their native lands. Both teams also managed theaters of their own – Harrigan managed the Theatre Comique and Weber and Fields owned and managed Weber and Fields' Music Hall. Gilbert and Sullivan and D'Oyly Carte had their home as well, the Savoy Theatre, which Carte founded for the purpose of producing the light operas of Gilbert and Sullivan. Did they flourish because they had theaters at their disposal, or did their artistic successes open up to them the possibility of shifting from artist to management, from tenant to landlord? There is a clear connection between their success as artists and their managerial careers, but which created the opening for the other?

The Syndicate

One of the most important shifts during this period was the development of a theatrical trust, a syndicate. The late 1800s was the time of the railroad trust, the oil trust, the steel trust, and the bank trust; consolidation and a thrust towards monopolies in various industries and ventures was the "hot" business model of the day. One big wave of trust formations occurred between 1898 and 1902, triggered by the recovery from the financial panic of 1893. One can see this urge towards consolidation reflected Henry Ford's famous assembly line approach to manufacturing the automobile, as late as 1908. In the world of business, consolidation was in the air.

Up until this time the booking of touring plays, musicals and artists was haphazard at best. Tours were usually sent out by actor/managers or by independent producers. Their booking practices frequently made little sense in terms of travel distances or times (which translated into expense) – tour producers and promoters took any dates they could get, frequently booking several theaters for the same night as a hedge against bookings falling through. Too often, this left theaters without their advertised attractions on very little notice. In August of 1896, Abraham Erlanger, Charles Frohman, Al Hayman, Marc Klaw, Samuel Nixon, and Fred Zimmerman, owners of theaters in New York and across the country, met in the Holland House Hotel to discuss the creation of a theatrical Syndicate, which would do away with the individual business managers in each theater and take over booking nationwide from a New York office. The Syndicate not only controlled the theaters of the six founders, but most of the others across the country. The Syndicate, controlling the theaters and the shows, represented a monopoly that required that actors and other theatrical professionals either work with the Syndicate, or not at all.

In retaliation, and in an attempt to maintain control over their own theatres, the Shuberts went to war against the Syndicate. The Shuberts proclaimed that they were fighting the good fight, in the name of fairness, but once they got a large enough circuit of their own to compete against the Syndicate, they too instituted a closed-door policy. The Shuberts and the Syndicate continued to battle for domination of the industry until Frohman's death aboard the *Lusitania* in 1915.

The new business model shifted everything in both production and booking and opened the way for a new generation of talents. Before this shift, artistic innovators needed to be producers/managers, or work in conjunction with one, like Gilbert and Sullivan – the business of production was now in the hands of businessmen, and the artists, for the most part, could focus on their art.

Just as all of this was going on, a new generation of creative musical theatre artists was about to arrive on the scene. Composer Victor Herbert made his debut with *Prince Ananias* (1894). Twenty-seven-year-old Florenz Ziegfeld made his debut producing a revival of Charles Hoyt's *A Parlor Match* (1896) and George M. Cohan began to make the transition from vaudeville to the musical theatre stage. But, more about these men in the next chapter, as we enter the twentieth century.

Chapter summary

- *The Black Crook* defines a new business model based on:
  - long run
  - female dancers appearing in flesh-colored tights

- ○ expanded audience with more women attending the theatre
- ○ nationwide touring made possible by the railroad system.

- The five dominant forms between 1865 and 1878:

  1 burlesques
  2 pantomimes
  3 pseudo-European imitators of *The Black Crook*
  4 plays with music
  5 variety entertainments/vaudeville.

- *HMS Pinafore* satirizes:

  - ○ class structure
  - ○ politics/politicians
  - ○ other rules of Victorian society.

- Defining English language comic opera, Gilbert was the first star lyricist.
- Gilbert and Sullivan, with producer Richard D'Oyly Carte, redefined the business model.
- Harrigan and Hart reigned from 1878 to 1885.
- *A Trip to Chinatown* – 657 performances.
- Weber and Fields.
- *A Gaiety Girl* featured an ensemble of attractive women scantily clad.
- The Syndicate formed in 1896.
- The Shubert Brothers begin to battle the Syndicate.

Notes

1 Raymond Knapp, *The American Musical and the Formation of National Identity*, Princeton, NJ: Princeton University Press, 2006, p. 24.
2 Raymond Knapp, *The American Musical and the Formation of National Identity*, Princeton: Princeton University Press, 2005. p. 24.
3 Gerald Bordman, *American Musical Theatre: A Chronicle*, New York: Oxford University Press, 1978, p. 20.
4 From the original program of *The Black Crook*.
5 "'The Black Crook' – New York Times review," *New York Times*, September 13, 1866.
6 It is an interesting footnote that in 1954 the musical *The Girl in Pink Tights* told the story of the creation of *The Black Crook*. *The Girl in Pink Tights* had a book by Herbert Fields and Jerome Chodorov, and a score by Sigmund Romberg, Romberg's final Broadway score, produced three years after his death.
7 Gerald Bordman, *American Musical Theatre: A Chronicle*, New York: Oxford University Press, 1978, p. 22.
8 Karen Hauser, *George L. Fox – IBDB: The Official Source for Broadway Information*, The Broadway League, 2001. Web, accessed June 21, 2009, http://ibdb.com/person.php?id=413885
9 Gerald Bordman, *American Musical Theatre: A Chronicle*, New York, NY: University of Oxford Press, 1978, p. 26.
10 Gerald Bordman, *American Musical Theatre: A Chronicle*, New York: Oxford University Press, 1978, p. 25.

11 Laurence Senelick, *The Age and Stage of George L. Fox, 1825–1877 (Studies in Theatre History & Culture)*, Ames, IA: University of Iowa Press, 1999, p. 142.

12 Mike Leigh directed an excellent film about Gilbert and Sullivan and the making of their opera *The Mikado* – the film's title is *Topsy Turvy*.

13 Colin Prestige, "D'Oyly Carte and the Pirates: The Original New York Productions of Gilbert and Sullivan," pp. 113–48 at p. 118, *Gilbert and Sullivan Papers Presented at the International Conference held at the University of Kansas in May 1970*, ed. James Helyar, Lawrence, KA: University of Kansas Libraries, 1971.

14 Denny Martin Flinn, *Musical! A Grand Tour*, Belmont: Wadsworth Group/Thomson Learning, 1997, p. 67.

15 E.J. Kahn, Jr., *The Merry Partners, The Age and Stage of Harrigan and Hart*, New York, NY: Random House, 1955, p. 7.

16 Richard Moody, ed., *Dramas from the American Theatre 1762–1909*, Boston, MA: Houghton Mifflin Company, 1966, p. 535.

17 E.J. Kahn, Jr., *The Merry Partners, The Age and Stage of Harrigan and Hart*, New York, NY: Random House, 1955, pp. 9–10.

18 Gerald Bordman, *American Musical Theatre: A Chronicle*, 2nd edition, New York, NY: Oxford University Press, 1992, pp. 43–44.

19 Robert Barde, Susan B. Carter and Richard Sutch, "Immigrants, by Country of Last Residence – Europe: 1820–1997," *Historical Statistics of the United States*, Table 106–120, Millennial Edition, vol. 1, ed. Susan B. Carter et al., New York: Cambridge University Press, 2006, pp. 561–563.

20 John Kenrick, *1879–1900: The First Musical Comedies*, 2003. Web, accessed June 25, 2009, http://www.musicals101.com/1879to99.htm

21 John Kenrick, *1879–1900: The First Musical Comedies*, 2003. Web, accessed June 25, 2009, http://www.musicals101.com/1879to99.htm

Further reading

The Black Crook

The musical was published as a novel under the title, *The Black Crook, a most Wonderful History: Now Being Performed in all the Principal Theatre Throughout the United States*. Philadelphia, PA: Barclay & Co., 1873. The PDF of this out-of-print book can be found online.

Reside, Doug. "Musical of the Month: The Black Crook." Library for the Performing Arts, New York Public Library, 2012. http://www.nypl.org/blog/2011/06/02/musical-month-black-crook

A PDF file of the script is available from the University of Maryland at: http://mith.umd.edu/mto/ebooks/BlackCrook.pdf

George Lafayette Fox

Senelick, Laurence. *The Age and Stage of George L. Fox, 1825–1877.* Iowa City, IO: University of Iowa Press, 1999.

Gilbert and Sullivan

Ainger, Michael. *Gilbert and Sullivan: A Dual Biography.* Oxford: Oxford University Press, 2009.

Leigh, Mike. *Topsy-Turvy*. Polygram, USA Video, 2000.

Williams, Carolyn. *Gilbert and Sullivan: Gender, Genre, Parody*. New York, NY: Columbia University Press, 2012.

Wren, Gayden. *A Most Ingenious Paradox: The Art of Gilbert and Sullivan*. Oxford: Oxford University Press, 2006.

As for internet sites, there are Gilbert and Sullivan societies all over the world, and many of them seem to have their own website.

Harrigan and Hart

Kahn, E.J., Jr. *The Merry Partners: The Age and Stage of Harrigan and Hart*. New York, NY: Random House, 1955.

Weber and Fields

Fields, Armond and L. Marc Fields. *From the Bowery to Broadway: Lew Fields and the Roots of American Popular Theatre*. New York, NY: Oxford University Press, 1993.

The Syndicate and the Shubert Brothers

Hirsch, Foster. *Boys From Syracuse: The Shuberts' Theatrical Empire*. Carbondale, IL: Southern Illinois University Press, 1998.

4   The turn of the century, 1900–07

A new era of great American songwriters begins

The twentieth century

As the twentieth century began, America came into its own, ... at least in the eyes of Americans; and in popular culture, American voices began to emerge to celebrate this fact. Senator Albert Beveridge proclaimed, "God has marked the American people as His chosen nation to finally lead in the regeneration of the world. This is the divine mission of America ... We are trustees of the world's progress, guardians of its righteous peace."[1] This was how Americans viewed themselves and their manifest destiny; for the most part expansion of the American West was complete and the next frontier was to share God's divine providence with the world.

There was little to dissuade this belief. America had healed from the Civil War, had survived the Spanish-American War, the Cuban War of Independence and the Boxer Rebellion. It had successfully defeated and displaced the Native Americans. The economic boom of the 1890s was still in evidence. America's gross national product exceeded those of Britain, France and their combined colonial empires. Horatio Alger, Henry Ford and Theodore Roosevelt embodied the American spirit and character; and America had its own aristocracy in the Astors, Vanderbilts and Morgans. Crowds of immigrants poured onto America's shores.

Wonderful new inventions made the 1900s feel futuristic, such as the internal combustion engine – the first cross-country trip by automobile took place in 1903, taking a little over two months. The movies and recorded sound were all invented in the 1890s and had begun to become popular – the first movie theater opened in Los Angeles in 1902. The Wright Brothers made their historic flight at Kitty Hawk in 1903 and Henry Ford raised $28,000 capital to found the Ford Motor Company.

A new breed of American composers with distinctly American voices appeared in the musical theatre. Throughout the nineteenth century, European writers, or those who imitated the European writers, predominated on Broadway; but that was about to change.

New York was a thriving, teeming metropolis and the theatre was thriving with more than thirty Broadway theaters. Brand new subway lines made the theatre easily accessible to tens of thousands of city residents who had not had easy access previously. With the ever-increasing number of tourists who came to New York by rail and steamship, the audience base allowed for more shows and longer runs than ever before.

The pulse of the twentieth century was fast, the rhythms sharp and ragged; and this new era needed a new sound that reflected that. Scott Joplin, the African-American composer responsible for refining and popularizing ragtime music, published his *Maple Leaf Rag*, the most famous ragtime piano piece, in 1900. By 1909 more than half a million copies of the sheet music had been sold. Ragtime embodied the energy of the early twentieth century; it would take a while for Joplin's ragtime to move from the juke joints and brothels onto the stages of the musical theatre, but it left popular culture and the musical theatre forever changed. The time was ready for American voices singing American songs.

But first, … *Florodora*

The biggest hit of the musical theatre stage in the 1900–01 season was an import. *Florodora* had opened in London the previous year where it ran for 455 performances; in New York it opened in 1900 and ran for 505 performances, making it the first hit of the new century. In addition to extensive touring, it received Broadway revivals in 1902, 1905 and 1920 – and in London in 1915, 1931 and 2006.

Florodora takes place on the Philippines Island of Florodora, where a perfume named Florodora is made from the florodora flower. The convoluted plot revolves around a greedy American who has stolen the factory and the island away from the rightful heir, the greedy American's six clerks, the daughter of the greedy American and her six friends, a British Lord traveling incognito and Lady Holyrood, a detective disguised as a traveling phrenologist. Ultimately, after much intrigue involving both love and business, all couples are rightly mated and the island and factory are restored to the proper hands. One easily sees the influence of W.S. Gilbert's topsy-turvy plotlines.

The story was silly and convoluted, the songs were pleasant but forgettable; but *Florodora*'s selling point was its female ensemble and, just like *The Black Crook* thirty-four years earlier, it became a massive success selling sex. Each girl of the ensemble stood exactly five feet four inches and weighed exactly 130 pounds. The hit of the show was the double sextet, "Tell Me Pretty Maiden," which was sung by the six maidens and the six clerks.

The "Florodora Girls," as they were known, garnered great attention and inspired reams of publicity. Each of the original girls were said to have left the show to marry millionaires; whether that is true or from the pen of a press agent, it inspired the imagination of the theatergoing public. To be a Florodora

Girl was to be an object of desire; they defined feminine beauty and allure and many of them did wind up marrying their "stage-door johnnies." In fact, girls married out of the chorus with such rapidity that more than seventy girls moved into the six ensemble positions over the initial New York run – on average, each played forty-seven performances before being whisked away to the altar. People followed the love lives of the Florodora Girls then in the same way that people follow the lives of their favorite reality television stars today. The most well remembered of the Florodora Girls today is Evelyn Nesbit, the notorious "girl in the red velvet swing,"[2] immortalized in the 1998 musical *Ragtime*. Nesbit was plucked out of the *Florodora* ensemble by architect Stanford White and became his longtime lover.

The success of the show and the popularity of the Florodora Girls did not escape the eyes of the advertising industry; and *Florodora* was used to market all sorts of products. Almost every home in America had a piano in the parlor and the primary means for a songwriter to see a profit from their work was the sale of sheet music. The sheet music from *Florodora* couldn't be printed fast enough; piano sheets and orchestral versions sold out as soon as they were available. Even though the recording industry was in its infancy (only 2 percent of households owned a cylinder player) the show's two hit recorded songs "Tell Me Pretty Maiden" and "In the Shade of the Palm" both had many best-selling "cover" recordings by various vocalists and instrumentalists. The Florodora Girls were used to advertise everything and anything – shoes, cookies, chocolates, tags, suits, scarves, and patent medicines, among others. *Florodora* was a national craze. Picking up where Gilbert and Sullivan's "Pinafore fever" left off, *Florodora* moved into the world of advertising, proving that there were revenue sources to be mined and great power in cross-promotion. Today every major Hollywood film released opens with a series of cross-promotions with fast food restaurants, soft drink companies, candies and so forth, thanks to the ground originally broken by *Florodora*.

Turn of the century vaudeville – a new business model

Just as in the 1890s, the Syndicate brought the theatre business into the age of trusts and corporations, the turn of the century saw a similar upheaval in vaudeville's business model. Tony Pastor's experiment in family entertainment had been a massive success; there was hardly a town of any reasonable size in the country that did not boast at least one vaudeville theater. Many of the great stars of the musical theatre and movies started out in vaudeville: George M. Cohan, Buster Keaton, W.C. Fields, Fanny Brice, and many more. At first theaters were independently owned and managed, leaving each act on their own to line up bookings and work out travel and routing arrangements between engagements.

Three businessmen, however, saw huge potential for profit in a different business model. Gustav Walter (1834–1910), an impresario who had built the Orpheum Opera House in San Francisco, in the west, and Benjamin Franklin

Keith (1846–1914) in partnership with Edward Franklin Albee, II[3] (1857–1930) in the east, started buying and building theaters in multiple cities, creating what would become two major vaudeville circuits, the Orpheum Circuit in the west and the Keith-Albee Circuit in the east. When Walter, Keith and Albee started empire building, they continued to have a manager in each theater, responsible for that theater's bookings. However, as their holdings grew, they began booking all their theaters out of a central office. They built on this idea, ultimately creating a centralized booking agency for *all* vaudeville houses, not just the ones that they owned; they signed up theaters across the country, taking a cut from everyone's end and creating a virtual monopoly in the booking of vaudeville acts.

In May of 1900 Walter, Keith, Albee and most of the independent vaudeville theater owners met, at the Hoffman House Hotel to sign the bylaws and constitution of the Vaudeville Managers Association of the United States – the VMA. The VMA functioned as a central booking house in New York, booking all acts for vaudeville theaters across the country – they would work out the most effective use and the most efficient routings for the various acts. Acts either signed an exclusive contract with the VMA or they did not work, and likewise vaudeville theaters either booked through the VMA or they had no access to any act under contract to the VMA. The VMA not only controlled all of the work, but they levied a 5 percent booking commission on each act for every engagement. If a vaudeville performer wanted to work, they not only had to sign exclusively with the VMA, but they also had 5 percent of their already meager salaries withheld and sent back to the VMA office by each local theater manager. The acts banded together to form the first performer's union in the U.S. called "The White Rats" ("rats" being "star" backwards). "The White Rats" attempted a work stoppage on Washington's Birthday in 1901 (traditionally a big box-office day), but were beaten down by the VMA and were reduced to minimal enrollment by the end of the year.[4] The trend towards trusts and consortiums, so prevalent in the U.S. at the time, became the rule in vaudeville, under the VMA.

Although vaudeville thrives, musicals need new voices

While vaudeville thrived, musicals had a rockier start to the decade. Of the forty-eight musicals that opened between 1900 and 1902, only ten ran more than 100 performances. *Florodora* was a huge hit, at 553 performances and Weber and Fields had good success with *Fiddle-dee-dee* (1900, 262 performances) and *Hoity Toity* (1901, 259 performances); but most other musicals offered in the first few years of the decade were either second-rate imports or pale imitations of second-rate imports. Figure 4.1 lists each show from the 1900–01 season along with the length of its run. Even the titles fail to promise exciting theatre, just the same warmed-over fare that Broadway had served up for years. Coming into the 1902 season the *New York Times* questioned if

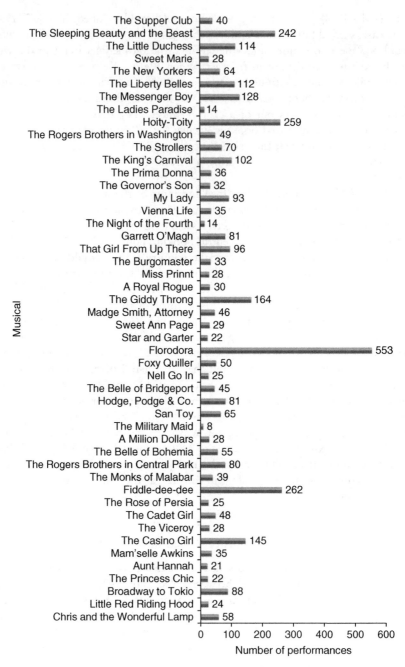

Figure 4.1 Musicals produced in the 1900–01 season and the length of their runs

musical theatre had just been a passing fad in an article titled "Musical Comedies' Vogue Said to be on the Wane."

> In the not far distant future the musical comedy and its kin will be found among the "have beens," so far as concerns New York. Nearly all agree that this cycle is dead; that the public is ready for a change toward the serious. Some assert that the change will be toward serious comedy. Others advance the idea of melodrama, and still others pick tragedy as the coming feature.[5]

Musical theatre had hit an impasse. The developing sense of national identity had begun to call for voices that spoke a clearly American idiom in America's popular culture. Some of these voices would speak through their art and some through their commerce, but speak they would.

Competition for the Syndicate – the Shuberts

Sam Shubert (1878–1905), Lee Shubert (1871–1953) and Jacob (J.J.) Shubert (1879–1963), born and raised in Syracuse, New York, worked their way up from poverty and founded what became the world's largest theatrical empire

Three brothers, sons of an abusive alcoholic father who had fled persecution in Poland to upstate New York, began a theatrical empire that would threaten and overwhelm the Syndicate.

Sam, Lee and Jacob Shubert began with little education or prospects, but quickly found themselves operating theaters in Syracuse, Buffalo, Rochester, Utica, Troy and Albany. In 1900, they moved into the territory of the Syndicate when Sam signed a three-year lease on the Herald Square Theatre. The Syndicate did not like these upstarts muscling in on their business and a war ensued. By 1901, the Brothers were producing their own plays in addition to managing the theater. Despite pressure from the Syndicate, by 1904 the Shuberts had acquired ten theaters including the Casino and the Princess in New York, the Hyperion in New Haven, the Dearborn in Chicago and the Colonial in Boston. By 1905, Sam Shubert had managed to broker an agreement with Erlanger, easing the tensions; but when Sam was killed in 1905 in a train accident Erlanger reneged on the agreement. Grief-stricken, Lee and J.J. recommitted themselves to building their own empire and tearing down Erlanger and the Syndicate.

Lee was known for his cold and emotionless demeanor and his ruthlessness in business matters, and J.J. was a violent and coarse man who made a number of headlines by "socking, slapping, chasing and swearing at stars and chorus girls."[6] He was known to hit chorus girls who complained about backstage conditions. Ruthless or not, the Shuberts were highly successful; and by 1924 they had eighty-six theatres and were making a million dollars a week in ticket sales. By the time the time the Depression hit, they owned, operated, managed or booked nearly a thousand theaters across the United States; they controlled 60 percent of the legitimate theaters in the United States; they owned their own ticket brokerage; a dancing and singing school and an enormous amount of real estate – and were producing one quarter of the plays in America.[7]

> **George Michael Cohan (1878–1942)**, the entertainer, playwright, compo-
> ser, lyricist, actor, singer, dancer and producer, represented a brash and
> brassy kind of American "can-do" spirit. He embodied the excitement and
> energy of his time, by playing the tough little guy who succeeds based on
> his guts, nerve and "never-say-die" spirit.

The man who owned Broadway

George M. Cohan captured the public imagination with his unabashedly proud American "can-do" attitude, his scrappy and self-confident swagger and his honest and genuine sentiments. He was "born in a trunk," raised on the road in vaudeville houses and knew the heart of the working man. His songs captured the imagination and pleased the ear with their simplicity and rousing sentiment.

Cohan was born on July 3, in a small hotel in Providence, RI, that catered to traveling theatre people. His parents were vaudeville entertainers, and George made his debut at age eight in velveteen pants, billed as "Master Georgie – violin tricks and tinkling tunes." By age eleven, he was doing a buck and wing dance act, and two years later, he transitioned from vaudeville to the legitimate theatre, playing the title character in the tour of *Peck's Bad Boy*. Henry Peck was a mischievous boy who liked to pull pranks just to create chaos and mayhem – as Cohan matured he never lost the scrappy, cocky, self-assured qualities that served him in the character of Henry Peck.

Throughout the 1890s, the Cohan family appeared together as "the Four Cohans" in minstrel shows, circuses and museums. They worked for Tony Pastor, where George learned the power of the patriotic anthem; a lesson he took to heart, going on to write such patriotic songs as "Yankee Doodle Boy," "Over There" and "You're a Grand Old Flag." Cohan was more successful at writing patriotic songs than anyone, except perhaps Irving Berlin.

In 1901, at age twenty-three, George wrote, composed, directed, produced and starred in his first Broadway musical, *The Governor's Son*. It was not hailed by the critics:

> As a comedy, the affair was not worth considering [...]. George Cohan,
> the youngest of the family, and the chief fun-maker in the combination is

the author. Josephine Cohan is about his age, and a very agile dancer. They are about all there is to the four Cohans. [...] The dull moments in the "musical comedy" were many, the opening of the first act being particularly stupid.[8]

George learned from every success or failure and three years later, in 1903, his first bona fide Broadway hit, *Little Johnny Jones*, opened, featuring two of his greatest songs, "Yankee Doodle Boy" and "Give My Regards to Broadway." Over the ten years between 1901 and 1911, George wrote, composed, directed, produced and starred in twenty-five new musicals on Broadway in addition to mounting five revivals – thirty productions in ten years. That does not include his touring – George always starred in the tours of his shows. He would go on the road with a tour and take the cast of his upcoming show on the road with him so that he could rehearse the new show during the day, perform in the current show in the evening and do his rewrites at night.

Cohan's adult stage persona was taken from his roots in *Peck's Bad Boy* and as a buck and wing dancer – buck and wing is a highly energized dance combining aspects of clogging and tap dancing. When Cohan and sister Josie danced together nothing got in their way – they would literally dance over the furniture. George's dancing never let up – powerful, grounded, aggressive and extremely masculine. His vocal style was strong as well; he would speak the lyrics clearly and loudly on pitch, punching out the words so that they were all clearly understood. Whether writing, composing, directing, producing or performing; energy, self-assurance and a willingness to stand up for himself or anyone else in need defined Cohan's work. These qualities made Cohan the quintessential American musical comedy persona at the turn of the century. At a time when the young country was feeling its adolescent prowess, Cohan displayed those qualities on the stage for all to see and cheer.

Every generation's star entertainers have personas that resonate with the public. Jimmy Stewart, Henry Fonda, Humphrey Bogart and John Wayne had film personas that spoke to the public in the 1930s through the 1970s. George Clooney, Russell Crowe, and Tom Hanks are more contemporary examples; these actors appeal to their audience just like Cohan appealed to his. The tough, pugnacious, loveable Irish-American patriot, a man who would defend his family and his country at every turn, was Cohan's image.

Of composer, conductor, cellist **Victor Herbert (1859–1924)**, biographer Neil Gould wrote, "Victor Herbert, as a musician, conductor, and, above all, composer ... touched every corner of American musical life at the turn of the century, ... His most enduring legacy is ... as one of the grandfathers of the modern musical theater."[9]

Composer, lyricist and orchestrator Victor Herbert who, like Cohan, was of Irish descent was another important new American voice on Broadway in the 1900s. Born in Ireland and trained at Germany's Stuttgart Academy, Herbert immigrated to New York in 1886, when his wife, a soprano, was offered a contract with the Metropolitan Opera. Herbert was immediately embraced by the musical community as a cellist and conductor upon arrival in New York. Although schooled in the classical European style, he held America and all things American close to his heart, which one hears in his soaring melodies and strong harmonies. Before ragtime and the foxtrot took over popular music, around the time of World War I, Herbert's was the most popular music in America. The only other composers of the time that came close to Herbert's success were Cohan and John Philip Sousa. While Cohan's songs were written for the working man, Herbert traveled in loftier circles with his background in classical and symphonic music. Herbert began his New York musical life working with conductor Walter Damrosch, ultimately becoming assistant conductor for the New York Philharmonic; he was also the principal conductor of the Pittsburgh Symphony for five years. Herbert's classical esthetic in combination with his flawless sense of melody and staunch patriotism made him the favorite of the operetta fans.

In 1894, his first operetta, *Prince Ananias* opened at the Broadway Theatre. *Prince Ananias'* immediate popularity spurred him on to write seven more operettas for Broadway before the end of the century, *The Wizard of the Nile* (1895), *The Serenade* (1897), *The Fortune Teller* (1898), *Cyrano de Bergerac* (1899), *The Singing Girl* (1899), *The Ameer* (1899) and *The Viceroy* (1900). He took three years off to focus on his symphonic works; but returned to Broadway with the operetta that would be one of his most lasting, *Babes in Toyland* (1903).

Herbert's output for the stage was prodigious. He wrote two operas, forty-three operettas, and incidental music for ten stage productions in addition to instrumental and symphonic works for the concert stage. Most of Herbert's operettas tell the story of the ability of simple honest American goodness to triumph over Old World ways.

Musically, Herbert's style can best be described as turn of the century eclecticism. Most theatre composers of the day imitated either the Viennese operettas or the operettas of Sir Arthur Sullivan, but Herbert was comfortable in many styles, and loved to take a particular tune through a variety of styles – brassy march, Italian folk tune, cakewalk, Irish, Indian, Egyptian music and so on. His embrace of the musical melting pot of America gives him his uniquely American sound.

In addition to fusing old-world classical training with an American sensibility, Herbert is responsible for composers' control over their own score. At the turn of the century, producers would slash scores to ribbons, taking out songs willy-nilly and interpolating songs by other composers as a matter of course. Herbert viewed a Broadway score as the unified vision of one composer. He insisted that no changes could be made in his scores without his permission, and helped to banish the era of cuts and interpolations. Starting with Victor Herbert, one composer would be responsible for the creation of a musical theatre score in its entirety, allowing for the rise of "star" composers.

Herbert worked hard on behalf of composers' rights. He lobbied and testified for the Copyright Act of 1909 and was a founding member of ASCAP (the American Society of Composers, Authors and Publishers), the guild that protects the rights of composers and lyricists. One day, when Herbert was in a restaurant and heard one of his songs played, it occurred to him that he should receive compensation. He sued the restaurant owner over the rights to perform his material; it was this lawsuit that led to the creation of ASCAP.

Herbert left a tremendous legacy in his catalog of operettas, operas and symphonic writings. Among Herbert's songs still sung today are "Toyland" from *Babes in Toyland*, "I Want What I Want When I Want It" from *Mlle. Modiste*, "Ah, Sweet Mystery of Life" from *Naughty Marietta* and "Art is Calling Me (I Want to Be a Prima Donna)" from *The Enchantress*.

> Writers, directors, stars and producers, **Bert Williams (1874–1922) and George Walker (1873–1911)** were the first successful African-American team in the musical theatre. Limited early in their careers to only portraying broad grotesque stereotypes, they developed African-American characters of increasing depth and dimension. In his solo career, after Walker's death, Williams went on to break many color barriers on the stage.

In 1893, Egbert "Bert" Williams and George Walker met in San Francisco, after solo careers performing in saloons, restaurants, road shows and blackface minstrel shows. After two years developing an act in San Francisco in which they did not play derogatory stereotypes of African Americans, they made their way to Chicago to join Isham's Octoroons, a minstrel troupe. They were let go after one week, after which they chose to embrace the prevalent racial stereotype; they put together a new act billing themselves as "The Two Real Coons."

> They based their act on standard minstrel routines reduced to a two-man performance: Walker played the part of a dandy and told the jokes, and Williams, dressed in mismatched, oversized clothes, played the straight man. After the audience reacted favorably to a performance in which he blackened his face, Williams donned the burnt-cork mask for the rest of his professional life.[10]

In 1896, they made a big splash in the musical farce *The Gold Bug*, in which their performance of the cakewalk is credited with keeping the show running for a thirty-six-week tour. This successful tour brought Williams and

Walker to New York, where they procured a booking in Koster and Bial's Music Hall. But their hope of transcending grotesque stereotypes had not died, and during this time and a subsequent engagement in London, Williams wrote:

> Long before our run terminated, we discovered an important fact: that the hope of the colored performer must be in making a radical departure from the old time "darky" style of singing and dancing. So we set ourselves the task of thinking along new lines. The first move was to hire a flat on 53rd St., furnish it, and throw our doors. ... The Williams and Walker flat soon became the headquarters of all the artistic young men of our race who were stage struck.[11]

On October 11, 1901, Williams and Walker became the first African-American recording artists, recording for the Victor Company. With twenty-eight recordings of songs like "The Phrenologist Coon," "When It's All Going Out and Nothing Coming In," "The Ghost of a Coon" and "My Little Zulu Babe," Williams was a hit as a recording artist in the fledgling industry and made many recordings over the next twenty years.

Meanwhile, the Williams and Walker flat on 53rd Street managed to produce several successful musical theatrical entertainments, song and dance and comedy shows with no particular plot – the best of these were *A Lucky Coon*, *Sons of Ham* and *The Policy Players*. In addition, in 1902 they produced *In Dahomey*, which had a profitable run on Broadway, a seven-month tour of England and a forty-week tour of the U.S. *In Dahomey* made the cakewalk an international dance sensation.

In Dahomey also featured a song that would become one of Williams' signature pieces, "I'm A Jonah Man." In this song, Williams found the essence of the character he would play for his entire performing life:

> Nearly all of my successful songs have been based on the idea that I am getting the worst of it. I am the "Jonah Man," the man who, even if it rained soup, would be found with a fork in his hand and no spoon in sight, the man whose fighting relatives come to visit him and whose head is always dented by the furniture they throw at each other. There are endless variations of the idea, fortunately; but if you sift them, you will find the principle of human nature at the bottom of them all.[12]

In 1906 Williams and Walker were active in organizing an African-American actors union called The Negro's Society. They followed up *In Dahomey* with two more successful shows. *Abyssinia* (1906) premiered the other song that Williams was associated with for the rest of his life, "Nobody." Williams' stage persona is the basis for the character of Amos in John Kander and Fred Ebb's musical *Chicago*, and the song "Nobody" is the model for Amos' song "Mr. Cellophane."

Williams and Walker's last show together, *Bandana Land* (1908), introduced a sketch that Williams continued to use for most of his career in which he pantomimed a game of poker in total silence. Using only facial expressions and body language he acted out a game of poker with changes of fortune coming on the turn of every card. *Bandana Land* was a success, but unfortunately, during the tour, in 1909, George Walker suffered a stroke, began to stutter and show the effects of memory loss, symptoms of tertiary syphilis, the disease that ultimately took his life in 1911. Bert Williams went on to a career as one of the great entertainers of the twentieth century. Williams and Walker left a significant legacy and opened the door for African-American writers, performers, directors, designers and producers.

Europe still hasn't lost its voice

European music theatre was still very much a part of the American musical theatre. Internationally the biggest hit since Gilbert and Sullivan's *HMS Pinafore* was a Viennese operetta, *The Merry Widow*, by unknown Austrian/Hungarian composer, Franz Lehár. *The Merry Widow* was so successful that it was translated into more than twenty-five languages; at one point it was running in five separate theaters in Buenos Aires, in five different languages. The 1907 London production ran for 718 performances and the New York production in the same year ran for 416. Originally produced on a shoestring in 1905 at the Theater-an-der-Wein in Vienna, using left-over sets and costumes, it is reported to have had more than 70,000 performances all told in various productions in cities around the world in the more than a century since its première.

The success of *The Merry Widow* is attributed to its ravishing melodies, the emotional depth of its music and the sophisticated use of harmony and orchestral color employed in the telling of a moving story. Emotional depth was not generally found in operetta at the time, nor was sophisticated use of harmony and orchestral color.

The Merry Widow is Hanna Glawari, a rich widow, and her countryman, Count Danilo Danilovitsch, who courts her in an attempt to keep her money in the principality. It is elegant, romantic, melodic, light, frothy and delicious, and people ate it up – and continue to today. One of the operetta's great moments is "I Love You So," the duet in which Glawari and Danilovitsch waltz – the song, known as "the Merry Widow Waltz," swept the world. Sheet music could not be printed fast enough. Cecil Smith described the opening night in New York:

> "The Merry Widow Waltz" appeared first in hints by the orchestra; Brian and then Miss Jackson began to hum it; tentatively and experimentally at first, then with a crescendo of fervor, the couple moved into the waltz. As their dance continued, they became faster and lighter, until it seemed that their feet scarcely touched the stage at all. With this single dance, this single tune, the aging musical theatre recaptured its youth. The audience

was transfixed as it watched the scene. At the end of the tumult of applause forced an encore, and another encore, and still another.[13]

"Merry Widow" products swept into the marketplace; most of them were unlicensed. Every woman wanted to be Hanna Glawari, and so there were "Merry Widow" hats (based on the hat worn in the London production), shoes, perfume and corsets (the Merry Widow corset is still sold in lingerie shops). There were also "Merry Widow" cigars, cocktails, chocolates, scallops, dogs, and anything else that could be sold using the name.

The Merry Widow's success initiated a wave of light romantic operetta with lush, melodic scores. While it appears to be a retreat to the older European model, *The Merry Widow* represents a step towards a musical theatre in which all elements are employed in telling the story, and it was a great leap forward for dance in the musical theatre. The swirl of the waltz across the stage brought the stage visually to life in a way never seen before. This animated waltz:

> presented in the intimate, gallant terms of the ballroom rather than the formal figurations prescribed by the established conventions. In "The Merry Widow," the ballroom dance was glorified as a symbol of romantic love and placed in the focus of attention. It dealt a deathblow to the marches, drills, and empty convolutions that had punctuated the musical-comedy performances until then. It opened the way for Vernon and Irene Castle, the tango, the turkey trot, and the fox trot. It humanized dancing, and made it warm, immediate and personal.[14]

Richard Traubner points out that it was "the beginning of a new wave of modern operettas in which the waltz was used for romantic, psychological purposes, and danced as much as sung."[15]

The success of *The Merry Widow* inspired an intense craze of new romantic Viennese operettas, including *The Dollar Princess* (1909) and *The Chocolate Soldier* (1909). However, none achieved the success or beloved reputation as *The Merry Widow*.

Why operettas, in 1907? First, they were extremely well written – the writers of operetta were craftsmen of the first degree. Franz Lehár, Jacques Offenbach, Johann Strauss – their music whips up a frothy lightness and sweeps the audience away in melodic splendor; additionally, *The Merry Widow* opened in America at exactly the right time. October 1907 saw a bankers' panic in which the New York Stock Exchange lost almost 50 percent from its highs the previous year. Panic occurred, many state and local banks and trust companies declared bankruptcy and collapsed and panic extended across the country. The panic would have been worse if banker and financier J.P. Morgan had not pledged large sums of his own money to keep the banking system afloat. *The Merry Widow* opened on October 21, 1907; what could be more desirable entertainment than a light, frothy, confection of a show to help people forget the troubles going on in their lives.

In *High Steel: The Daring Men Who Built the World's Greatest Skyline*, Jim Rasenberger sums up the ethos of the first decade of the twentieth century. "I think that Americans were at this stage where they had enough confidence scientifically and technologically to think that anything was possible but not enough knowledge to realize that, in fact, everything was *not* possible. So there was this wonderful sense of limitlessness."[16] The national character was embodied by such success stories as Horatio Alger, Henry Ford and Theodore Roosevelt. This is the same "can-do" spirit that we have been looking at in the work of Cohan, Herbert, the Shubert Brothers, Keith, Albee, Walter, Scott Joplin and Walker and Williams and others.

Chapter summary

- *Florodora.*
- Three new voices:

  1 George M. Cohan
  2 Victor Herbert
  3 Bert Williams and George Walker.

- Keith, Albee and Walter develop the VMA.
- The Shubert Brothers begin building their empire.
- *The Merry Widow.*
- Growing audiences for both the Broadway and vaudeville.
- American voices singing American songs rather than copying Europe.

Notes

1 Lois Gordon and Alan Gordon, *American Chronicle: Year by Year Through the Twentieth Century*, New Haven: Yale University Press, 1999, p. 6.
2 "The girl on the swing" refers to one of Stanford White's favorite "games," to have Nesbit perched nude on a swing above him, which was common knowledge at the time. After Nesbit's husband killed White in a fit of madness and jealousy, Nesbit, in need of an income, was reduced to performing a vaudeville act on a swing to exploit her sordid past.
3 Adoptive grandfather to the great American dramatist, Edward Albee, playwright of *Who's Afraid of Virginia Woolf.*
4 Arthur Frank Wertheim, *Vaudeville Wars: How The Keith-Albee and Orpheum Circuits Controlled the Big-Time and Its Performers*, New York: Palgrave, Macmillan, 2009.
5 *New York Times*, September 7, 1902. Web, accessed June 23, 2011, http://query.nytimes.com/mem/archive-free/pdf?res=F40715F63A591B728DD-DAE0894D1405B828CF1D3
6 Foster Hirsch, *The Boys From Syracuse: The Shuberts' Theatrical Empire*, Carbondale, IL: Southern Illinois University Press, 1998, p. 109.
7 Encyclopedia of World Biography, 2nd edition, 17 volumes, Gale Research, 1998. Reprinted on *Broadway: The American Musical. Stars over Broadway. Shubert Brothers PBS*. Web, http://www.pbs.org/wnet/broadway/stars/shubert-brothers

8 "'The Governor's Son,' The Four Cohans Produce a 'Musical Comedy' at the Savoy," *New York Times*, February 26, 1901. Web, accessed June 22, 2011, http://query.nytimes.com/mem/archive-free/pdf?res=FA0B17FA3F5B11738DDDAF0A94DA405B818CF1D3

9 Neil Gould, *Victor Herbert: A Theatrical Life*, New York: Fordham University Press, 2011. Web, Project MUSE, accessed May 5, 2014, http://muse.jhu.edu

10 Thomas L. Morgan, Jass.com: Bert Williams & George Walker, 1992. Web, accessed June 30, 2011, http://jass.com/w&w.html

11 Bert Williams, quoted by Mary White Ovington, *Half a Man: The Status of the Negro in New York*, New York: Longmans, Green, and Co., 1911, pp 130–1.

12 Bert Williams, "The Comic Side of Trouble," *American Magazine 85*, January 1918, pp. 33–34.

13 Cecil Smith and Glenn Litton, *Musical Comedy in America*, London: Routledge, 1987, p. 88.

14 Cecil Smith and Glenn Litton, *Musical Comedy in America*, London: Routledge, 1987, pp. 88–89.

15 Richard Traubner, *Operetta: A Theatrical History*, Garden City, NY: Doubleday & Company, 1983, p. 321.

16 Jim Rasenberger, quoted by Carey Winfrey in "Pulled by Bears: In 1908 Anything Was Possible," *Smithsonian Magazine*, January 2008. Web, Smithsonian.com, accessed July 11, 2011, http://www.smithsonianmag.com/history-archaeology/editors-200801.html

Further reading

Florodora

Lamb, Andrew. *Leslie Stuart: Composer of Florodora (Forgotten Stars of the Musical Theatre)*. London: Routledge, 2002.

Vaudeville

Travis, S.D. *No Applause – Just Throw Money: The Book that Made Vaudeville Famous*. London: Faber and Faber, 2006. An excellent book chronicling the history of vaudeville.

Wertheim, Arthur Frank. *Vaudeville Wars: How The Keith-Albee and Orpheum Circuits Controlled the Big-Time and Its Performers*. New York, NY: Palgrave, Macmillan, 2009. An excellent history of the machinations of the businessmen who ran vaudeville.

The Shubert Brothers

Hirsch, Foster. *The Boys From Syracuse: The Shuberts' Theatrical Empire*. Carbondale, IL: Southern Illinois University Press, 1998. This biography does not attempt to "prettify" any of the Shuberts' shortcomings; an excellent resource.

George M. Cohan

McCabe, John. *George M. Cohan: The Man Who Owned Broadway*. Boston, MA: Da Capo Press, 1980.

Victor Herbert

Gould, Neil. *Victor Herbert: A Theatrical Life*. New York, NY: Fordham University Press, 2008. This biography is comprehensive and exceptionally well written.

Walker and Williams

Forbes, Camille F. *Introducing Bert Williams: Burnt Cork, Broadway and the Story of America's First Black Star*. New York, NY: Basic Civitas Books, 2008. An excellent and well-researched biography, almost 100 pages devoted to Williams' work with Walker.

The first act

5 The Princess and the great revues, 1907–20

The operetta craze

Early twentieth-century operettas were confections – light and airy musically and in subject matter. At the turn of the century, operettas were the rage throughout Europe; the two centers being Paris, home to composer Jacques Offenbach (*The Tales of Hoffman, Orpheus in the Underworld*) and Vienna, home to composer Johann Strauss (*Die Fledermaus, The Gypsy Baron*). Gilbert and Sullivan's work represents English-language operetta. However, the most successful and influential operetta of the time was Franz Lehár's *The Merry Widow*.

The Merry Widow, by the unknown Lehár, had taken Europe by storm with successful productions in: Vienna, Hamburg, Berlin, Budapest, London and Paris. By 1907 it had also become the reigning smash hit of New York. Because success breeds imitation, European operetta became the vogue. Its success was so definitive, that for seven years the most successful musicals in New York and across the U.S. were either European imports or imitations of them. In the wake of the economic chaos of the 1907 Bankers' Panic, these operettas offered middle-class audiences a window onto the world of dukes, barons and Grand Balls held in embassies in a swirl of glorious music and comic turns. Audiences wanted to escape into a world of European royalty, and these shows offered them that opportunity. Just as people during the Great Depression would flock to see Fred Astaire and Ginger Rogers whirl around on the silver screen in top hat and tails, people of the late 1900s and 1910s thronged to operettas.

Operettas were melodic, beautifully sung, set in ballrooms, castles, and places that most people would never see. Musically sumptuous, beautifully constructed and fun to watch, operettas were the highest culture that Europe had to offer. *A Waltz Dream* (1908), *The Dollar Princess, The Chocolate Soldier* (both 1909), *The Spring Maid* (1910), *The Rose Maid* (1912), and a string of Lehár's operettas were just some of the many operettas imported from Europe during this period.

The most successful American operetta writer was Victor Herbert. His output was prodigious; including twelve new operettas during the seven-year stretch between 1907 and 1914, including some of his most successful: *Mlle.*,

Modiste (1907), *Naughty Marietta* (1910) and *Sweethearts* (1913). Born in Dublin, Ireland, and trained in Stuttgart, Germany, Herbert was grounded in a European sensibility, but passionately loved his adopted country and all things American. Melding his European training with an American energy and verve, Herbert created a tradition of American operetta.

George M. Cohan managed a prodigious output during this period, composing, writing lyrics and books, producing, directing and starring in seven musicals in these seven years, plus taking on the same duties for five plays, writing and producing two minstrel shows, and producing another twelve plays with his partner Sam Harris. In all, Cohan mounted twenty-six new productions on Broadway – plus several revivals and many touring companies – all in a seven-year period.

But Cohan was the exception that proved the rule. For the most part, by 1907, America was crazy for operettas about European aristocracy. The most successful operettas between 1907 and 1914 include: *The Merry Widow*, *The Dollar Princess*, *The Chocolate Soldier*, *Naughty Marietta* and *Sweethearts*.

There were a few musicals that dealt with American subject matter. But shows like *The Alaskan* (twenty-nine performances), *Miss Pocahontas* (sixteen performances), and *Little Miss Fixit* (sixty-four performances) were less successful. The smart money was on operetta.

> **Rudolf Friml (1879–1972)** – Born and trained in Prague, Friml embraced his adopted homeland. He found success with his first operetta, *The Firefly*, but his greatest successes would be in the 1920s with *Rose-Marie*, *The Vagabond King* and *The Three Musketeers*. His career as a concert pianist lasted into his nineties.

The king and the two crown princes of American operetta

While Victor Herbert was the king of American operetta between 1907 and 1914, the other two great American operetta composers were Rudolf Friml and Sigmund Romberg. Friml was born in Prague, Czechoslovakia, and Romberg in Nagykanizsa, Hungary; both immigrated to the United States, embraced their new homeland and fused old-world traditions with American energy; European classicism joined to the optimistic sense of twentieth-century America. Romberg had studied in Vienna, while Friml had studied composition with Dvorak at the Prague Conservatory; both carried the European sensibility prized by American audiences of the time. By the time of their earliest successes on Broadway, both were firmly established in the upper echelons of classical music in New York; bridging the two worlds made them simultaneously accredited and accessible.

Friml's *The Firefly* opened at the Lyric Theatre in 1912, produced by Arthur Hammerstein (Oscar II's uncle), where it ran for 120 performances. Victor Herbert was originally to have written *The Firefly*, but had had an argument with the fiery diva, Emma Trentini, and left the project. Hammerstein turned to the unknown Friml to compose the score. The story was about a poor young woman who sings on the streets for coins, who disguises herself as a boy in order to serve as a cabin boy on a ship to Bermuda. She falls in love, complications arise and she ultimately becomes a grand opera diva. *The Firefly* brought instant success to Friml:

> [Friml] has written one of the most popular scores imaginable. For once it was possible to be patient with the encore fiends. They were not content with repetitions of practically every number, but had the little Trentini out after the curtain had fallen on the second act and would not let her go until she sang a verse of the particularly insinuating number, "Gianini," with which, in the first act, she had made the rafters ring.[1]

Friml had visited the United States from his native Prague in 1901 and in 1904 before immigrating to the U.S. in 1906. Of his twenty-one Broadway scores, the most well remembered today are *Rose Marie* (1924, with lyricist Oscar Hammerstein II), set in the Canadian Rockies, and *The Vagabond King* (1925), set in fifteenth-century France. Friml was particularly successful at evoking distant places and times musically. Friml also wrote a large body of concert work and many film scores.

Born in the Austro-Hungarian Empire, **Sigmund Romberg (1887–1951)** studied engineering and composition in Vienna. Having immigrated to the U.S. in 1914 he was hired by the Shuberts as their house composer. Although he wrote for many different formats, his most enduring are his operettas, like: *Blossom Time*, *The Student Prince*, *The Desert Song*, *Rosalie* and *The New Moon*, which still appear on the schedules of light opera companies across the world.

The Shubert Brothers hired Romberg to write songs for their revue *The Whirl of the World* in 1914, which ran for 161 performances. *The Whirl of the World* was created for the Shuberts' Winter Garden Theatre, known for housing spectacles, lots of scenery, big casts, big orchestras and special effects. The headline of the New York Times review read, "Brilliant Show at the Winter Garden; Color, Dance, Song, and Fun, with an Added Touch of Effective Spectacle. Girls and Gowns Galore."[2] People sought out the latest Winter Garden show for the scenic spectacle in the same way that people go to see the latest Cirque show. *The Whirl of the World* delighted critics and audiences alike and immediately put Romberg in demand. The Shubert Brothers hired him as a staff writer and within the year he was averaging four to five new shows on Broadway every season. He was one of the most prolific Broadway composers ever; in 1924 he premiered seven new musicals, including one of his most popular, *The Student Prince*.

Romberg wrote for Broadway through the 1920s, moving to Hollywood in the 1930s as many Broadway artists did, looking for work. He returned to Broadway only briefly and sporadically. During his Broadway days, Romberg wrote scores for more operettas, book musicals and revues than practically any other composer. Even at a time when composers, lyricists and book writers would churn out a show, having it ready to go into rehearsal in six to eight weeks, Romberg's body of work is astounding. Putting Romberg's name above a title usually guaranteed an audience, and Romberg had a voracious appetite for his work.

Most musicals of the time were based on previously existing source material – just as most musicals are now. Today many musicals are based on films; the musicals of the 1900s and 1910s were often based on popular plays, other musicals or novels. Operettas were driven by beautiful voices singing soaring melodies rather than by plot. This meant that a composer could store a bunch of great tunes in his "trunk" and pull out a couple for every production. Being able to write during times of inspiration and use the material later helped these composers to seem so astoundingly prolific by today's standards. The love songs had to be lush and soaring (as in "Ah, Sweet Mystery of Life") and the comic songs had to allow the comics and character actors to ham it up a bit. Beyond that, not much else mattered, so structuring and writing a musical then was substantially simpler than it is today.

Herbert, Friml and Romberg dominated American operetta. Operettas continued to be popular through the 1920s, although other more contemporary musicals overtook them in popularity after 1920 or so, as ragtime and jazz became the rage and the intoxicating economic boom of the 1920s ushered in the Jazz Age. Still there would be a place in the hearts of the audiences for operettas, revivals continued through the 1970s and light opera or operetta companies keep these works alive today.

The world order shifts

Until the 1914–15 season American culture tended to be imported or copied from Europe. Musical theatre came most often from Vienna, Paris or London; and most American musicals were adaptations of European pieces, or written in the style of European musicals or operettas. In the mid 1910s, however, a unique confluence of events created the perfect environment for the Americanization of the musical theatre.

In June 1914 Archduke Franz Ferdinand of Austria, heir apparent to the Austro-Hungarian throne, and his wife were assassinated. This set in motion events that resulted in the outbreak of World War I, one month later. Within months, the German Navy, fearing that transatlantic ships might be transporting weapons and troops, began shutting down transatlantic shipping lanes.

In May 1915, a German U-boat sank the *Lusitania*, a passenger ship traveling from New York to Liverpool; 1,195 of the 1,958 passengers aboard the *Lusitania* died. This halted all non-essential transatlantic travel for the duration of the war. Suddenly the open importation of everything – including musical theatre – was shut down.

Importing a show became impossible; even going to London to scout new shows and acquire rights was potentially deadly. In addition, most of the younger generation of European musical theatre artists were off fighting the war, and older writers, too old to go off to war, were aging and either dying off or becoming less and less relevant; so there was substantially less new European material available.

As America watched the War in Europe, the nation was swept up in a surge of national pride the likes of which it had never known. As it geared up to enter the War, America was ready for American voices speaking in American idioms, using the imagery of newly emerging American myths and archetypes. By the end of the War, America felt like the world's savior, and the U.S. economy had shifted from that of a debtor nation to being lender to the world.

> By 1919, New York had displaced its last and greatest rival, London, as the investment capital of the world, and money was flowing into the city, one British observer remarked, "as water flows downhill."[3]

New York was thriving. There was money to produce theatre, there was money to see theatre and the Jazz Age lay just ahead.

New composers with distinctly American voices

As Herbert, Friml and Romberg reigned over the worlds of Broadway, operetta and popular music in America, two important new American composers arrived on the scene. These composers' musical vocabulary was distinctly American, informed by the tempo and rhythms of the city, by the influence of ragtime and jazz, and by the energy, verve and can-do spirit of the American heroes of the day.

Irving Berlin (1888–1989). Born in Russia, Berlin immigrated to New York at age five. Throughout an eighty-year career his music spoke directly to people's hearts. Berlin wrote the kind of jazzy syncopated tunes that the country was ready for, and achingly sweet, simple ballads. Cole Porter has been quoted saying "Irving Berlin does not have a place in American music, he *is* American music."

Born Israel Isidore Baline in Tyumen, Russia, the Jewish Berlin grew up impoverished in New York's Lower East Side, one of eight children. Forced by necessity to work as a youngster, Berlin did anything he could, including working as a waiter at a Chinatown café. When the house pianist at a competing café successfully published a song, copies of which were on sale by the cash register, Baline's boss called for a song that *he* could publish. Baline and his house pianist wrote "Marie, From Sunny Italy." In printing the music, a typesetter's mistake transformed Israel Baline to Irving Berlin – and Berlin was a published songwriter. Although he never learned to read music, he composed over 3,000 songs, many of which are still popular today. These include: "Alexander's Ragtime Band," "I Love A Piano," "Blue Skies," "Puttin' on the Ritz," "Cheek to Cheek," "Easter Parade," "Heat Wave," "Top Hat, White Tie and Tails," "God Bless America," "There's No Business Like Show Business," "White Christmas" and many more.

African-American composer/pianist Scott Joplin (1867–1917) had been instrumental in taking ragtime music from the barrooms and the brothels and legitimizing it as early as the 1893 Chicago World's Fair, but Berlin turned ragtime into an international craze. In 1911, Berlin published "Alexander's Ragtime Band," which became an international hit. The song made Berlin world famous and legitimized ragtime; Berlin's song made it all right for people of all races to listen to ragtime. Thanks to Berlin, ragtime, and the jazz that descended from it, defined the pulse of urban America early in the twentieth century.

Berlin and Cohan were the two greatest American composers of patriotic songs during World War I. Speaking to this Berlin said, "a patriotic song is an emotion and you must not embarrass an audience with it, or they will hate your guts."[4]

Berlin was the primary composer and lyricist for several revues, including *The Ziegfeld Follies,* and contributed songs to various musicals and plays between 1910 and 1914. His first complete score for a musical was the successful *Watch Your Step,* starring the dance team of Vernon and Irene Castle. The program described the show as "a syncopated musical," and reviews ascribed much of the credit for the show's success to Berlin.

> More than to any one else, "Watch Your Step" belongs to Irving Berlin. He is the young master of syncopation [...]. For it, he has written a score of his mad melodies, nearly all of them the tickling sort, born to be caught up and whistled at every street corner, and warranted to set any roomful a-dancing. Berlin has always enjoyed capturing a strain of fine, operatic music and twisting it to suit his own ragtime measures, [...] "Watch Your Step" affords this song writer a rare opportunity. He has availed himself of it. In this new attack Berlin has found New York defenseless and captured it.[5]

Berlin was one of the most prolific writers on Tin Pan Alley[6] and on Broadway, writing original musicals and revues through 1933. He was responsible for writing songs for eight Ziegfeld shows, and all-told contributed to forty-eight Broadway shows between 1910 and 1933.

In 1918, Berlin enlisted in the Army to fight in World War I. They requested that he write a show for his camp, Camp Upton in Yaphank, NY. The show, *Yip, Yip, Yaphank* was performed by soldiers at the camp, and was such a hit that it moved to Broadway where it continued to be performed exclusively by soldiers. During World War II, Berlin's updated version of the show, re-titled *This*

Is the Army, was successfully revived on Broadway, and became a successful movie. Berlin also produced his own shows. With partner, Sam Harris, their Music Box Theatre housed Berlin's own series of revues, the *Music Box Revues*, in the early 1920s. After Harris' death in 1941 one half ownership of the Music Box would go to the Shubert Organization and the other half to Berlin. The period 1933 to 1940 saw Berlin in Hollywood, writing film scores, but by 1940 he had returned to Broadway, with *Louisiana Purchase*. Although so many of his successes had been in the pre-Rodgers and Hammerstein age, his greatest success, *Annie Get Your Gun*, came after, running for 1,147 performances.

Jerome Kern (1885–1945) was born in New York, and trained in New York and Heidelberg, Germany. Not content to simply write some of the greatest contemporary music of his day, Kern's music served the stories and characters; he was the first great musical dramatist.

Jerome Kern wrote over 700 songs and worked on over 100 stage works. He collaborated with every major lyricist and book writer of his time including: Guy Bolton, P.G. Wodehouse, Otto Harbach, Oscar Hammerstein, II, Dorothy Fields, Johnny Mercer, Ira Gershwin and E.Y. "Yip" Harburg.

Before Kern, most Broadway dance music was in waltz time, but Kern began writing music in the jazzier 4/4 time, leading to the inclusion of the jazz dance vocabulary onto the Broadway stage. Kern's work led to the rage of ballroom dance acts like Vernon and Irene Castle, and opened the door for Irving Berlin, Blake and Sissle and other great composers who came after. Today most non-balletic musical theatre dances are written in 4/4 time, or variations thereof. Alec Wilder claims, "All the prominent American composers of modern theatre music, living and dead, have acknowledged Kern to have been the first great native master of this genre. Without exception they consider his songs a greater inspiration than those of any other composer, and his music to be the first that was truly American in the theatre."[7] Although Kern's melodic gift was profound and his harmonic choices continue to sound fresh to listeners today, Kern also believed music in the theater should be a dramaturgical tool to further the action or to add to character development – a revolutionary concept at the time.

Born in New York, to Jewish German immigrant parents and raised in Newark, New Jersey, Kern began writing songs at the age of sixteen. To discourage him from writing music his father took him to work in the family store; but when the younger Kern accidentally bought 200 pianos rather than the two he was supposed to buy, his father relented and Kern matriculated at the New York College of Music.

Early in Kern's career, he contributed songs to other composers' shows, usually British imports, for which he would write a couple of "American" sounding songs. His career as a Broadway composer began in 1904, and by 1914, he had contributed to thirty-four Broadway musicals. Successful as he was, Kern was anxious to compose a full score, to put into practice the dramaturgical beliefs he had started to develop through his early years. That chance would come soon.

The Princess musicals

Kern, Guy Bolton and P.G. Wodehouse have been dubbed "the men who invented musical comedy." It began with the Princess musicals, a new model of musical theatre which developed to meet the requirements imposed by the economics and finances of a very small production budget and the tiny Princess Theatre.

Producer Ray Comstock had built the 299-seat Princess Theatre to house a repertoire company that would play a series of short dramas in rotation. Within two years, the repertoire company failed and Comstock, needing some attraction to keep his theater open, consulted with Elizabeth Marbury, an agent. They attempted to produce a ten-year-old British operetta, *Mr. Popple of Ippleton*, but as rehearsals began, the producers feared the piece would never work for an American audience. Marbury suggested creating a small musical in the little theater, but with so few seats to sell, they would never be able to afford to hire any of the leading writers. Comstock and Marbury talked to Kern, who brought Bolton onboard to write the book and lyrics. Seeing very little chance to recuperate any kind of substantial investment, and trying to hedge their bets, Comstock and Marbury agreed to produce the Kern/Bolton show for a budget of $7,500. Kern and Bolton were given just over a month to write their show, titled *Nobody Home*, but they were required to write their show to fit sets and costumes which had already been ordered for *Mr. Popple of Ippleton*. *Nobody Home* opened, and two months later, the demand for tickets was so high that it had to move to the much larger Maxine Elliott Theatre (935 seats) across the street to accommodate the need.

Why were *Nobody Home* and the other "Princess" musicals that followed so successful? A typical musical of the 1910s was driven by spectacle and entertainment; funny comedians and beautiful songs, usually in a traditional arioso style, made up a musical. The scenery would be spectacular enough to attract an audience. No matter what the subject matter there would have been a large chorus of beautiful girls dressed as provocatively as the setting would allow. Specialty acts would be hired and contracted to perform their specialty at a specific time, allowing them to keep other engagements during the evening – these contractual matters would all have to be taken into account in the writing of the show. For instance, for *Sunny*, in 1925, producer Charles Dillingham contracted entertainer Cliff Edwards, whose stage name was Ukulele Ike, to perform his ukulele specialty between 10:00 and 10:15. Book writer Oscar Hammerstein, II had the challenge of writing a script that would accommodate this and other contractual obligations.[8] The characters tended to be royalty or fantastical characters – lords and ladies, enchantresses, gypsies, student princes or Canadian mounties – and they employed large orchestras, based on the European model. The financial circumstances surrounding *Nobody Home* stripped the show of any possible spectacle or scenic splendor. The number of seats required that the weekly expenses be held to a minimum – therefore, there could be no chorus and the orchestra had to be as small as absolutely possible. However, having stripped away from Bolton and Kern all the things that made a musical work (in 1910's terms), they had to entirely reconceive the art form.

However, in the small Princess Theatre, where there was only room for a minimal chorus onstage or backstage, no room for anything approaching scenic spectacle and the audience was all situated within a few rows of the stage, the only option left open to Bolton and Kern was to drive the evening's entertainment with the characters and the story. The story was slight by today's terms, but all of the elements of the show, the melodies, the lyrics, the structure, the jokes and dialog, were driven by the thrust of the narrative. The music not only revealed Kern's exquisite sense of melody, it revealed character and helped to move the story forward. For the first time, there was dramatic need behind every aspect of the show. Stripped of all the trappings of the contemporary musical, Kern and Bolton offered recognizable, contemporary characters acting out a story that the audience would recognize from their own lives. The music was accessible; the jokes were snappy and contemporary. We see some of the same comic tropes that we saw in the comedies of ancient Rome – henpecked husbands, domineering wives, and ditzy or conniving maids – but here they were recognizable and contemporary. And people loved it.

> Our musical comedies ... depend as much upon plot and the development of their characters for success as upon their music, and ... they deal with subjects and peoples near to the audiences. In the development of our plot ... we endeavor to make everything count. Every line, funny or serious, is supposedly to help the plot continue to hold.[9]

For the subsequent Princess musicals, Kern and Bolton were joined by P.G. Wodehouse, and in short order *Nobody Home* was followed by *Very Good Eddie* (1915), *Have A Heart* (1917), *Oh Boy!* (1917), *Leave It to Jane* (1917), *Oh, Lady! Lady!* (1918) and *Oh, My Dear!* (1918). In addition to these seven shows, Kern wrote fifteen other shows between 1915 and 1920. Kern continued to turn out hit after hit through the 1920s and at the end of the decade he composed the score for one of the greatest and most pivotal and groundbreaking musicals, *Show Boat*, which will be dealt with in a later chapter.

As prolific as Kern's work was, he was also an activist for composers' rights. In the 1910s any song could be performed without compensation for the song's writers. In response to this, Kern co-founded ASCAP (The American Society of Composers, Authors and Publishers) along with Irving Berlin, John Philip Sousa and Victor Herbert. The Society collected royalty payments from restaurants, bars, nightclubs and other venues where music was performed, to distribute to their members based on the number of times the members' works were performed. Ultimately this coverage extended to radio and television and a competing guild, BMI (Broadcast Music, Inc.), was formed in the 1930s, as was its European counterpart, SESAC (the Society of European Stage Authors and Composers).

A new American art form, the revue

In the 1910s, Broadway saw a new American form of musical theatre, the musical revue. A revue is an evening of songs, comic sketches, dance, variety acts and choruses of beautiful girls wearing costumes that displayed their beauty to maximum effect. The revues of the 1910s and 1920s were known for lavish scenic spectacle. The material was topical and frequently satirical.

Revue had been seen earlier, but financial and cultural conditions were right for this opulent and ornate form to take off. It was a vital time and America was experiencing financial, technological and industrial expansion, thanks to the likes of J.P. Morgan, John D. Rockefeller, Thomas Edison, Henry Ford, the Wright Brothers and others. Ford's assembly line and mass-production, the Wright Brothers' airplane, Edison's electric light, all manner of electrical appliances and the wiring up of America – all helped move America forward in the economic recovery from the 1907 Bankers' Panic, with a uniquely American never-say-die spirit. European-inspired operetta continued to be popular; but the time was right for new voices, American voices, speaking a contemporary American idiom. And the revue provided a natural place for people to go hear those voices; with its short pieces, joined together to make an evening of song, dance, comedy, and always lots of pretty girls on display, it was the perfect venue for new, young writers to get heard.

The revues hold some similarities and some differences to vaudeville. In both there is no narrative, no plot; the evening's entertainment was comprised of a series of acts of different sorts – song, dance, comedy, specialties and so on. The acts that comprised an evening of vaudeville would change regularly; and individual acts were individually booked from theater to theater – there was no set "show." The performers in revues usually did not change from week to week; they would stay with the show. The revue was often created with an overarching shape, a distinctly organized "running order" that made theatrical sense, even though it was not driven by any narrative.

Since the revue audience tended to be more upscale, a bit more sophisticated than the vaudeville audience, the revues tended to be a bit more risqué, a little more socially and politically satirical and a little less traditional in their values. Vaudeville producers insisted on strictly family fare, but the material in the revues was often racier, more socially and politically outspoken.

Revues had been around for a while, but as their popularity increased in the 1910s, it was the producers whose work the audience came to see; as one would have gone to see the latest Gilbert and Sullivan show in the previous quarter century, one would go see the latest revue by Ziegfeld, George White, Earl Carroll or the Shuberts. These shows boasted the finest composers and lyricists (Berlin,

Kern, Gershwin all wrote for Ziegfeld), and the most popular performers (Fanny Brice, Will Rogers, Eddie Cantor and W.C. Fields,), but the real stars, the names above the title, who filled the seats, were the producers.

The first successful revue had been George Leaderer's *The Passing Show of 1894*, which burlesqued popular theatrical productions from the previous season. *The Passing Show of 1894* played at the Casino Theatre for 145 performances with a cast of over 100 and had an extensive and successful tour after its New York run.

With Leaderer's 1894 success at the Casino Theatre, 1895 saw a new "review" (the French spelling had not yet caught on), called *The Merry World* followed the next year by *In Gay New York*. In March of the same year Koster and Bial's Theatre, known for producing comic opera, tried their hand at review and offered *In Gayest Manhattan or Around New York in Ninety Minutes*; it only ran a couple of weeks. Every other year or so, a review would appear in the New York season, but the genre really hit its stride in 1907, when Florenz Ziegfeld opened his *Follies of 1907*.

> **Florenz Ziegfeld (1867–1932)** was one of the great showmen of the early twentieth century. In addition to the Follies, he produced several other series of revues and many plays and musicals. Ziegfeld was known as the glorifier of the American Girl.

The most famous revues were *The Ziegfeld Follies*. In 1907 Florenz Ziegfeld, Jr. was a successful Broadway producer, having already produced twelve plays and musicals in just over ten years. He had grown up in Chicago, and began his career as an impresario by promoting a strongman, Eugen Sandow. Ziegfeld had booked Sandow to appear at his father's failing nightclub in Chicago, the Trocadero. Audiences liked Sandow, but when Ziegfeld invited several high society matrons backstage to see Sandow flex his fifty-eight inch chest up close, making sure that photographers and reporters were waiting to capture and report the story, Sandow's popularity caught fire. This stunt single-handedly saved the Trocadero and taught Ziegfeld a valuable lesson in showmanship. Ziegfeld took Sandow on a two-year vaudeville tour, made a small fortune with him and lost most of it gambling. The lesson of selling Sandow's beautiful physique was not lost on Ziegfeld, who would make his name selling beautiful physiques and "glorifying the American Girl."

While preparing his first Broadway play, *A Parlor Match* (1896), Ziegfeld fell in love with his leading lady, Anna Held. Held had been a star of the *Folies Bergère* in Paris; she had a charming French accent (although the daughter of a Polish Jewish glove-maker), an hourglass figure with an eighteen-inch waist and a charming and flirtatious way. Ziegfeld won her heart and bought out her *Folies* contract. To create a publicity buzz around Held's appearance in *Parlor Match*, Ziegfeld "leaked" word to the press that Held kept her creamy complexion by taking daily baths in milk; when the buzz began to slow down he brought suit against a dairy for sending sour milk. To create a need for tickets for *Parlor Match*, Ziegfeld limited the run of the show and withheld tickets from sale in order to assure that demand outweighed supply. Then, while the show was still very popular in New York, he shut it down to take it on the road, only to return it to New York for a lengthy run after the tour. Between 1896 and 1907 Ziegfeld produced twelve shows on Broadway, seven of them starring Held.

In July 1907, Ziegfeld opened the *Follies of 1907* on the roof garden of the New York Theatre. It was, quite literally, a "review" of the season just passed. The "book" was a series of satiric sketches by Harry B. Smith, who published a newspaper column called "Follies of the Day." Ziegfeld and Held thought the title would evoke a feeling of the French *Folies Bergère*, and so they rechristened the New York Theatre roof the *Jardin de Paris* and the *Follies* was born. The 1907 edition was produced for $13,800, a modest sum even in 1907 dollars, and earned a profit of more than $130,000.

That edition of the *Follies* included a satirical impression of Teddy Roosevelt "wearing his Rough Rider uniform and displaying a spectacular array of teeth."[10] One sketch took place in Grand Central Station (then under construction for four years, with six still to go), in which the "Misinformation Department" was overseen by a character named Chauncey Depot (Chauncey Depew was the name of the lead attorney of Cornelius Vanderbilt's railroad interests). The two big rivaling opera impresarios in New York, Oscar Hammerstein I and Heinrich Conried were represented in a scene in which they fought an operatic duel. Another sketch satirized the first celebrity trial of the century from the year before, when the opera singer Enrico Caruso was jailed for molesting a woman in the monkey house of the Central Park Zoo, "annoying" her as it was reported in the newspapers of the time. Other sketches satirized Victor Herbert, John D. Rockefeller, Andrew Carnegie, Commodore Perry and other celebrities. Musical numbers included: "Budweiser's a Friend of Mine," "I Think I Oughtn't Auto Any More," "In The Surf," "The Ju-Jitsu Waltz" and "The Gibson Bathing Girls" which featured the first Ziegfeld chorus of fifty beautiful chorus girls in revealing bathing costumes.

Ziegfeld, Erlanger and Klaw, who had backed the production and whose theater housed it, had planned the *Follies of 1907* as a limited run, mounted to put the roof garden to some profitable use over the summer. The show was so successful, however, that after its initial seventy performances at the *Jardin de Paris* it moved to the Lyric Theatre for two additional weeks, went out on a two-month tour, returned to New York and played at the Grand Opera House for another week and then played for an entire month in Philadelphia. Despite critical indifference, people adored it and it made a substantial profit, convincing Ziegfeld that there was a future for this kind of entertainment (see Figure 5.1).

Ziegfeld glorified the American Girl. In what would become his trademark, he presented the most beautiful girls in the most exquisite costumes. Bedecked with massive headdresses, some weighing up to fifty pounds or more,

Figure 5.1 American dancer Marna Darby (© Underwood & Underwood/CORBIS)

sometimes wearing shockingly revealing costumes, Ziegfeld had his girls parade around the stage displaying their costumes and their beauty.

The *Follies* became a yearly tradition. The 1908 edition featured the beautiful chorus of girls as curvaceous New Jersey mosquitoes, commuting through the Holland tunnel (still under construction) and as sexy taxicabs (taxis had just been introduced to the city) with actual electric lights indicating that they were "on duty." It also introduced the popular song "Shine On Harvest Moon." The 1909 edition introduced the song "By The Light of the Silvery Moon," featured the chorus girls as battleships and offered a number in which several of the girls flew overhead in a replica of the Wright Brothers' airplane. The typical Ziegfeld show was two acts long, each act comprised of a number of lavish musical numbers featuring the Ziegfeld girls, scenes featuring the featured comics and other specialty performances. The program from the 1911 *Ziegfeld Follies* on tour in Washington, DC indicates the following scenes:

Act I: Scene I "The Customs", including two songs, "New York" and "The Widow Wood"

Act I: Scene II "Jardin de Paris, featuring a German singer from Hamburg and his "Saengerbund" (choral singers)

Act I: Scene III "A California Poppy Field", including a dance, "The Bumble Bee"

Act I: Scene IV "Everywife" (A Symbolic Play in Four Scenes) including the songs "The Girl In Pink," "The Imitation Stage," "Take Care Little Girl," "Texas Tommy," "Ephriam" and an undisclosed song

Act I: Finale – Special Musical Number

Act II: Scene I "H.M.S. Vaudeveel" Featuring a choral selection from "Pinafore"

Act II: Scene II "Tad's Daffydils"

Act II: Scene III "New York Central Depot" (Now in course of construction)

Act II: Scene IV "Exterior of New York Central Depot" (Now in course of construction) featuring songs by Bert Williams

Act II: Scene V "A Fifteen Minute Peep at 'The Pink Lady'" featuring a cakewalk dance and the song "My Beautiful Lady"

Finale[11]

In 1910, Ziegfeld introduced comedienne Fanny Brice, whom he co-starred with Bert Williams (now without Walker); it was the first time that an African-American actor appeared onstage with a white company. When several members of the company refused to appear onstage with Williams, Ziegfeld informed them that they were replaceable, while Williams was not; the complainers quickly acquiesced – Williams was a big star and became a staple of Ziegfeld's revues. In 1911 the *Follies* became *The Ziegfeld Follies*. In 1913, the series moved to the beautiful new art nouveau New Amsterdam Theatre on 42nd Street.

The Ziegfeld Follies of 1915 introduced one of the great scenic designers of the American musical theatre, Joseph Urban. His art deco design for the 1915 edition opened on showgirls "swimming" in waves of blue light, and massive golden elephants spouting actual water through their trunks. An architect and decorator turned designer, Urban developed color schemes that would take the audience through a theatrical journey based on progression of color. He developed the concept of stippling, breaking up solid surfaces with small dots of other colors, which would be appropriately mixed in the eye of the viewer, not on the artist's palette – much as Georges Seurat did with his pointillist paintings on canvas. Urban was a driving force behind the success of the many later Ziegfeld shows.

There was a yearly edition from 1907 to 1924; the 1924 edition was so successful that it ran through the 1925 season. The 1926 edition was very uneven. Ziegfeld opened the show, but didn't want to risk damaging the name of *The Ziegfeld Follies*, so he opened it as *No Foolin': Ziegfeld's American Revue*; it ran for 108 performances. Ziegfeld's maddening attention to detail and his compulsive need to give every element of production his personal attention were well documented. When a costume designer suggested that Ziegfeld provide his chorus girls with less expensive underwear than the imported silk he had been providing, claiming that no one would ever know the difference, Ziegfeld told him that he would know and the girls would know; the imported underwear stayed.

Ziegfeld glorified the American Girl and he sold the allure of the sexual.

> Ziegfeld knew the subtle line between desire and lust, between good taste and vulgarity, and never crossed it. He came close a few times but he never quite crossed it. [...] the exhibitionism which was part of his private life was not contrived. It was an integral part of him, part of the personality mechanism that made him what he was: a gambler who had an almost childish irresponsibility toward the value of money and an equally childish conviction that he could always get some more when he wanted it. [...] And finally, he had a sense of showmanship and of female beauty that was the despair of his competitors.[12]

The final edition Ziegfeld created was in 1931, two years after he had been wiped out by the stock market crash. Very different from the initial $13,000 production, the 1931 edition cost over $250,000. However, the *Ziegfeld Follies of 1931* was more an act of desperation than anything else; it lost its entire investment. Audiences of the Depression were not able to support such an opulent show. Less than a year later Ziegfeld died.

Ziegfeld's competition – George White (1891–1968) and Earl Carroll (1893–1948)

> **George White (1891–1968)** – Ziegfeld's stiffest competition, White presented his *George White's Scandals* between 1919 and 1939.

George White began his career as a performer, appearing in the *Ziegfeld Follies of 1911* and *1915*. White learned from Ziegfeld and created his own series of revues called *George White's Scandals,* which ran from 1919 to 1931. After 1931 White went to Hollywood, returning to Broadway to create a *Scandals* in 1936 and again in 1939. Ziegfeld had his chorus of beautiful girls and White had his "George White Girls." While the Ziegfeld Girls were idealized American Girls, beautiful but austere, George White's girls were more accessible and contemporary, the hot modern jazz baby. White's material was a little edgier than Ziegfeld's, fresher and newer. While working on *George White's Scandals* in the early 1920s, *Scandals'* conductor Paul Whiteman commissioned George Gershwin to write his *Rhapsody in Blue*. Many great entertainers including The Three Stooges, Ray Bolger, Helen Morgan, Ethel Merman, Ann Miller, Bert Lahr, Rudy Vallée, Louise Brooks and Eleanor Powell got their start in the *Scandals*. A dance called "The Black Bottom" had appeared uptown in a Harlem show called *Dinah,* but it was when Ann Pennington introduced it to

Figure 5.2 Actress Ann Pennington dancing (© John Springer Collection/CORBIS)

Broadway audiences in *George White's Scandals of 1926* that it became a national dance craze (see Figure 5.2).

Earl Carroll (1893–1948) – The other great revue creator, Earl Carroll was a producer/director/performer/composer/lyricist. He presented *Earl Carroll's Vanities*.

The other great revue producer, Earl Carroll, began his series of *Earl Carroll's Vanities* in 1923. Carroll produced a new edition yearly until 1931. Carroll delighted in testing the boundaries of decency and morality. Like his competitors, his shows were spectacle based and offered comedians and singers; but Carroll lived up to his nickname, "the body merchant." Carroll's shows included more nudity than his competitors' shows, and his personal life included more outrageous behavior than Ziegfeld or White. Reportedly, in 1926 an orgy was held in the theater after the performance for the entertainment of Carroll's backers and supporters, at which Joyce Hawley was hired to sit nude onstage in a bathtub filled with champagne. Unfortunately, Prohibition was in effect. Carroll was found guilty of providing alcohol and of perjury, paid a fine of $2,000 and served one year and one day in jail, but was paroled after nine months. He found himself in and out of court and jail regularly, but never changed his behavior or his production standards; and his shows remained extremely popular. The Great Depression ended Carroll's New York career and he moved to Hollywood, where he opened an Earl Carroll Theatre in Hollywood, where he continued his New York traditions. In 1948 Carroll died in an airplane crash.

By 1911, it was clear that the revue held the potential for great financial success. That season, in addition to Ziegfeld's show, the Shuberts presented *The Revue of Revues* at their new theater, The Winter Garden. Despite the poor showing of *The Revue of Revues*, in July 1912 the Shuberts presented *The Passing Show of 1912* in order to compete directly with Ziegfeld. *The Passing Show* was very successful and had annual editions for the next ten years. After their success with *The Passing Show*, the Shuberts added another yearly revue, *Artists and Models*, created to compete for Earl Carroll's audience.

> Last night, at the opening of "Artists and Models" at the Shubert, the audience realized, with appropriate gasps a few moments after the curtain had risen, that the girls of the ensemble were entirely unclothed from the waist up. [...] The show itself is for the most part a very good revue. There are several beautiful settings – among them Japanese prints designs, porcelain statuettes and a pastoral scene by Watson Barrett – and one or two really comic sketches. [...] The girls of the chorus were young and pretty.[13]

In an effort to stay competitive, George M. Cohan created and produced minstrel shows and revues during this period. *Cohan and Harris Minstrels of 1908* and *1909, Hello Broadway* (1914), *The Cohan Revue of 1916* and *1918* were some of Cohan's entries into this arena.

Producer/performer Raymond Hitchcock, who had some estimable success producing musicals on Broadway, created his own series of very successful revues titled *Hitchy-Koo*. They ran from *Hitchy-Koo of 1917* to *Hitchy-Koo of 1924*.

With 5,200 seats, The Hippodrome offered several musical spectacles each year from 1905 to 1921. Some of these included: *Circus Tournament* (1905), *A Yankee Circus on Mars* (1905), *Society Circus* (1905), *Neptune's Daughter* (1906), *The Auto Race* (1907), *The Battle of the Skies* (1908), *The International Cup, The Ballet of Niagara, and the Earthquake* (1910), *Wars of the World* (1914) and so on. As these titles suggest, the emphasis was on spectacle. In this case, the theatre, rather than the producer, was the star.

Between 1919 and 1928, John Murray Anderson created a series of revues called *The Greenwich Village Follies*. Other revues played during this time as well: *From Broadway to Paris* (1912), *Odds and Ends of 1917*, *The Garrick Gaieties* (1926 and 1930), *The Shubert Gaieties of 1919*, *Frivolities of 1920*, *Silks and Satins* (1920) and so on.

Actors' strike of 1919

The actors' union, Actors' Equity, was formed in 1913, in response to unfair treatment and conditions rained down upon actors by producers. Before the union, "it was common practice for producers to make actors pay for their own costumes, to rehearse them for weeks without pay, and to fire them without notice."[14] In addition, the "casting couch" was used as chorus girls were hired in exchange for sexual favors and sometimes offered to investors and other powerful people as escorts and playmates. The union was formed in 1913, but had waited until after the war to press its demands against the producers. Fortunately, for the union, the previous year's flu had crippled the producers, so the actors went on strike in 1919. When the stagehands' union honored the strike, the producers were broken; they had no choice but to accept the union's demands. While the formation of the union did not directly affect the types of shows that were produced, it changed the way in which Broadway musicals were produced, and the economic conditions surrounding these shows. The union initiated pay for rehearsals, the provision of appropriate costumes, rules regarding rehearsal hours, and overtime pay when those hours were infringed upon, casting conditions, touring conditions and so on. George M. Cohan, who had always prided himself on treating his employees as family, felt personally betrayed by the union's behavior, a betrayal he never got over; he never joined the union.

Chapter summary

- Operetta became the vogue.
- The three greatest American operetta writers:

  - Victor Herbert
  - Rudolf Friml
  - Sigmund Romberg.

- World War I impacts American musical theatre:

  - younger European composers off fighting the war/older composers were diminishing in their powers or becoming out of date
  - transatlantic shipping lanes were shut down.

- New American ethos develops. Thomas Edison, Teddy Roosevelt and Henry Ford represented the "can-do" spirit of America. There was a need to see this character onstage.
- Two important new composers:

  - Jerome Kern
  - Irving Berlin.

- The Princess musicals.
- Revues: Florenz Ziegfeld's *Follies* are so successful that they are copied by the Shubert Brothers, George White, Earl Carroll and others. The revue becomes a staple of Broadway through the 1920s.

- Theatrical seasons between 1908 and 1920 were rich and varied. The economy was strong after the war, as we headed into the Jazz Age of the 1920s.

Notes

1 "The Firefly Bright: Trentini a Live Wire," *The New York Times*, December 3, 1912. Web, accessed July 12, 2011, http://query.nytimes.com/mem/archive-free/pdf?res=9402E4DF1730E233A25750C0A9649D946396D6CF

2 "Brilliant Show at the Winter Garden; Color, Dance, Song, and Fun, with an Added Touch of Effective Spectacle. Girls and Gowns Galore," *The New York Times*, July 11, 1914. Web, accessed July 12, 2011, http://query.nytimes.com/mem/archive-free/pdf?res=F30810FE355D13 738DDDA80994D9405B848DF1D3

3 Ric Burns and James Sanders, *New York: An Illustrated History*, New York: Alfred A. Knopf, 2003, p. 315.

4 Irving Berlin, quoted in *Jewish Heroes and Heroines of America: 150 True Stories of American Jewish Heroism*, Hollywood, FL: Lifetime Books, 1996, pp. 162–3.

5 "'Watch Your Step' is Hilarious Fun: Irving Berlin's Revue at the New Amsterdam is Festivity Syncopated," *The New York Times*, December 9, 1914. Web, accessed July 20, 2011, http://query.nytimes.com/mem/archive-free/pdf?res=940CE6DE1438E633A 2575AC0A9649D946596D6CF

6 Tin Pan Alley is the area of New York, on West 28th Street between Broadway and 6th Avenue, where the music publishing offices were. The sound of all of those composers banging out their tunes for potential publishers throughout the neighborhood at the same time sounded like people banging on tin pans.

7 Alec Wilder, *American Popular Song: The Great Innovators 1900–1950*, New York: Oxford University Press, 1972, p. 31.

8 William Zinsser, *Easy to Remember: The Great American Songwriters and Their Songs*, Jeffrey, NH: David R. Godine, 2006, p. 18.

9 Gerald Bordman, *American Musical Theatre: A Chronicle*, New York: Oxford University Press, 1978, p. 330.

10 Gerald Bordman, *American Musical Theatre: A Chronicle*, New York: Oxford University Press, 1978, p. 231.

11 "Ziegfeld Follies" program, The New National Theatre, Washington, DC, February 26, 1912. Web, accessed July 18, 2011, http://memory.loc.gov/cgi-bin/ampage?collId=varspbk&fileName=brnn62/brnn62.data&recNum=1&itemLink=r%3Famm em%2Fvarstg%3A%40field%28NUMBER%2B%40band%28varspbk%2Bbrnn62% 29%29

12 Marjorie Farnsworth, *The Ziegfeld Follies*, New York, Bonanza Books, 1961, p. 11.

13 "'Artists and Models' in Scant Adornment," *The New York Times*, August 21, 1923. Web, accessed July 20, 2011, http://query.nytimes.com/mem/archive/pdf?res=FB091 3F83B5417738DDDA80A94D0405B838EF1D3

14 John Kenrick, "History of the Musical Stage 1910–19 Part III," 2003. Web, accessed July 20, 2011, http://www.musicals101.com/1910bway3.htm

Further reading

Rudolf Friml and Sigmund Romberg

Everett, William. *Rudolf Friml*. Urbana, IL: University of Illinois Press, 2008.
Everett, William. A. *Sigmund Romberg*. New Haven, CT: Yale University Press, 2007.

Jerome Kern

Banfield, Stephen. *Jerome Kern*. New Haven, CT: Yale University Press, 2006. Banfield's biography tends to be more analytical than Bordman's.

Davis, Lee. *Bolton and Wodehouse and Kern: The Men Who Made Musical Comedy*. New York, NY: James H. Heineman Publisher, Inc., 1993.

Irving Berlin

Furia, Philip. *Irving Berlin: A Life in Song*. New York, NY: Schirmer Trade Books, 1998.

Jablonski, Edward. *Irving Berlin: American Troubadour*. New York, NY: Henry Holt & Co., 1999.

Magee, Jeffrey. *Irving Berlin's American Musical Theatre*. New York, NY: Oxford University Press, 2012.

Revues

Mordden, Ethan. *Ziegfeld: The Man Who Invented Show Business*. New York, NY: St. Martin's Press, 2008.

Murray, Ken. *The Body Merchant: The Story of Earl Carroll*. Los Angeles, CA: Ward Ritchie Press, 1976.

6 The Jazz Age, 1920–29

A period of great songwriters

American musical theatre prior to the turn of the century had been driven by dynamic individuals or teams who wrote, produced, directed, starred in and more; the 1910s was the time of the great impresarios. In the 1920s, the musical theatre begins to be driven by great songwriters who started building the American songbook, the canon of great popular songs of twentieth-century America.

The 1920s in America

In 1918, World War I ended, leaving America, now a leader among nations, continuing its transition from an agricultural economy to an industrial one, from a rural society to an urban one. Amazing new popular inventions made the 1920s feel futuristic: airplanes, automobiles, movies, radios, phonographs, trucks all changed the way Americans lived. Prohibition, which came into effect in 1919, did not stop the sale or consumption of alcohol; it just made it more fun. Speakeasies flourished, the hooch flowed and the Jazz Age was born.

America experienced a sexual revolution in the late 1910s and 1920s, initiated by Margaret Sanger, who smuggled diaphragms into the country and distributed them, putting the means of birth control in the hands of women for the first time. In 1921, Sanger founded the American Birth Control League. Making unwanted pregnancy controllable, sexual behavior outside of marriage surged. Adding fuel to the fire, automobiles helped young people move the dating scene out from under the watchful eyes of their parents' parlor. One of the places where young people liked to go was the theater. Following a brief period of economic uncertainty after the war, America saw an economic boom. Reflecting the ethos of these times was the new cultural rhythm, the sexy pulse of jazz, making the 1920s known as "The Roaring Twenties" or "The Jazz Age."

Because of increased audiences, low production costs and the availability of investment capital, the 1920s saw a spike in the production of musical theatre. More productions were mounted than ever before – or ever since (see Figure 6.1).

The average number of new musicals produced in the 1910s was twenty-five per season. An increase in productions correlated to the economic boost of

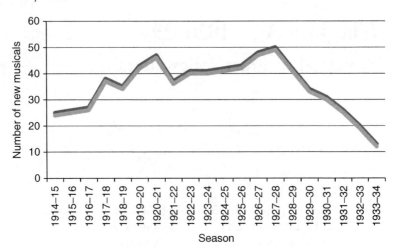

Figure 6.1 Number of new musicals produced on Broadway from the 1914–15 season through the 1933–34 season

America's entry into World War I; and by the 1919/1920 season, there were forty-two new musicals produced on Broadway; the average stayed at forty-two through the next nine seasons. By the 1929/1930 season, with the Depression under way, the number dropped yearly – thirty-three new musicals, thirty, twenty-five, nineteen, and finally twelve new musicals in the 1933/1934 season.

In the 1920s, however, the musical theatre roared along with the rest of the decade. The number of productions was up, the length of the runs was up, profits were up and the quality of these shows was way up. Within one week of Thursday, September 16, 1925, four of the biggest and most important shows of the 1920s opened. *No, No, Nanette*, Rodgers and Hart's *Dearest Enemy*, Rudolf Friml's *The Vagabond* and Kern and Hammerstein's *Sunny* all opened in that week.

No, No, Nanette is one of the best remembered of the 1920s musical comedies. Tours, subsequent productions and revivals continue to this day, helped in part by the successful 1971 Broadway revival. The Vincent Youmans, Irving Caesar and Otto Harbach score is chock full of hits, including "I Want to Be Happy" and "Tea for Two."

While *No, No, Nanette* defined the quintessential musical of the 1920s, *Dearest Enemy* stretched the paradigm; subtly nuanced lyrics, jazzy and musically challenging score, and an above-average book. It tells the story of an American woman using her feminine wiles to stall the British soldiers for almost two hours during the Revolutionary War. It announced that new youthful and exciting voices would be heard, and new writers (Richard Rodgers and Lorenz Hart) would find new forms for the musical. *Dearest Enemy* ran for 286 performances.

The Vagabond King was Rudolf Friml's greatest successes, playing 511 performances and becoming a staple of the operetta repertoire. It was the end of the great age of operetta, but *The Vagabond King* ushered it out with a bang.

Sunny topped *The Vagabond King*'s run at 517 performances. *Sunny* was written by Jerome Kern, Oscar Hammerstein, II, eighteen years before he began working with Rodgers, and Otto Harbach, who was opening *Sunny*, at the New Amsterdam Theatre on 42nd Street, and *No, No, Nanette*, at the Globe Theatre on 46th Street.

> The blaze of fall colors gave way to a "riot" of every conceivable hue in *Sunny*. Its curtain rose on an extravagantly colorful circus set filled with freaks, snake-charmers, barkers and roustabouts. As the evening progressed, the circus was supplanted by a brilliant hunting scene [...], an ocean liner, and an elegant ballroom (with George Olsen's jazz musicians onstage to supplement the pit orchestra). *Sunny* happily reunited Marilyn Miller and Jerome Kern, but they were only the most prominent names in a splendid array of talent.[1]

New voices in the 1920s

Empowered on many fronts, women broke free from traditional roles of behavior and dress – smoking, drinking, dancing suggestive dances such as the Charleston and the Black Bottom, new hairstyles, new skirt lengths, a sexual revolution was underway. It was the age of the flapper and the "jazz baby." People were getting out of the house, there was a huge surge in attendance at theaters, clubs, restaurants, speakeasies, bowling alleys, miniature golf courses – the search for fun, excitement and sophistication was on.

People hungered for new entertainment, and ticket prices were affordable. Just when the need for more musicals to fill the theaters surged, there was a wave of exciting new American writers. They used the new jazzy sounds to write their new shows, and established what has become known as the American songbook. These writers defined the American musical theatre.

Music and lyrics were hip, angular, jazzy, urban and urbane, and spoke in the voice of the contemporary person like no music or lyrics ever had. Jerome Kern, of course, continued to push the envelope, as did Irving Berlin – both were finely attuned to the pulse and the sound of America throughout their lives. Other new voices entered the scene as well. The 1920s was a Golden Age of songwriting in the musical theatre.

In the 1920's Oscar Hammerstein, II, Richard Rodgers, Lorenz Hart, Cole Porter, George Gershwin, Ira Gershwin and Noël Coward all entered the scene just when production money was plentiful. With the middle class expanding and people clamoring for entertainment, it was the perfect recipe for growth in the musical theatre. Shows were written and mounted very quickly by today's standards, and, although most are light and fairly superficial, there is a high degree of craftsmanship to the musicals of the 1920s. Other composers and lyricists that arrived on Broadway in the 1920s, include: Vincent Youmans, Eubie Blake, B.G. "Buddy" DeSylva, Lew Brown, Ray Henderson, Jimmy McHugh, Dorothy Fields and E.Y. "Yip" Harburg.

> **Oscar Hammerstein, II (1895–1960)**, lyricist and book writer, was born in New York. The pinnacle of the spectacular first half of his career, writing mostly operettas, was *Show Boat*, written with Jerome Kern.

The means to produce shows inexpensively gave producers the ability to put a lot of product on the market, some of it imitative and derivative and some of it new and innovative. This market condition allowed the musical theatre to thrive and develop. So many people creating so much musical theatre led to some amazing experiments, brilliant successes and dazzling failures.

Oscar Hammerstein, II was one of the few great lyricists who wrote the book as well as the lyrics. Writing both allowed Hammerstein to write the script *into* the song, rather than *up to* it, and the song out of the script. This explains the seamlessness in Hammerstein's writing not found in most others. Even his earlier works display clarity and simplicity, and are marked by the elegance of his workmanship as a wordsmith. Take, for example, the lyric to refrain of the well-known "Indian Love Call" from *Rose-Marie* in 1924:

> When I'm calling you-oo-oo oo-oo-oo!
> You will answer too-oo-oo oo-oo-oo!
> That means I offer my love to you to be your own.
>
> If you refuse me, I will be blue
> And waiting all alone;
> But if when you hear my love call ringing clear,
> And I hear your answering echo, so dear,
> Then I will know our love will come true,
> You'll belong to me, I'll belong to you![2]

The sentiments could not be clearer; the syntax could not be more concise. There are only seven two-syllable words and only one three-syllable word; no line contains more than one polysyllabic word. Notice the internal rhyme in the third line, "to you to," which connects back to the long melismatic "oo"s at the end of the first and second lines. In less capable hands the rhyme would feel contrived, yet in such neatly constructed phrases the final "oo" words seem inevitable.

Hammerstein was born, in 1895, into a highly successful if volatile theatre family. His grandfather, Oscar I, a hugely successful theatre impresario, produced theatre, musical theatre, variety arts and opera. The elder Oscar Hammerstein built and owned eight theaters, at various times.

Although young Oscar's father William managed the Victoria Theatre for his father, he was against his son's entering the family business, and saw to it that Oscar, II was enrolled in Columbia University followed by Columbia Law School. However, when William passed away, Oscar could no longer resist the call of the theatre. He quit law school and began his theatrical career working for his Uncle Arthur as an assistant stage manager, then a production stage manager. At the same time he began writing English translations of European plays, operas and musicals, as well as contributing rewrites on scripts that were being developed. He learned from his translations and script "doctoring" and ultimately mastered the form, becoming a leading operetta writer.

His first success was *Wildflower* (1922, 477 performances) for which he co-wrote the book and lyrics with Otto Harbach to a score by Herbert Stothart and Vincent Youmans. Hammerstein began regularly supplying books and lyrics to productions, working regularly with Romberg, Friml, Stothart, and Harbach, who became his mentor. Hammerstein's groundbreaking works from the 1920s were with Jerome Kern, including *Sunny* (1925), *Sweet Adeline* (1929) and *Show Boat* (1927).

In the 1920s Hammerstein wrote twenty-two new musicals and operettas, and had greater and more regular success than practically anyone else writing for Broadway. Hammerstein's great operetta successes were: *Rose-Marie* (1924), *The Desert Song* (1926) and *The New Moon* (1928).

Richard Rodgers (1902–79), composer and producer, was born to a prosperous German Jewish family in Queens. With his first collaborator, Lorenz Hart, he moved the American musical theatre forward in both form and content. He would drive the American musical even further ahead with his second great collaborator, Oscar Hammerstein.

Richard Rodgers wrote music and occasionally lyrics for more than 900 songs for more than forty-three Broadway shows and composed music for movies and television. Rodgers was the first person to win an Emmy Award, a Grammy Award, an Oscar and a Tony Award – in addition, he won a Pulitzer Prize for *South Pacific*. Rodgers had two of the greatest collaborations in the history of the musical theatre with Lorenz Hart in the 1920s and 1930s and Oscar Hammerstein in the 1940s and 1950s. In addition to writing music, Rodgers produced plays and musicals, ran his own music publishing company and was one of the most successful businessmen in the theatre.

Born into a prosperous German Jewish family in Queens, New York, Rodgers was the son of a prominent physician. He began to study the piano at age six and at the age of fifteen wrote his first score for a show, called *One Minute*

Figure 6.2 Composers Richard Rodgers (left) and Lorenz Hart (right) posing together (© Bettmann/CORBIS)

Please, which was performed by his older brother's social club in the Ballroom of the Plaza Hotel. Two years later his second show, *Up Stage and Down* played in the Grand Ballroom of the Waldorf-Astoria. Several lyrics for *Up Stage and Down* were written by Arthur Hammerstein, a patient of his father's, and father of Oscar Hammerstein, II.

While studying at Columbia University, Rodgers, looking for a lyricist, was introduced to Lorenz Hart, seven years his senior, a recent Columbia graduate (see Figure 6.2). Rodgers describes that first meeting:

> The total man was hardly more than five feet tall. He wore frayed carpet slippers, a pair of tuxedo trousers, an undershirt and a nondescript jacket. His hair was unbrushed, and he obviously hadn't had a shave for a couple of days. All he needed was a tin cup and some pencils. But that first look was misleading, for it missed the soft brown eyes, the straight nose, the good mouth, the even teeth and the strong chin. Feature for feature he had a handsome face, but it was set in a head that was a bit too large for his body and gave him a slightly gnomelike appearance.[3]

Lorenz Hart (1895–1943), lyricist, was also born in New York. Rodgers and Hart were the cutting edge of musical theatre writing in the 1920s and 1930s. Hart's lyrics are at once clever and beautifully crafted, filled with internal and polysyllabic rhymes, and touchingly human.

Lorenz Hart, who was born in Harlem, the son of immigrants of German Jewish descent, attended Columbia University's School of Journalism for two years, and began his theatrical career writing varsity shows and translating German plays into English for the Shuberts.

Hart may have suffered from a minor form of dwarfism. He was homosexual, at a time when homosexuality was considered a mental illness and homosexuals had to stay in the closet. Uncomfortable about physical appearance and tormented about his sexuality, his personal demons led him to a life of unhappiness and alcoholism. Hart would disappear for days, drinking and engaging in rough sex only to reappear bruised and hung over. Despite this, or perhaps because of it, his work was unmatched; his lyrics are a hallmark of craft and insight into the human psyche. Hart's lyrics display wit, fun, and playfulness, while articulating truths of the human condition. An outsider, he looked deep within himself to access and articulate essential human experiences. In "Where or When," Hart articulates the feeling of déjà vu and the rush of meeting someone special for the first time:

VERSE
Sometimes you think you've lived before
All that you live today
Things you do come back to you
As though they knew the way
Oh, the tricks your mind can play!

REFRAIN
It seems we stood and talked like this before
We looked at each other in the same way then,
But I can't remember where or when.
The clothes you're wearing are the clothes you wore.
The smile you are smiling you were smiling then,
But I can't remember where or when.

Some things that happen for the first time,
Seem to be happening again.
And so it seems that we have met before
And laughed before
And loved before,
But who knows where or when.[4]

Here Hart resists extraneous rhymes, choosing instead to approach his subject with simplicity, grace and restraint.

Rodgers and Hart wrote more than twenty-eight musicals and more than 500 songs between 1919 and 1943. Their first song on Broadway was "Any Old Place With You," sung in *A Lonely Romeo* (1919). They had individual songs appear in a variety of shows, but their first complete score (except for one song) and breakthrough success was *The Garrick Gaieties* (1925), scheduled as a two-performance fundraiser for the Theatre Guild. It was so successful that it was extended and ran for 211 performances. A second edition the following year ran for 174 performances. Rodgers and Hart quickly became the toast of the town.

Lorenz Hart's lyrics were hip, urbane and contemporary and often racy; and Rodgers' melodies were the cutting edge of contemporary music, swingy, jazzy, urban and sophisticated. Some of their popular 1920s songs include: "Mountain Greenery," "Thou Swell," "My Heart Stood Still," "You Took Advantage of Me," "With A Song In My Heart" and "A Ship Without A Sail."

They wrote a dazzling array of shows during the 1920s that captured the bright and jazzy feel of the times without ever falling into a formula. Adventurous, forward thinking, never settling into a mold or model; looking back at their accomplishments, a 1943 *Time Magazine* story described Rodgers and Hart's success:

> Their services to musicomedy [...] rests on a commercial instinct that most of their rivals have apparently ignored. As Rodgers & Hart see it, what was killing musicomedy was its sameness, its tameness, its eternal rhyming of June with moon. They decided it was not enough just to be good at the job; they had to be constantly different also. The one possible formula was: Don't have a formula; the one rule for success: Don't follow it up.[5]

Rodgers and Hart were busy. Their fifteen Broadway shows of the 1920s included three in 1925 (*Garrick Gaieties*, *June Days* and *Dearest Enemy*), three in 1926 (*The Girl Friend*, *Peggy-Ann* and *Betsy*), and three in 1928 (*She's My Baby*, *Present Arms* and *Chee-Chee*). They worked fast and they dazzled the audiences with wit, sly sexual innuendo and the ability to crystallize essential human experiences and feelings.

Composer **George Gershwin** (1898–1937) and lyricist **Ira Gershwin** (1896–1983) were born to Russian-Jewish immigrant parents in Brooklyn, NY. George would straddle the worlds of classical and popular music in a way the world had never seen; and Ira, a brilliant wordsmith, fitted words to his brother's melodies seamlessly.

George Gershwin was a star composer simultaneously in the musical theatre, popular music, jazz and classical music. Two years younger than Ira, George was the second of four children. His parents bought a used piano so that Ira could take lessons, but George sat down at the piano and could not be pulled away. At age fifteen he left school to work as a song plugger for Jerome H. Remick and Company, a publishing firm, for $15.00 a week. Song publishers paid "pluggers" to sit in their show rooms and play songs for customers to interest them in buying the sheet music. By age seventeen George was paid $5.00 for the rights to publish his first song, "When You Want 'Em You Can't Get 'Em." The following year he had his first commercial success with a song called "Rialto Ripples," and two later, at age nineteen, he became a star composer when his song "Swanee" was published.

Gershwin claimed that he and Irving Caesar wrote "Swanee" on a New York City bus in about ten minutes. It was originally a production number for a short-lived revue called *Demi-Tasse*. The number made very little impact until Al Jolson, the biggest star of the day, heard it and insisted on putting it into his show *Sinbad*, already running at the Winter Garden Theatre. Jolson made the song an international hit. It was on the charts for eighteen weeks in 1920 holding the number one position for nine weeks. It sold millions of copies of sheet music and two million records.

George had songs in Broadway shows like *Ladies First* (1918), *Good Morning, Judge* (1919) and *The Lady in Red* (1919); and finally wrote his first full score for *La, La, Lucille* in 1919. Much of George's early success was in contributing songs to Broadway revues like *Morrie Gest's Midnight Whirl* (1919), *Demi-Tasse* (1919), *George White's Scandals* (1920, 1921, 1922, 1923, 1924 and 1926), *Broadway Brevities of 1920*, *Snapshots of 1921* and *The Broadway Whirl* (1921).

Until 1924 George's primary lyricist was Buddy DeSylva; but in 1924 George teamed up with his brother Ira to write the musical *Lady Be Good*. George and Ira were hired for *Lady Be Good* by producers Alexander Aarons and Vinton Freedley who had been influenced by the Princess musicals and established their own manifesto:

> Aarons-Freedley musical comedies included everyday characters caught in comic situations, snappy contemporary dialogue, no intrusive "star turns," and songs arising from plot and character. Wishing to fill larger theaters, the producers used a larger chorus and youthful stars, relying on comics such as Victor Moore. The Gershwins became virtual "house composers." Gershwin biographer Edward Jablonski remarked, "The kind of 'smart show' that Aarons and Freedley aimed at provided [them] with the chance to compose songs for a knowing, literate, contemporary audience.[6]

Aarons and Freedley produced most of the Gershwins' musicals, building the Alvin Theatre (now named the Neil Simon Theatre) for the Gershwin musical *Funny Face*. Joining forces with Aarons and Freedley, George shifted his focus from writing revue songs to writing book musicals. George and Ira wrote nine musicals from 1924 to 1929.

George infused his popular and symphonic music[7] with the jagged rhythms and dissonances of jazz. In any of these pieces, you can hear the hustle and bustle of 1920s Manhattan. He joined blues notes from African-American music with the minor-keys and melismas of traditional Jewish music and infused this potent cocktail into both classical and popular music.

Some of the Gershwins' enduring songs of the 1920s include: "Fascinating Rhythm," "Embraceable You," "How Long Has This Been Going On," "I've Got A Crush On You," "The Man I Love," "'S Wonderful" and "Someone To Watch Over Me." The Gershwin Brothers' greatest successes lay ahead in the 1930s, but the body of work they produced in the 1920s is astounding.

Popular song hits

In the Gershwins' and Rodgers and Hart's 1920s musicals, the chance to insert a great song trumped considerations of plot and storytelling. Songs that didn't work in one show were removed and later placed in another, frequently to terrific result. Many great songs got second and third chances to become popular hits. While musical comedies had stronger plots and more clearly defined characters than they had in the previous decade, thanks to the Princess musicals, they were still light and breezy entertainments in which a great musical or comic moment could sidetrack the plot until the book writer found their way back. Characters in these musicals tended to be urban, recognizable and contemporary, people you might meet on the street. They spoke in contemporary slang, although filtered through the pens of great wordsmiths – first or second generation Jewish, European immigrants putting their idea of 1920s New York up on the stage.

A popular song was a valuable commodity – it could sell sheet music, recordings and tickets at the box office. They were prized, and it was the composers and lyricists who became popular – audiences always want to see the latest Rodgers and Hart or Gershwin musical. Sometimes a proven popular song would be placed in a new musical to help assure its success.

Revues of the 1920s

The revue dominated through much of the 1920s. There were, of course, the big yearly revues: Ziegfeld produced not only the *Follies*, but others like the *Ziegfeld Frolics*; George White's *Scandals* and Earl Carroll's *Vanities*; the Shubert's *The Passing Show* and *Artists and Models*; Irving Berlin's *Music Box Revues*. Other revues appeared and disappeared from season to season with titles like: *Bad Habits of 1926, Bunk of 1926, Nic Nax of 1926, Bare Facts of 1927, Padlocks of 1927*. In 1924 British producer and director André Charlot created a compilation of his London revues from the past several seasons and presented them in New York as *Charlot's Revue*. *Charlot's Revue* introduced Americans to Jack Buchanan, Gertrude Lawrence, Beatrice Lillie, Jessie Matthews and to the songs of Noël Coward. A smash hit, *Charlot's Revue* ran for just under 300 performances.

Revues in the 1920s were a vital component of the musical theatre and an excellent training ground for the up-and-coming generation of artists. The revue was topical and satirical. Revues provided a great training ground for young writers. Every sketch had to be well structured and establish exposition quickly; every joke or "bit" had to land properly and finish with a "button." And every song had to work without benefit of story or character – they just had to be great songs – beautiful, funny or revelatory. The music of the revues tended to be hip and contemporary, tinged with jazz; and the lyrics were contemporary and edgy. In the 1950s, the writers' room of Sid Caesar's television show *Your Show of Shows* spawned the great comic writers of the 1960s and 1970s (Woody Allen, Mel Brooks, Carl Reiner, Neil and Danny Simon and Larry Gelbart). In the same way, the revues of the 1920s spawned Rodgers and Hart, the Gershwins, and most of the other great writers of the 1920s and 1930s.

In the early 1920s, revues were the most successful musical theatre form. They were large and lavish, including massive spectacular scenery and huge choruses of beautiful girls in scanty attire. Revues provided great training grounds for entertainers as well as writers; Fanny Brice, W.C. Fields, Will Rogers, Bill "Bojangles" Robinson, Eddie Cantor, Sophie Tucker, Al Jolson, Ed Wynn, all cut their teeth as entertainers performing in revues.

Revues of the 1920s relied heavily on scenic spectacle. Every song and sketch was an independent short story, requiring a new setting. The sets and costumes were lavish and great designers were prized and fought over.

Every revue boasted the most beautiful and most scantily clad women. To be a Ziegfeld girl or a George White girl was an entrée into society and offered many beautiful young women the chance to meet and marry wealthy men. For a wealthy man to have a beautiful chorus girl as a trophy bride was considered a coup. Onstage the girls were clothed in as little as producers could get away with, but always at great expense – lavish headdresses, silks and chiffons, beads and boas were all in vogue.

In one season, 1919–20, Broadway saw seventeen new original revues. Writers of these revues included: Irving Berlin, Joseph McCarthy, Harry Tierney, Victor Herbert, John Murray Anderson, Walter Donaldson, Sigmund Romberg, Buddy DeSylva, Cole Porter and twenty-one-year-old George Gershwin. The seventeen revues of this season, in New York and on tour, employed thousands of artists; they had substantial runs entertaining millions of patrons and almost all turned substantial profits.

The 1920/1921 Broadway season saw 157 shows open, 45 musicals and 112 plays.[8] Broadway in the 1920s was thriving; it was inexpensive to produce a Broadway musical, even a lavish revue; and the amount of time required to recoup investment and show a profit was a matter of weeks in the 1920s.

Irene, *Sally* and the Cinderella musicals

Two of the biggest hits of 1919 and 1920 respectively were *Irene* (675 performances) and *Sally* (561 performances). They share a basic storyline, and both shows define the model for the Cinderella musicals. The Cinderella musicals were extremely popular through the 1930s and continued to crop up through 1960s – and even today.

The Cinderella musicals tell a rags-to-riches story. A poor immigrant girl, usually Irish, falls in love with a rich successful man; or he falls in love with her. She opts to make it on her own, and by dint of her plucky immigrant spirit, hard work, and a bit of luck, she succeeds, and by the end of the musical, she also marries the rich, handsome man, usually her boss or benefactor. It is the story of the indomitable will of the plucky immigrant. Home to so many first and second-generation immigrants, New York had an audience hungry for these shows; it was their story, or their parents'. All of these musicals tried to spin variations on the theme, but ultimately only so many variations existed. It didn't matter though; audiences loved these shows – in the same way that television sitcoms recycle the same basic stories, so the Cinderella musical was revisited time and time again.

Just like George M. Cohan's persona, the bold and brassy, slightly pugnacious, fiercely patriotic and justifiably egotistic hero, was embraced twenty years earlier, the Cinderella story appealed to "the American dream" as it existed for so many recent immigrants in the 1920s. Cohan's persona, *Peck's Bad Boy* grown up, the scrappy little immigrant guy who succeeds by dint of his energy and drive, is a piece of the dream that touched people. Audiences were touched in the same way by the plucky little immigrant girl in the "Cinderella" musicals, from the 1920s forward.

Irene is the most often produced of these shows today thanks to a successful 1973 revival. Poor Irish shop girl, Irene O'Dare, is sent on an errand to the Long Island estate of the Marshalls. The handsome and wealthy Donald Marshall immediately falls in love with Irene. He finds her a job as a model with the famous couturiere, Madam Lucy. Irene manages to steal everyone's heart, causing her mother and Donald to both set aside their class prejudices, allowing them to marry by the final curtain. These musicals offered variations on the basic theme, but ultimately helped to define "the American dream." As audiences happily sat through incarnation after incarnation of this story, the trope became a part of the American story.

Sally, with a book by Guy Bolton, music by Jerome Kern, lyrics by P.G. Wodehouse, ballet music by Victor Herbert and scenic design by Joseph Urban, was produced by Florenz Ziegfeld, and starred twenty-two-year-old *Follies* girl (and off-again-on-again mistress of Ziegfeld), Marilyn Miller. Sally, a poor dishwasher, realizes her dream and becomes a famous ballerina. Miller, one of the biggest stars of the 1920s, starred in *Sally* for two years, toured the country for another year and made an early movie version for Hollywood in 1929. She also starred in *Sunny* (1925) and *Rosalie* (1928); *Sally*, *Sunny* and *Rosalie* were three of the biggest hits of the 1920s.

Some of the most successful "Cinderella" musicals include: *The O'Brien Girl* (1921), *Good Morning Dearie* (1921), *Sally, Mary and Irene* (1922), *Little Nellie Kelly* (1922) and *Sunny* (1925). Others include: *Elsie, Cinders, Little Miss Charity, The Half Moon, Poppy, Mary Jane McKane, The Rise of Rosie*

O'Reilly, Lollipop, Plain Jane, Princess April, Kosher Kitty Kelly, Betsy, Bye Bye Bonnie, Naughty Cinderella – the list goes on and on.

Leisure-time musicals

In the 1920s, the working and middle classes were expanding and moving up. They were able to attend the theater on a regular basis; the average orchestra seat at $5.00 may have been out of their reach, but the average balcony seat, which cost between 50¢ and $1.00, was within the means of the shop-girls and secretaries depicted in the Cinderella musicals. John Bush Jones identifies a 1920s trend that he terms "leisure-time musicals" – musicals whose plots "invariably remained true to the boy-meets-girl formula," that were set in the world of the same sports and leisure-time activities that the audiences were engaging in: the race track, the golf course, the boxing arena.

In June 1919, a horse named Man o' War captured the public imagination as he began an incredible winning streak. Winning his first race by six lengths and winning nine out of ten races in his first year, Man o' War "effectively turn[ed] the 'sport of kings' into mass entertainment."[9] May 1920 saw the opening of *Honey Girl*, a musical set in the world of horse racing. *Honey Girl* was based on a 1903 melodrama called *Checkers*, by Henry Blossom, which was based on an 1896 book of the same title, also by Blossom. The title for the 1920 musical version had originally been *What Are the Odds*, but producer Sam Harris took over the failing production out of town, brought in a new writer to rewrite the book and changed the title. *Honey Girl* is the story of a young racetrack gambler, Checkers, who ultimately wins the girl he loves by betting on a 25-to-1 long shot, a nag named Honey Girl. Honey Girl wins the race, giving Checkers the $25,000 he needs to claim the girl he loves from her father. The show featured an actual horse race onstage with the horses on a treadmill. *Honey Girl* is only one in a number of highly successful musicals set in the locales of sports and leisure-time activities. Other horse-racing musicals appeared, including 1922's *Red Pepper* and 1925's *Big Boy* with Al Jolson.

Man o' War had brought attention to horse racing; Jack Dempsey created a fervor for boxing. In 1919 Jack Dempsey knocked out the current champion, Jess Willard, winning the heavyweight title and the nickname "the Manassa Mauler." He defended his title in six fights over seven years and finally lost it to Gene Tunney in 1926. Dempsey's power and aggressive style made him a crowd favorite and one of the most popular boxers in history. In 1923 *Battling Butler*, an Americanized version of a British musical, opened, very successfully exploiting this interest. In 1928 *Hold Everything*, with a score by DeSylva, Brown and Henderson, made a star out of Bert Lahr, who played a punch-drunk boxer.

No 1920s professional man or businessman could compete socially without playing golf. This national craze for golf found its way on the musical stage as well. *Kid Boots* opened in 1924, produced by Florenz Ziegfeld and starring

Eddie Cantor playing a dishonest caddy who sells crooked golf balls and illegal booze. *Top Hole* opened less than a year later.

A six-day bicycle race was the setting for *The Girl Friend,* with a book by Herbert Fields (son of Lew Fields, of Weber and Fields, and brother to emerging lyricist Dorothy Fields) and a score by Rodgers and Hart.

One of the most successful leisure-time musicals took place on the college football field. DeSylva, Brown and Henderson's *Good News* is "the quintessential musical comedy of the era of wonderful nonsense. The decades' jazzy sounds, its assertive, explosive beat, its sophomoric high jinks were joyously mirrored in a hilarious, melody-packed evening."[10] The story revolved around tutoring the football hero so that he'll pass his exams and be allowed to play in the big game. The score includes songs that have become standards: "The Best Things In Life Are Free" and "The Varsity Drag," which became the hit of the show, and a national dance craze. *Good News* is another one of the 1920s musicals more frequently performed today.

Musical theatre librettos in the 1920s

The 1920s is a popular era in which to set musicals – *Chicago, Thoroughly Modern Millie, The Boy Friend, Sugar* or the musical-within-the-musical in *The Drowsy Chaperone* to mention a few. The Jazz Age offers great musical possibilities; the dances of the day offer great choreographic possibilities; the fads, crazes and headlines of the 1920s offer a panoply of story and plot ideas. Despite the setting of contemporary musicals in the 1920s, we see very few revivals of actual musicals from the 1920s today. Broadway saw successful revivals of *No, No, Nanette* and *Irene* in the 1970s. In 1993, the Music Theatre of Wichita produced *Good News*, with a revised book. These three shows see occasional productions. On the whole, however, musicals of the 1920s are rarely produced today.

Theaters wanting to produce a Gershwin musical tend to choose *Crazy For You*, a very loose adaptation of *Girl Crazy*, with a new book by Ken Ludwig in 1992, or *My One and Only*, an original musical from 1983 by Peter Stone and Timothy Mayer that simply used the catalog of great Gershwin songs.

Why do the musicals of the 1920s, so popular in their own day with scores by the great songwriters and songs that we still love, so rarely get produced? Structurally, books serve the great songs, rather than the other way around. This is a reversal of the musical theatre of today. The stories of the 1920s seem silly and frivolous to us because of this.

For instance, *Good News* is about Tom, the football hero of Tait College, failing his astronomy final, having to be tutored so that he can pass his makeup exam and be allowed to play in the big game on Saturday and falling in love with his tutor – will Tom choose the tutor or the debutante? Will Tate come from behind and win the big game? Along the way are a bunch of great 1920s songs. Compare the emotional stakes in *Good News* to those in *A Chorus Line*, *Sweeney Todd, Next To Normal* or *Rent*. Unfortunately the musicals of the

1920s don't play well for contemporary audiences except as a sort of nostalgic artifact of historic camp.

Books of 1920s musicals were frequently comprised of contemporary topical humor, which connected one song to the next. Topical humor quickly fades in relevance. While the ancient Greek and Roman comedies, the comedies of Shakespeare and Molière are eminently producible today, being situational, the topical humor of the 1920s musicals has passed us by, making them very difficult to play for a contemporary audience.

One of the defining issues of the 1920s was prohibition. It was in the newspapers, on people's minds and on the musical theatre stages. Prohibition was ratified on January 29, 1919. That year's *Ziegfeld Follies* featured Bert Williams singing Irving Berlin's "You Cannot Make Your Shimmy Shake On Tea" and "When The Moon Shines on the Moonshine." The show also featured the Berlin songs "Prohibition," "A Syncopated Cocktail" and the song "You Don't Need the Wine to Have a Wonderful Time." *The Greenwich Village Follies* featured the song "Moonshine (Is in the Mountain Still)." *The Passing Show of 1919* at the Winter Garden Theatre opened with a "Wine Ballet."

Once Prohibition became a way of life, bootlegging, bootleggers, rum-runners, hip flasks and prohibition agents became standard fare for books of musicals and part of the fun for audiences. Some shows made passing reference just for the sake of a laugh or two and others made it a central issue of the plot. In *Kid Boots* Eddie Cantor played a crooked caddy who sells alcohol on the side. *My Girl* is about a dry wedding at which a bootlegger, trying to hide his wares, accidentally mixes the drinks. The Gershwin's *Oh, Kay!* is about the impoverished Duke of Durham and his sister Lady Kay who have turned to rum-running to bring in an income; they have hidden hundreds of cases of illegal booze in the cellar of a house that they believe is empty, until the owner returns and they have to try to get it all out.

Another issue that showed up in musicals with some frequency was the Florida land boom. In the early 1920s and through 1925 Florida experienced a land boom as Americans had, for the first time, disposable time and money – an educated American middle class with paid vacations, pensions and fringe benefits. Also, new technologies in landfill and widespread ownership of the automobile had filled in the wetlands and made Florida accessible. It was a time of prosperity when anyone could get rich by owning the right investment, and Florida property was perfect. Those who didn't have money got credit – the economy was good, what could go wrong? By the end of 1925 the Florida real estate bubble began to burst as *Forbes Magazine* wrote that Florida property values were not based on any reality of the land; they were based on the assumption that the bubble would continue forever.

References to Florida land and to real estate speculation are peppered through musicals of the 1920s. Jokes about Florida became more pointed after the bubble burst, but they appeared both before and after. The *Ziegfeld Follies of 1921* featured the Richard Whiting song "While Miami Dreams." *Gay Paree of 1925* featured the song "Florida Mammy." *No Foolin'* featured the song

"Florida, the Moon and You" and many others. *It's Up To You* is about a wild real estate scheme; *Kid Boots*, the golf musical, takes place in Palm Beach; Jerome Kern's *Sitting Pretty* takes place in Florida; *The Florida Girl*, the Gershwin's *Tip-Toes* and *The Coconuts* (starring the Marx Brothers) were all set in Florida.

Backstage musicals

Stories of chorus girls who step in for ailing stars on opening night and become stars themselves are as much a part of our cultural mythology as the Cinderella story. Musicals of the 1920s told this story frequently. Victor Herbert's 1920 *The Girl In The Spotlight* was set in an opera company where the mousy young girl who works in the composer's boarding house has learned all of the music by hearing him rehearse – good thing too, since the diva throws a fit and refuses to perform. Also in 1920, Rodgers and Hart's *Poor Little Ritz Girl* told the story of a chorus girl who falls in love with the rich young man whose apartment she has sublet. Later that season in Ziegfeld's *Sally*, the title character, a dishwasher in a Greenwich Village inn, steps in for a missing prima ballerina and ultimately winds up a Ziegfeld star. *Blossom Time* was a different kind of backstage story, a musical biography of Franz Schubert. Also in 1921 *Love Dreams* tells the story of a musical comedy star whose notorious persona has been made up by her press agent; although a nice girl at heart, she allows the myth to exist so long as she can use it to make money to support her ailing sister. Theatergoers had to wait four years for the next backstage musical, *Merry, Merry* (1925), followed by *Footlights* (1927) in which a burlesque star manages to get a rich backer to produce a Broadway show. It isn't until the movies start using this story in 1927's *The Jazz Singer* that this popular story becomes a money-maker. The movies exploited this story, very successfully, for decades.

African-American musicals of the 1920s

There had been African-American musicals before the 1920s – minstrel-based theatrical entertainments, many of which had extremely successful touring productions. Shows like *The Creole Show* (1890), *The Octoroons* (1895) and *Black Patti's Troubadours* (1896) led the way to the first full-length New York musical written, directed and produced by African-Americans, Bob Cole's *A Trip To Coontown* (1898) – a spoof of the hit musical *A Trip to Chinatown*. Cole followed this up with *Clorindy, the Origin of the Cakewalk* in 1898, which ran successfully at the Casino Theatre's rooftop, concurrent with the run of *A Trip to Coontown*. As discussed earlier Walker and Williams were the great African-American musical theatre stars at the turn of the century, and Bert Williams continued well into the twentieth century, becoming a major star for Ziegfeld and crossing the color barrier by performing on the stage with a white company.

Noble Sissle (1889–1975), composer, lyricist, bandleader, singer and playwright, was born in Indiana. **Eubie Blake (1887–1983)**, composer and lyricist, was born in Baltimore to former slaves. They were the most successful African-American team of songwriters of the 1920s.

Noble Sissle and Eubie Blake met in Baltimore in 1915, began collaborating on songs and formed a vaudeville act, "The Dixie Duo." The team met the book writers Flournoy Miller and Aubrey Lyles in Philadelphia. The two teams joined forces to write the musical *Shuffle Along* and mounted it in New York on a shoestring. Although African-American shows had appeared in New York earlier, discrimination had heated up since the war. Despite this Sissle, Blake, Miller and Lyles played a few songs for Harry Cort, whose theatrical empire was crumbling. They convinced Cort to give them some sets and costumes left over from *Roly-Boly Eyes* and *Fables*, which had just both closed, and let them play in his run-down lecture hall far away from the theater district, which was quickly renamed the 63rd Street Music Hall, in exchange for giving Cort's son a financial interest in the show. On 63rd Street, there was no chance of getting single-ticket sales from passersby; people would need to seek this show out.

All shows at the time tried out, out of town, but when it came time for *Shuffle Along*, which had rehearsed in Harlem, to travel to their first stop, Trenton, NJ, it was discovered that no one had the money for the company's train fare. Quickly some money was raised from a shabbily dressed man who had been hanging around rehearsals – everyone assumed that he was a sad old derelict, come to ogle the showgirls.[11] The company managed to put together a series of one- or two-night stands which "traced a helter-skelter course, jumping and doubling back over town, hamlet, theatre, auditorium, barn, movie house throughout New Jersey and Pennsylvania"[12] until they were too far in the hole financially to continue. In debt to the amount of $18,000, they brought *Shuffle Along* into New York.

The plot was very thin – just enough of an excuse to get from song to song. The story, which was an expanded version of Miller and Lyles' vaudeville sketches, and characters were slight and would be considered more than slightly offensive today. Three men, Steve Jenkins, Sam Peck and Harry Walton, are all running for the office of Mayor of Jimtown. Jenkins and Peck, partners in a grocery business as well, promise each other that if either is elected they will name the other Chief of Police – and each is stealing from the store to finance their campaign and have hired the same detective to spy on the other one. Jenkins' underhanded campaign manager wins the office for his client. Peck discovers that the job of Chief of Police is to salaam to the mayor, but he confuses "salaam" with "slam" and the two get into a dancing fight. Ultimately Walton manages to throw the other two out and reform and justice prevail in Jimtown.

They had to tread a very careful line in presenting African-American characters – there were certain expectations that white audiences had and in order to create a show that was salable those expectations had to be met. The players in the orchestra pit for *Shuffle Along* played without music, having committed the entire score to memory because, Eubie Blake remembered in an interview, "it was expected of us. People didn't believe that black people could read music – they wanted to think that our ability was just natural talent."[13] In truth the players in the pit were highly trained musicians, many of whom went on to long and important careers.

> African American audiences realized that a certain degree of bowing and scraping was necessary for the success of the performer, and so they accepted performers of their own race blacking-up [putting on blackface makeup]. "Shuffle Along" was one of the first shows to provide the right mixture of primitivism and satire, enticement and respectability, blackface humor and romance, to satisfy its customers.[14]

Opening in May 1921, *Shuffle Along* was the second biggest hit of the season with 484 performances. Critics adored the show and singled out the title song and "In Honeysuckle Time," "I'm Craving For That Kind of Love" and "Love Will Find A Way" as exceptionally good songs – although they made almost no mention of the show's most enduring song, "I'm Just Wild About Harry." Even in its out of the way location the demand for tickets was intense. The police had to change 63rd Street to one-way traffic in the block of the theater to accommodate the traffic flow caused by the show. *Shuffle Along* did several very important things:

- It began a trend of African-American musicals that would create a boom of employment for African-American writers, actors, singers, dancers, designers, directors and producers.
- It broke the color-barrier in the audience. Prior to *Shuffle Along*, people of color sat in sections to which they were relegated, but on opening night African-American patrons were seated as far down as the fifth row of the orchestra.
- *Shuffle Along* was the first show in which a genuinely sincere love duet, "Love Will Find A Way" was sung by two persons of color. Up until this time the only love songs sung by African Americans were either satirical or parodies. The Broadway audience got its first experience of African-American people of depth with whom they could empathize.
- *Shuffle Along* launched the careers of a whole generation of great African-American entertainers including: Josephine Baker, Florence Mills, Adelaide Hall and others.
- Unfortunately, despite the advancement represented by "Love Will Find A Way," *Shuffle Along*, in its effort to appeal to white audiences, depicted African-American characters as the same kind of grotesque caricature that had been seen since the minstrel shows. The overwhelming success of *Shuffle Along* insured that this would continue throughout the decade. The shiftless,

lazy conniving black man became all too familiar a type on the musical theatre stage.

In the wake of *Shuffle Along*'s success the first show of the 1922–23 season was Henry Creamer and Turner Layton's *Strut Miss Lizzie* followed by the *Plantation Revue* produced and directed by Lew Leslie, a white writer and director famous for producing African-American shows on Broadway and at Harlem's famous Cotton Club. Four months later *Liza* opened at Daly's Theatre which once again took place in Jimtown and dealt with a monument being erected to the late mayor and the shenanigans of the town's dandies as they filch from the monument funds. The end of this season saw *How Come?* which was "billed as 'a girly musical darkomedy,'" its high-stepping black dancing was tied together with a thin plot in which Rastus Stuntom Lime endeavors to embezzle funds from the Mobile Chicken Trust Corporation."[15] None of these musicals achieved anything like *Shuffle Along*'s success; *Liza* had the longer run at 172 performances, while *Plantation Revue* eked out a meager 33 performances. However, this did not stop the trend.

October 1923 saw *Runnin' Wild*, which harkened back to the musicals of Walker and Williams – once again Miller and Lyles had written the book and were playing Steve Jenkins and Sam Peck, the characters they had created in *Shuffle Along*. *Runnin' Wild* took place back in Jimtown again and with many of the same actors from *Shuffle Along* it had a successful run of 228 performances. The following season brought a lavish new musical revue by Sissle and Blake, *Chocolate Dandies*, which, despite boasting a cast that included Blake, Sissle, Josephine Baker and Elizabeth Welsch, closed after a disappointing ninety-six performances. Robert Kimball and William Bolcom ascribe the show's failure to the extravagant running costs – salaries alone cost the production $7,500 per week, as opposed to $3,700 for *Shuffle Along*. Two months later *Dixie to Broadway* opened at the Broadhurst Theatre featuring an all black "March of the Wooden Soldiers" and the final stage appearance of Florence Mills, who stopped the show every night performing "Jungle Nights in Dixieland." That June saw *Lucky Sambo*, which offered all the expected degrading racial stereotypes. The curtain opened in front of Aunt Jemima's cabin and the plot told the story of how Rufus Johnson and Sambo Jenkins are tricked into bogus oil investment by Jim Nightengale, but the plan backfires when Rufus and Sambo actually strike oil. "One reviewer wrote, 'These negro musical shows vary in titles and principals but they all have one glorious feature in common – a genuine and spontaneous hilarity which can't be surpassed by the most elaborate troupe on the other side of the cotton line."[16] Despite this critic's mirth *Lucky Sambo* only ran for seven performances.

African-American musicals continued to be produced through the end of the decade – most of them closed a lot faster than they had hoped. One hit African-American musical was *Blackbirds of 1928*, produced and directed by Lew Leslie and marking the Broadway debut of the composer-lyricist team of Jimmy McHugh and Dorothy Fields. *Blackbirds of 1928* starred Adelaide Hall, Elizabeth

Welsch and Bill "Bojangles" Robinson and featured the songs "Diga Diga Doo" and "I Can't Give You Anything But Love."

Amidst all the gaiety, the high-stepping, the shuffling along, the "spontaneous hilarity" and blackface of the African-American musicals of the 1920s, there was a musical that came along and honestly dealt with issues of race and racial identity. And it came from the most unlikely of places.

Show Boat

The most well known and most often revived musical of the 1920s is Kern and Hammerstein's 1927 *Show Boat*. In addition to its initial run of 575 performances at the Ziegfeld Theatre, *Show Boat* had successful revivals in 1932, 1946, City Center revivals in 1948 and 1954, a successful tour produced by the Houston Grand Opera company which played on Broadway in 1983, and Hal Prince's 1994 revival which ran for 947 performances.

Show Boat had been a successful novel by Edna Ferber. Kern ran into Ferber at an opening night and asked for her permission to musicalize the work; although Ferber thought that the book defied musicalization, she agreed. Kern enlisted Hammerstein to write the book and lyrics, and after having written the bulk of the first act Kern and Hammerstein played their score for Ziegfeld, who they felt was the only producer able to mount a show that large with a cast of ninety, a large orchestra and massive scenic requirements. Once Ziegfeld was onboard, instead of taking the traditional six to eight weeks to write the musical, Kern and Hammerstein took almost a year, spending time along the Mississippi River to pick up authentic local color, dialects and regionalisms.

Show Boat sprawled – the story was epic, taking place over more than forty years, in locales along the Mississippi River from Natchez to Chicago. The musical followed the separate story lines of four separate couples: Gaylord Ravenal and Magnolia, Steve and Julie, Captain Andy and Parthy, and Queenie and Joe. The original production was a spectacle, with so many far-flung locales and sets by Joseph Urban.

Show Boat was unlike any other musical to date. It dealt with real and serious social issues: relations between the races, miscegenation, spousal abuse and abandonment, the ravages of alcoholism, addictive gambling. *Show Boat* featured a full white company and a full black company including full and separate choruses as well. Most musicals of the 1920s opened with a bright and peppy up-tempo number that marked time until late-comers could be seated and introduced the audience to the world of the musical, an energetic musical number that presented the characters and the locale or situation of the story. As the curtain rose on *Show Boat*, the audience heard the black stevedores singing Hammerstein's lyric:

> Niggers all work on the Mississippi,
> Niggers all work while the white folk play.
> Loading up boats wid de bales of cotton,

Gittin' no rest 'til de judgement day.

An audience used to light-hearted musicals was not ready for this opening. Subsequent revivals have softened this opening to: "Darkies all work on the Mississippi," "Colored folk work on the Mississippi," and ultimately "here we all work on the Mississippi," but clearly the thrust of the musical was to confront issues head-on. For the first time characters of color were portrayed with respect and treated as people of depth and substance. Although, while racial issues lie at the heart of the musical, and the portrayal of characters of color was treated with respect, the pivotal role of Queenie was played by a White Italian woman named Tess Gardella who performed in blackface under the stage name Aunt Jemima.

Norma Terris, the twenty-two-year-old ingénue who created the role of Magnolia, talked about the opening of the show in New York:

> "We all knew we were involved in something special. We wanted the audience to go out feeling they had seen something magnificent and new." But, she says, the opening night audience in New York was not quite prepared for what it saw. "After the show was over, there was no applause, no curtain calls, people were just dumbfounded. They sat there. Mr. Ziegfeld thought he had the biggest flop on his hands." Not so, of course. The reviews were unanimous in pronouncing "Show Boat" a masterpiece. "The next day, there was a line of people three blocks long. They were all there trying to get to the box office."[17]

The show was so successful that in 1928, Ziegfeld announced that he was putting together a second company for New York so that he could run the show in two theaters at the same time.

Show Boat is the next important step after the Princess musicals on the evolutionary path toward the integrated musical, in that fewer elements of the production than ever are present simply for their entertainment value. In an 1849 essay, opera composer Richard Wagner had created the term *Gesamtkunstwerk*, to describe a piece of art that is whole and complete unto itself, all embracing and with nothing extraneous. He applied that principle to the opera in his work, and by the end of the 1920s the musical theatre was following slowly down the same path.

Based on its success artistically and commercially *Show Boat* should have set the next trend for the musical theatre, establishing a model that other musical theatre artists would eagerly copy. Unfortunately while *Show Boat* was running, America was felled by the Great Depression, and the few people left who could afford theater tickets had little interest in dealing with weighty issues, they wanted to be transported to a land of magic and fun. In addition, producers could not afford to mount productions as large as *Show Boat*. Times were bad, but *Show Boat* had shown what was possible.

Chapter summary

- Jazz captured the wild abandon of the times as America roared into the 1920s.
- A period of great musical theatre songwriters includes:
    - Oscar Hammerstein, II
    - Richard Rodgers
    - Lorenz Hart
    - Cole Porter
    - George Gershwin
    - Ira Gershwin
    - Noël Coward
    - Vincent Youmans
    - Eubie Blake
    - B.G. "Buddy" DeSylva
    - Lew Brown
    - Ray Henderson
    - Jimmy McHugh
    - Dorothy Fields
    - E.Y. "Yip" Harburg.
- Revues of the 1920s were highly topical and many were very successful.
- Book musicals included: Cinderella musicals, Leisure-time musicals, Backstage musicals.
- A look at the African-American musicals of the 1920s.
- *Show Boat* provides a new model, but also ushers in the Great Depression.

Notes

1 Gerald Bordman, *American Musical Theatre: A Chronicle*, New York: Oxford University Press, 1992, p. 405.
2 Oscar Hammerstein II, lyric of the song "Indian Love Call" from *Rose-Marie*, 1924. Reprinted in *The Complete Lyrics of Oscar Hammerstein, II*, New York: Knopf Publishing, 2008, p. 55.
3 Richard Rodgers, *Musical Stages: An Autobiography*, New York: Random House, 1975, p. 27.
4 Lorenz Hart, lyric of the song, "Where or When," from *Babes In Arms*, 1937. Reprinted in *The Complete Lyrics of Lorenz Hart*, New York: Knopf Publishing, 1995.
5 "Theatre: The Boys From Columbia," *Time Magazine*, Monday September 26, 1938. Web, accessed August 21, 2011, http://www.time.com/time/magazine/article/ 0,9171,788806,00.html
6 James Ross Moore, *American National Biography*, Oxford: Oxford University Press, 1999. Web, accessed August 25, 2011, http://www.nytimes.com/books/first/g/garraty-biography.html
7 George's most popular symphonic works of the 1920s include *Rhapsody in Blue*, *Concerto in F* and *An American in Paris*.
8 Compare this with the 2000–1 season with twenty-eight Broadway openings, twelve musicals and sixteen plays.

9 John Bush Jones, *Our Musicals, Ourselves: A Social History of the American Musical Theare*, Waltham, MA: Brandeis University Press, 2003, p. 61.
10 Gerald Bordman, *American Musical Theatre: A Chronicle*, New York: Oxford University Press, 1978, p. 427.
11 Robert Kimball, liner notes for the CD, *Sissle and Blake's Shuffle Along*, New World NW260, 1976. Adapted from Robert Kimball and William Bolcom's *Reminiscing With Sissle and Blake*, New York: The Viking Press, 1973. Web, accessed August 27, 2011, http://www.dramonline.org/content/notes/nwr/80260.pdf
12 Ibid.
13 Ibid.
14 David Krasner, *A Beautiful Pageant: African American Theatre, Drama and Performance in the Harlem Renaissance, 1910–1927*, New York: Palgrave MacMillan, 2002, pp. 263–67.
15 Gerald Bordman, *American Musical Theatre: A Chronicle*, New York: Oxford University Press, 1978, p. 378.
16 Gerald Bordman, *American Musical Theatre: A Chronicle*, New York: Oxford University Press, 1978, p. 400.
17 Steve Metcalf, Hartford Courant, October 28, 1988. *Los Angeles Times*, Web, accessed September 9, 2011, http://articles.latimes.com/1988-10-28/entertainment/ca-146_1_show-boat

Further reading

The new voices of the 1920s

Furia, Philip. *Ira Gershwin: The Art of the Lyricist*. New York, NY: Oxford University Press, 1997.
Marmorstein, Gary. *A Ship Without A Sail: The Life of Lorenz Hart*. New York, NY: Simon and Schuster, 2012.
McBrien, William. *Cole Porter*. New York, NY: Vintage Press, 2000.
Pollack, Howard. *George Gershwin: His Life and Work*. Berkeley, CA: University of California Press, 2007.
Secrest, Meryle. *Somewhere for Me – A Biography of Richard Rodgers*. New York, NY: Applause Books, 2002.

Intermission

Intermission.

7 A double whammy, 1929–39

The Great Depression and talking movies threaten the Broadway musical

The Great Depression

On Wednesday, October 30, 1929, *Variety* reported a two-day drop in the stock market of 23 percent in the lingo of show business with the headline, "Wall Street Lays an Egg." Wall Street had in fact laid an egg, and the heady days of the 1920s when the money had flowed more freely than the bootleg hooch abruptly ended.

During the post-war boom of the 1920s money was available like never before for both the production of musical theatre, and to buy tickets. When the economy crashed, in 1929, that all dried up. In the 1920's Ziegfeld and others were able to put hundreds of beautiful girls on stage wearing spectacular costumes of the finest imported silk and lace, expensive headdresses and jewelry amidst opulent and spectacular sets, large orchestras and expensive stars. In a market that allowed for higher ticket prices and longer runs, producers were reasonably able to recoup those costs. But the crash meant fewer patrons at lower prices; those days were gone.

Talking pictures sweep the nation

In 1927, Warner Brothers released *The Jazz Singer* with Al Jolson, the first full-length film to include sequences of talking, and singing; up until then movies were silent, usually accompanied by music played live in the theater. *The Jazz Singer* revolutionized the entertainment industry. By 1929 every major studio had jumped on the bandwagon and geared up for the production of "talkies." With *The Jazz Singer*'s success, four movie musicals were released in 1928, sixty in 1929 and fifty in 1930. By 1933 the craze had stabilized, and throughout the rest of the 1930s Hollywood pumped out a steady stream of more than thirty new movie musicals each year.

These movie musicals were in direct competition for the audience of the American musical, on Broadway and on the road. The movies could provide all the spectacle audiences had come to look for onstage, including stars, in local theaters across the country for a fraction of the cost of a theater ticket. A top price theater ticket for a Broadway musical was $3.00, but a movie could be

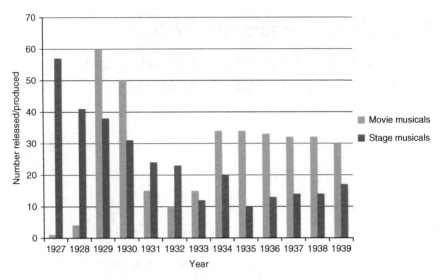

Figure 7.1 Movie musicals released vs. Broadway musicals produced 1927–39

seen for 50¢. As production of musicals was going gangbusters in Hollywood, the production of stage musicals in New York and around the country dried up (see Figure 7.1).

Now that movies had sound, Hollywood needed people to write the music, lyrics and dialog, and Hollywood studios looked to New York to fill this need. With production of new stage musicals down to almost a quarter of what it was in the previous decade, movies provided a source of income for the great musical theatre writers just when productions in New York were getting harder and harder to come by. For instance, during the Depression George M. Cohan had six shows open in New York (no musicals) while his songs appeared in forty movies.

The Jazz Singer had included Irving Berlin's song "Blue Skies." Between 1930 and 1939 Berlin had three musicals on Broadway while his songs appeared in forty-one movies. These include: *The Cocoanuts* (1929), *Puttin' on the Ritz* (1930), *Mammy* (1930), *Alexander's Ragtime Band* (1931), *Top Hat* (1935), *Follow The Fleet* (1936) and *Carefree* (1938).

Jerome Kern's five new Broadway musicals in the 1930s could not compare to his twenty-four Hollywood movies, including: *Show Boat* (1929 and again in 1936), *Sally* (1929), *Sunny* (1930), *The Cat and The Fiddle* (1934), *Music in The Air* (1934), *Roberta* (1935), *Swing Time* (1936) and *The Story of Vernon and Irene Castle* (1939).

Rodgers and Hart were more successful in New York in the 1930s than most, with twelve new musicals on Broadway; even so, their songs appear in twenty-six movies, including: *Spring is Here* (1930), *The Phantom President* (1932), *Hallelujah, I'm A Bum!* (1933), *Manhattan Melodrama* (1934) and *Babes in Arms* (1939).

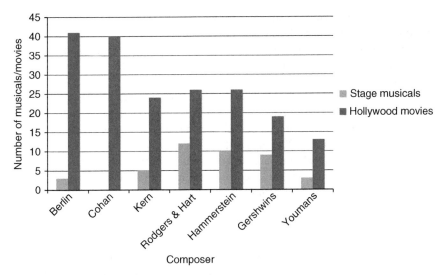

Figure 7.2 Number of new stage musicals vs. number of Hollywood movies 1929–39

Hammerstein also had ten new musicals produced on Broadway, while his songs appeared in twenty-six movies, including: *Show Boat* (1929 and 1936), *Sunny* (1930), *New Moon* (1930), *Music in the Air* (1934), *Sweet Adeline* (1934), *Rose-Marie* (1936) and *The Great Waltz* (1938).

George Gershwin had nine new musicals on Broadway, while nineteen movies featured his music, including: *St. Louis Blues* (1929), *Girl Crazy* (1932), *A Damsel in Distress* (1937), *Shall We Dance* (1937) and *The Goldwyn Follies* (1938). (See Figure 7.2.)

The potential for profit in movies was higher than that of the stage. With the ability to put multiple copies of movies in hundreds or thousands of theaters around the world simultaneously at minimal additional expense, movies operated on an entirely different financial scale than Broadway musicals. Writers needed to make a living during the Depression, and Hollywood needed product that they could package and sell around the world – it was a perfect match.

One of the great success stories of the movie musicals was the team of Harry Warren and Al Dubin. Warren and Dubin had each separately contributed songs to three Broadway musicals in the 1920s. When the Depression hit they moved to Hollywood, and began their collaboration. Their songs appeared in hundreds of movies during the decade. They were contracted as house writers for Warner Brothers from 1932 to 1938; although they were paid very well, Warner Brothers owned everything they wrote outright. In 1944 Warner Brothers bought Leon Schlesinger's cartoon production unit, which featured Bugs Bunny and Porky Pig, to directly compete with the successful Disney cartoons. Needing music for their cartoons, they decided to use Warren and Dubin's songs, which they already owned outright. This made Warren and Dubin's songs some of the best known of the 1930s – although they never received additional compensation or royalties. They finally made it back to Broadway in 1980, thirty-five years after Dubin's death and one year before Warren's, when producer David Merrick and director/choreographer Gower Champion combined two of their movies and brought them to Broadway as *42nd Street*.

The musical theatre not only lost audience and writers to the movies, but other talents moved from New York to Hollywood during the Depression; many never came back. Busby Berkeley, who had choreographed seventeen Broadway shows in the 1920s, moved to Hollywood and developed an entirely new choreographic vocabulary based on symmetry and camera position. Ruby Keeler, Al Jolson, Eddie Cantor, Fred Astaire and others left the musical theatre stage for the sound stages of Hollywood.

Stars of the 1930s

Like today, stars were used to drive business at the box office. Unlike today the stars were made on Broadway and then went on to Hollywood and the movies. While a strong Hollywood résumé can open doors on Broadway today, in the 1930s it was the reverse. With the production of stage musicals down, and the production of musical movies up, some of Broadway's great stars transitioned to the silver screen. Fred Astaire moved to Hollywood and became a movie star. The unique comic style of The Marx Brothers could never have worked in silent film, but was perfect for the "talkies." Bert Lahr, Ed Wynn, Bob Hope, Ray Bolger, Jimmy Durante, Ann Miller and Betty Grable, all transitioned from Broadway to the movies during the 1930s.

Many Broadway stars of the time who didn't transition to film are less familiar to us since there is little filmed record of their work, stars like William Gaxton, Victor Moore, Ethel Waters, Marilyn Miller and Bea Lillie. A few we know well despite the fact that the bulk of their work was onstage, stars like Ethel Merman (Broadway debut 1930) and Mary Martin (Broadway debut 1938).

Revues and vaudeville in the 1930s

Lavish stage spectacles could no longer make a go of it, financially. Costs to mount them were exorbitant and running expenses – with huge casts, orchestras and crews – placed them out of reach in the 1930s. Ziegfeld tried to continue as he had before, but had to withdraw from producing by 1932. The business model that had served Ziegfeld so well in the 1920s failed during the Depression. Ziegfeld's *Simple Simon*, featuring Ed Wynn's comic performance and Ruth Etting singing "Ten Cents a Dance," ran for 135 performances, but failed to pay back its expenses. *Smiles*, despite performances by the Astaires, Marilyn Miller, Eddie Foy, Jr. and Bob Hope, only ran for sixty-four performances due to the labored story, which crept "laboriously along, without cracking anything louder than a smile."[1] Of the *Follies of 1931*, Brooks Atkinson wrote, "There is a bankruptcy of ideas in this 'Follies.'"[2] Ziegfeld's final show, *Hot-Cha!*, managed to run for 119 performances, but lost money due to high expenses.

Earl Carroll opened successful 1930 and 1931 editions of his *Vanities*, at 215 and 300 performances respectively. Carroll gave the audience upbeat songs like "Out of a Clear Blue Sky" and "Parasols on Parade." The material was light and breezy, the chorus girls were more scantily clad than ever, but it wasn't enough. The 1932 edition took a huge loss, only running for eighty-seven performances. Carroll created a backstage musical murder mystery called *Murder at the Vanities* in 1933, but despite a run of 207 performances it closed at a loss. *The New York Times* review said, "the heart is out of this 'new romantic mystery comedy' which bears the 'Vanities' label. Without opulent scenery an elevator orchestra pit and all the gew-gaws of flamboyant showmanship, Mr. Carroll is a lonely watchman of the night."[3]

George White also tried to produce through the Depression, but by 1932 his productions ran out of steam. *George White's Music Hall Varieties of 1932* with Bert Lahr and Harry Richmond only ran for forty-seven performances, after which White closed it down, rewrote and reopened it for a disastrous twenty-four performances. He attempted editions in 1936 and 1939 but unsuccessfully.

As for vaudeville, competition with the "talkies" finally did it in. In an attempt to keep vaudeville alive, Keith and Albee increased the number of performances per day in each theater, but they couldn't stem the tide. In a desperate move in 1932 they even increased the number of shows a day at their flagship theater, the Palace in New York, to four, but even that wasn't enough. In November the Palace was renamed the "RKO Palace" and converted to a movie theater.

Despite the death of the large 1920s style revues and of vaudeville, there was still a place for variety musical entertainment throughout the 1930s – it just needed a new format, a different model. The successful revues of the 1930s were smaller and smarter. Gone were the huge choruses of beautiful girls and massive scenery, and in their place were strong scores, smart writing, clever staging ideas and smaller casts. Creativity and invention overtook opulence as the model for variety entertainments in the 1930s.

> **Hassard Short (1877–1956)**, actor, director, set and lighting designer. Born in England, Short brought a designer's eye to the director's chair. His revues of the 1930s set the standard for replacing opulence with wit, humor and charm.

Smaller revues

Leading the shift in how a revue was put together was British-born director and designer Hassard Short. Short made his Broadway debut as an actor in 1902. He had early successes as a director, staging Irving Berlin's *Music Box Revues* in 1921, 1922 and 1923. By 1928 he was lighting all of his shows as well. His 1930 *Three's a Crowd* was one of the hits of the season, with great praise lavished on the cleverness of both the material and the execution; with a relatively small cast of thirty-two (small considering the revues of the 1920s), it relied heavily on the talents of the three principals, Fred Allen, Clifton Webb and Libby Homan. The following year saw Short's greatest success, the quintessential 1930s musical revue, *The Band Wagon*, with music by Arthur Schwartz (1900–84), lyrics by Howard Dietz (1896–1983) and book by Dietz and George S. Kaufman (1889–1961). Dietz and Schwartz would become the top revue writers of the 1930s. *The New York Times* review of *The Band Wagon* read:

> Something went out and something came in with the arrival of "The Band Wagon" ten or eleven days ago. What went out was the overstuffed musical show.[4]

Short's design innovations included the introduction of the light bridge, and the revolving stage. His revues were the cleverest and the most popular of the 1930s. They included *Face the Music* and *As Thousands Cheer*, both by Irving Berlin, and he would continue to direct musical revues up through *Michael Todd's Peep Show* in 1950.

Arthur Schwartz (1900–84) and **Howard Dietz** (1896–1983) were one of the most successful composer and lyricist teams of the 1930s on Broadway. Their greatest successes were in the revue form; they excelled at writing great songs that stood on their own.

As Short was the pre-eminent director of 1930s revues, Dietz and Schwartz were the leading revue writers. Their 1930s shows include: *The Second Little Show* (1930), *Three's A Crowd* (1930), *The Band Wagon* (1931), *Flying Colors* (1932), *Revenge With Music* (1934), *At Home Abroad* (1935), *The Show Is On* (1937) and *Between the Devil* (1937). They were masters of writing brilliant songs that stood on their own, without character or plot, and played to the strengths of their stars. Their songs include: "By Myself," "Dancing in the Dark," "I Guess I'll Have to Change My Plan" and the perennial showbiz anthem, "That's Entertainment."

One of the longest runs of the decade was Olsen and Johnson's *Hellzapoppin'*. Ole Olsen and Chic Johnson had struggled in vaudeville for twenty-four years until it gave out from under them. In 1938 they compiled the material they had developed through those years and put it all into a revue-style Broadway entertainment. The result, *Hellzapoppin'*, was crazy, frenetic, silly and highly insulting – but the insult was part of its charm. Despite poor critical response, the show ran for 1,404 performances. There was a revival of *Hellzapoppin'* produced in 1977 starring comedian Jerry Lewis and actress Lynn Redgrave, but it closed out of town before reaching Broadway.

African-American revues in the 1930s

The 1930s saw many successful African-American revues. With a great many talented African-American performers in need of work, producers realized that they could pay African-Americans substantially lower salaries. The 1930s saw shows with titles like: *Brown Buddies* (1930), *Lew Leslie's Blackbirds* (1930), *Rhapsody in Black* (1931), *Blackberries of 1932* (1932), *Shuffle Along of 1932* (1932) and many more.

These shows featured great stars like Ethel Waters, Flournoy Miller, the Nicholas Brothers and the dance team of Buck and Bubbles. While these artists had work, they were relegated to playing stereotypes and rarely allowed a moment of genuine emotion. Outside of these shows, employment for African-American actors was limited to roles as maids, butlers, shoeshine boys and train porters.

Musical revues grow a social conscience

Despite the need for escapist entertainment, as the Depression deepened, revues, which had always dealt with topical material, began to become more political in nature. The song that became the anthem of the Great Depression, "Brother Can You Spare a Dime?," was written for the 1932 revue *Americana*. The *New York Times* review said "Brother Can You Spare a Dime?" "has expressed the spirit of these times with more heart-breaking anguish than any of the other prose bards of the day."[5]

Irving Berlin's 1933 hit, *As Thousands Cheer*, directed and lit by Short, was a solid hit at 400 performances. One of the standouts was Ethel Waters, of the 1930s great African-American singers, singing "Supper Time." As Waters sang the lyric: "Supper time, I should set the table, cause it's supper time, Somehow I'm not able, 'cause that man o' mine, Ain't comin' home no more," the silhouette of her husband hanging from the tree where he had been lynched informed the scene from behind. America was deeply in need of escapism, but the time was right for social and political statements on the stage of musical revues.

Pins and Needles, the second longest running show of the 1930s (after *Hellzapoppin'*), was commissioned by the International Ladies Garment Workers' Union (ILGWU). It was to have been an in-house union show, mounted for its members at the rented Princess Theatre. Harold Rome wrote the songs, and sketches were solicited from many writers. The actors were all ILGWU members – cutters, basters and sewing machine operators – who could only rehearse evenings and weekends. The show took a light-hearted pro-union look at current events. Only scheduled for a few performances, it caught the attention of theatergoers, ultimately moving to the Labor Stage and then to the Windsor Theatre, eventually playing for 1,108 performances. Throughout its entire run the cast was comprised of members of the ILGWU, most of whom continued to work at their day jobs during their time in the show, and for most of whom this was their only venture in professional theatre. By 1938, despite the Depression, the time was right for material with a political bent – even as gentle as this material was. Songs and sketches changed through the course of the run as current events came and went. Songs included: "It's Better With a Union Man" and "One Big Union For Two."

Book musicals of the 1930s

Book musicals of the 1930s tended to be light, breezy entertainments designed to take the audience's mind off their troubles for a few hours. They had learned the lessons of the Princess musicals; without lavish spectacle and huge casts, the shows had to be driven by plot, story and character. Throughout the decade the plot-driven musical continued to evolve, the level of integration of elements grew deeper – all the elements of production were used more and more to service the story. The specialty acts of the earlier musicals had no place in the musicals of the 1930s – instead characters with conflicts to be resolved drove the evening and informed the music, lyrics, dialog, structure, costuming, scenic elements, choreography and all other elements of production.

Most of the 1930s plots would be considered silly today: they were peopled by stowaways, gangsters, society matrons, American expatriots, French Ambassadors and the like. They spoke the language of everyday people but their position in life was heightened a little from the average American, helping audiences forget their troubles for a couple of hours, by offering characters whose problems seemed relatively simple.

The economic realities of the 1930s dictated that fewer shows were produced, but the political and social realities saw the introduction of social and political satire into the musical theatre. The book musicals of the 1930s were all light and funny, but they fell into two categories, the escapist entertainment musical comedies or the topical satirical musicals.

Musical comedy of the 1930s

Hot off the success of *Show Boat*, Jerome Kern weathered the Depression in New York better than most. Although he was in Hollywood supervising the 1929 movie of *Sally* and the 1930 movie of *Sunny*, he returned to New York for the October 1931 opening of *The Cat and the Fiddle*, for which he wrote the music, and co-wrote the book and lyrics with Otto Harbach. This love story about an American woman composer jazz musician and a classical Romanian composer ran for 395 performances at the depth of the Depression.

Music in the Air, with book and lyrics by Oscar Hammerstein, II, opened in the fall of 1932 and ran for 342 performances. A young composer and his love travel from rural Bavaria to Munich seeking a music publisher. Once in the city they fall in love with other people, but ultimately learn that their place is at home, together; they return and reunite. Although the plot sounds hackneyed today, Brooks Atkinson wrote:

> At last the musical drama has been emancipated. [...] No precision dancing troupes, no knock-about comedians; no flamboyant song numbers; no grandeous scenic play – none of the hackneyed trumperies. Having a music box filled with tunes in all of his most alluring genres Mr. Kern has found a way to sing them spontaneously, and Mr. Hammerstein has spun him a sentimental adventure that warms the vocal chords.[6]

Stripped of spectacle by the practicalities of producing a musical in the Depression, Kern and Hammerstein focused on telling their story. The result was true musical drama uncluttered with extraneous dances, massive scenic effects, comedians and other specialty acts thrown in to divert and amuse. In *Music in the Air*, Kern and Hammerstein arrived at a truer musical play than had yet been seen on Broadway.

Roberta, from 1933, with book and lyrics by Harbach, was successful at 295 performances. The story of an American fullback who inherits his aunt's dress shop in Paris, he loves an American girl but a Russian girl loves him. In the hands of director Short, *Roberta* pleased Depression audiences.

After *Roberta*, Kern moved to Hollywood where he worked on dozens of movies with old New York friends like Hammerstein, Busby Berkeley and Fred Astaire. After suffering a heart attack his doctors advised him to focus on writing for movies, which was less stressful and demanding. However, in 1939 he again teamed up with Hammerstein for his final Broadway musical *Very Warm for May,* which only ran for fifty-nine performances.

In 1945 Richard Rodgers and Oscar Hammerstein, who were producing the Broadway musical *Annie Get Your Gun*, asked Kern to write the score. Kern returned to New York, but had forgotten to bring his heart medication. While crossing the street, trying to get to a pharmacy, he suffered a cerebral hemorrhage. Hammerstein was with Kern at the end – he is said to have hummed Kern's favorite of his songs "I've Told Every Little Star" into Kern's ear, and when Kern did not respond Hammerstein knew he was dead.

Of the great songwriters of the 1930s, **Cole Porter** (**1891–1964**) was the one Midwestern gentile amongst the Broadway composers and lyricists. Born wealthy, Porter's lifestyle informed, but never diminished his art. His songs, born of a life of wit and the mad social whirl, appealed to an audience looking for fantasies into which they could escape during the Depression. But as a closeted homosexual, his work is also informed by his struggle for identity, and reveals the depth of his humanity as well as his wit and sophistication.

Cole Porter was born in Peru, Indiana, to a Baptist family, grandson to the wealthiest man in the state. He was raised in great wealth and coddled by his mother. Violin lessons started at age six, piano at eight, and at ten his mother helped him write his first operetta. Graduating as valedictorian of his high school class, his grandfather sent him on a tour of Europe and then to Yale University, where Porter discovered that writing songs was key to his popularity. He supposedly wrote 300 songs at Yale, including the fight song "Bingo Eli Yale," still played at Yale football games today. Cole began graduate studies at Harvard Law School, but bored by law, he switched to music before ultimately leaving Harvard.

In 1915 Porter had a song in the Broadway revue *Hands Up*. The next year his first full Broadway production, *See America First*, opened, a dismal failure. A "patriotic comic opera," *See America First* closed in less than two weeks.

To recover from this disappointment, Porter moved to Paris, where he maintained a luxurious apartment as a base for his travels throughout Europe and where he regularly entertained. His scandalous parties were famous for "much gay and bisexual activity, Italian nobility, cross-dressing, international musicians, and a large surplus of recreational drugs."[7] Porter met and married Linda Lee, a wealthy American divorcee; that Porter was a homosexual didn't matter, they were deeply committed to each other in all other ways. In 1919 many homosexual men married women to maintain an appearance of "normalcy;" the marriage legitimized Porter in the eyes of the world.

Although thought to be a jet-setting partier, Porter actually worked hard throughout the 1920s, building a catalog of songs; several had appeared in London and Broadway revues. After an almost ten-year hiatus from Broadway, Porter returned in 1928 with the musical *Paris*. The critics had trouble following the silly and incidental plot which was mostly an excuse for beautiful costumes and terrific songs, particularly "Let's Do It, Let's Fall In Love." The show made a star of Irene Bordoni and Porter's triumphant return to Broadway ran for 195 performances.

Despite opening mere days after the collapse of the stock market in 1929, his next show was a huge success. *Fifty Million Frenchmen* was energetic, witty, whimsical and set in a beautiful place among beautiful people. It succeeded for the same reasons that the movies of Busby Berkeley or Fred Astaire and Ginger Rogers did; they let people escape to a frivolous place. Porter was the most successful Broadway songwriter of the 1930s, with more hits than anyone else. The lavish lifestyle he lived allowed him to depict a world onstage into which people struggling through the Depression wanted to escape.

Porter spent the rest of the 1930s shuttling between Hollywood, which he loved for the relaxed, open homosexual lifestyle it allowed him to lead, and New York. He created ten Broadway musicals between the market crash and the end of the 1930s, two revues and eight book musicals – all but one turned a profit. Almost all of these shows received productions in London, where Porter was immensely popular.

In 1932's *Gay Divorce* (which became the 1934 movie *The Gay Divorcee*), Fred Astaire sang "Night and Day" in his final Broadway musical. It ran for 248 performances.

For *Anything Goes* (1934), producer Vinton Freedley lined up all of the talent – stars Ethel Merman, William Gaxton and Victor Moore, book writers

P.G. Wodehouse and Guy Bolton, and songwriter Porter – by claiming the others had already agreed. The musical was to have been about a shipwreck; tragically, just before rehearsals began, a major shipping accident occurred, causing many deaths and rendering the musical far from funny. Last minute rewrites resulted in one of Porter's greatest hits, and one of the most often revived musicals of the 1930s. The original 1934 production of *Anything Goes* ran for 420 performances. Porter's score included "I Get a Kick Out Of You," "All Through the Night" and "You're the Top." Ethel Merman became one of Porter's favorite leading ladies – they did four more shows together.

Jubilee was written with Moss Hart while the Harts and the Porters were on an around-the-world cruise in 1935. Directed and lit by Hassard Short, it ran for 169 performances. Songs included "Begin the Beguine" and "Just One of Those Things." *Jubilee* recouped its investment, but Porter was disappointed in the response it received and vowed to write less literate songs from then forward. In an interview he said, "Sophisticated allusions are good for about six weeks … more fun, but only for myself and about eighteen other people. … Polished, urbane and adult playwriting in the musical field is strictly a creative luxury."[8]

Red, Hot and Blue (1936) starred Jimmy Durante, Ethel Merman and Bob Hope. The flimsy plot revolved around a former manicurist, Nails O'Reilly Duquesne, who organizes a benefit to raise money to rehabilitate convicts with her sidekick, an ex-con, and her boyfriend, Bob Hale. Together they search for Bob's old girlfriend; but the lottery that they start up is deemed unconstitutional. Porter's songs included: "Down in the Depths on the 90th Floor," "It's Delovely" and "Ridin' High." *Red, Hot and Blue* ran for 183 performances.

In 1937, while riding, Porter's horse threw him and then fell on him, crushing his legs, leaving him crippled and in pain for the rest of his life. He spent the first seven months after the accident in the hospital. In tremendous pain, and distraught over the thought of losing one or both of his legs, Porter put his energies into his writing. His first show after the accident, *You Never Know* (1938), was not a success, but Porter quickly regained his professional stride in 1938's *Leave It to Me*. This show introduced audiences to a young Mary Martin singing "My Heart Belongs to Daddy," and also featured William Gaxton, Victor Moore and Sophie Tucker. The plot revolved around an aging businesswoman, Alonzo "Stinky" Goodhue, who is named American ambassador to the Soviet Union.

Porter's last musical of the 1930s was *DuBarry Was a Lady* (1938), which ran for 408 performances. A men's room attendant, in love with the nightclub singer, is accidentally knocked unconscious by a spiked cocktail. He dreams that he is King Louis XV of France and she is Madame du Barry. Despite poor critical response, audiences loved it, thanks to Porter's score and stars Bert Lahr and Ethel Merman. The hit of the score was the great Porter list song, "Friendship."

Much of the musical theatre during the Depression was light comic enter-tainment. Cole Porter's shows represent the pinnacle of those shows. Funny and clever list songs and patter songs, deeply felt emotion, risqué innuendo, all combined with elegance and sophistication, define the work of Porter through the 1930s. His were unquestionably the best of the escapist musicals.

> Theatrical renaissance man, **Sir Noël Coward (1899–1973)**, was a play-wright, actor, director, composer and lyricist. Coward, like Porter, represented flamboyant wit and sophistication. British by birth, Coward's career was international.

Noël Coward had been introduced to New York audiences in 1924 when British revue producer André Charlot introduced two Coward songs, "Parisian Pierrot" and "There's Life in The Old Girl Yet," to Broadway. Even though he remained equally active in London and New York, Coward wrote, directed and sometimes starred in eight productions on Broadway in the late 1920s, six plays, one musical revue, *This Year of Grace,* and one operetta, *Bitter Sweet.*

Throughout the 1930s Coward wrote, directed and starred in plays like *Private Lives* and *Design for Living* and contributed songs to revues like *Ziegfeld Follies of 1931.* Although the bulk of his work in the 1930s was on plays rather than musicals, many of his plays included songs and underscoring, all of which he wrote himself. In the 1930s he wrote the operetta *Conversation Piece* (1934), the musical *Operette* and the revue *Set to Music* (1938). Perhaps his most impressive achievement of the 1930s was the show *Tonight at 8:30* (1936) which was a series of ten short plays played in rotation, three or four in an evening to make up an entire evening at the theater. Included in these was the musical *The Red Peppers* (1936), in which Coward and lifelong friend Gertrude Lawrence played a bickering husband and wife music-hall team.

Known more for his songs than his musicals in the 1930s, titles include: "Mad About the Boy," "Mad Dogs and Englishmen," "Someday I'll Find You" and "(Don't Put your Daughter on the Stage) Mrs. Worthington." Many con-sider Coward to have been the wittiest and most literary facile lyricist since W.S. Gilbert and his musical range stretched from turn-of-the-century Victorian popular to music hall to operetta to the rumbas, sambas and bossa novas of the 1950s and 1960s. His artistic scope was so wide that he defies being categorized as simply a playwright, a composer, a director or a star.

Cutting edge 1930s book musicals – further integration and political/social satire

The large revues had died off and were reimagined as more streamlined enter-tainments by Berlin, Dietz and Schwartz, Short and others. Bright and breezy diversionary book musicals by Kern, Porter, Coward and Hammerstein were successful. Simultaneously, a small contingent of artists were pushing book musicals in new directions, further integrating production elements into moving the story forward. Social and political issues were central to their work, frequently through the use of satire. Just as the revue had shifted from topicality to political and social commentary, some book musicals addressed these issues.

The Gershwins in the 1930s

The Gershwins saw great success throughout the 1920s, at first separately, and then together. Shows like *Lady, Be Good!*, *Tip-Toes*, *Oh, Kay!* and *Funny Face* had made their producers, Aarons and Freedley, rich, and made the Gershwins two of the hottest writers of the 1920s. George Gershwin's sound was unique and contemporary – urban and wildly popular – while Ira's lyrics were unmatched in their wit and their sense of fun – their sheer wordplay.

The first Gershwin show of the 1930s, *Strike Up the Band,* was originally produced in 1927, with a book by George S. Kaufman, but closed out of town before Broadway. In 1930, book writer Morrie Ryskind worked with Kaufman rewriting the book. Originally, Horace J. Fletcher, a cheese tycoon, maintains his grip on the American market by getting the government to declare war on Switzerland in response to a tax on cheese. In the revised version Fletcher is a chocolate manufacturer and a romantic plot was emphasized. The mood of the country, three months after the stock market crash, had become more accepting of a darker political musical; the show was successful, running for 191 performances and inspiring two sequels. Bobby Clark, the reigning comic actor of the day, played Fletcher to rave reviews. Prior to *Strike Up the Band*, the Gershwins had written many terrific songs, but for *Strike Up the Band* they consciously set out to write a score as integrated as those of Gilbert and Sullivan, whose work they used as a model. While there still are terrific songs, including "Strike Up the Band" and "I've Got A Crush on You," the Gershwins use extended and shortened song forms, underscoring, leitmotif and recitative. It was new for a new day, and audiences loved it.

Later that year the Gershwins' *Girl Crazy* opened at the Alvin, starring two young actresses both soon to become stars; Ginger Rogers and, in her Broadway debut, Ethel Merman. Another notch on their belts, *Girl Crazy* ran for 272 performances. In 1992 *Girl Crazy* was revised as *Crazy For You*. The premise of the plot remained the same; a rich young playboy is sent out west by his father to put him out of reach of gold-digging women, but he goes and falls in love.

Two months later the Gershwins saw their biggest hit to date with rave reviews and 441 performances at the Music Box Theatre, *Of Thee I Sing*, the sequel to *Strike Up the Band*. With a book once again by Kaufman and Ryskind, *Of Thee I Sing* was the first musical to win a Pulitzer Prize. *The New York Times* wrote:

In "Of Thee I Sing" […] George S. Kaufman and Morrie Ryskind have substituted for the doddering musical comedy plot a taut and lethal satire of national politics, and George Gershwin has composed a score that sings in many voices, simmers with ideas and tells the story more resourcefully than the book. [...] "Of Thee I Sing" is no Gilbert and Sullivan palimpsest, for the humorous elegances of Gilbert and the idyllic melodies of Sullivan belong to an era that is dead. "Of Thee I Sing" is shrill and galvanic. It is written and produced in a nerve-twanging key. It attacks with the rapier and the club indiscriminately. [...] "Of Thee I Sing" has very nearly succeeded in liberating the musical comedy stage from the mawkish and feeble-minded formula that has long been considered inevitable.[9]

In *Of Thee I Sing*, Presidential candidate, John P. Wintergreen, runs on a platform of love, holding a beauty contest to select his first lady (satirizing the recently inaugurated Miss American Pageant). As the review indicated, the score was integrated in the telling of the story in addition to being tuneful.

After a hiatus in Hollywood, *Pardon My English* opened in January 1933. The show was in trouble out of town, suffering from a number of star replacements and rewrites until it arrived in New York, a cobbled-together mess.

October 1933 brought the third political musical by the Gershwins, Kaufman and Ryskind, *Let 'em Eat Cake*. This time Wintergreen and his Vice-President, Throttlebottom, fail to be elected for a second term, so they form a Fascist movement to overthrow the elected government. The material was exceedingly dark, and the show closed after a mere ninety performances.

The Gershwins turned their attentions towards a project that had been on the back burner for several years which became the first great American opera, *Porgy and Bess*. Based on the play *Porgy* by DuBose and Dorothy Heyward, *Porgy and Bess* takes place in Charleston, South Carolina, and tells the story of a poor African-American cripple named Porgy who falls in love with a cocaine-addicted prostitute named Bess. Porgy's love transforms Bess, but when she is led back to her former street life by Sportin' Life, Porgy vows to follow them to New York to win Bess back. Gershwin spent the summer of 1934 on a small island near Charleston to get a feel for the locale, vocal and speech patterns of the local people.

When the opera opened in 1935 it ran well over four hours. Praised by some and decried by others, to this day scholars and critics argue over whether it is an opera or a musical. In *Porgy and Bess* the Gershwins abandoned satire; what continued was development of the score as the driving mechanism of storytelling. Their earlier 1930s musicals helped them evolve as dramatists to the point where they could write an opera in an American vocabulary in which the action of the play is driven forward by every note and word. The score includes the hits "Summertime," "I Got Plenty of Nothin'" and "It Ain't Necessarily So." *Porgy and Bess* opened, at the Alvin Theatre, produced by the Theatre Guild. The original production of *Porgy and Bess* ran for only 124 performances, but a highly successful touring production, which had stripped the show of its recitative and simply replaced it with dialog, came back to Broadway in 1942 and ran for 286 performances.

Porgy and Bess was George Gershwin's last Broadway musical; while in Hollywood working on several film scores he tragically died less than two years later at the age of thirty-nine of a brain tumor.

The WPA and *The Cradle Will Rock*

In 1935 President Franklin Roosevelt created a massive employment initiative called the Works Progress Administration (WPA). The WPA spent $13.4 billion dollars funding different projects, between 1935 and 1943, offering employment to three-million people in 1938 alone. One branch of the WPA, the Federal Theatre Project (FTP), funded theatre across the country – new works, touring productions, children's theatre, "living newspapers" – it ran the gamut.

Perhaps the most notorious project supported by the FTP was Marc Blitzstein's musical *The Cradle Will Rock* (1937). Produced by John Houseman, directed by Orson Welles, *The Cradle Will Rock* is an allegory of corporate greed and hypocrisy. The musical is set in "Steeltown, USA," and revolves around the evil owner of the mill, the town and everything else, "Mr. Mister," his wife "Mrs. Mister," their children "Junior Mister" and "Sister Mister," newspaper editor "Editor Daily," the minister "Reverend Salvation," the union organizer "Larry Foreman" and "the Moll," a prostitute. The musical equates the Moll's prostitution with the town fathers prostituting themselves for wealth and power.

The day before *The Cradle Will Rock* was scheduled to open, the WPA closed the production and shuttered the theater. Welles, Houseman and Blitzstein, along with the cast, met the opening night audience in front of the theater and paraded them uptown to another theater, procured at the last minute. Actors' Equity had forbade their members from appearing onstage, as had the musicians' union; but nobody could stop them from sitting in the house and chiming in with their parts when the time came. The curtain opened on Blitzstein sitting alone at the piano, and as he began to speak and sing the show by himself, the cast joined in from where they sat scattered throughout the house. The result was one of the most electric evenings in the history of the American musical. The buzz caused created a clamor for tickets, and the production ran for 108 performances – as it had been performed on that first night, from the audience, with Blitzstein alone onstage at the piano.

The Cradle Will Rock has received several off-Broadway revivals and many regional productions; it is customarily staged with just an onstage piano and a group of actors sitting in chairs lined up across the stage.

Rodgers and Hart in the 1930s

Rodgers and Hart had found their initial success on Broadway from 1925 to 1931. The Depression drove them to Hollywood, as it did so many other Broadway artists, where they spent 1931 to 1934. Upon their return to Broadway in 1935 they wrote many of the songs that would become the foundation of the American songbook while they pushed the book musical forward with every show. Audiences of the 1930s were always excited to see the newest show by "the boys;" they represented the hottest and the most current on Broadway.

Jumbo (1935), the circus musical produced by Billy Rose, played for 233 performances at the 5,000-seat Hippodrome Theatre. Songs included "The Most Beautiful Girl in the World," "My Romance" and "Little Girl Blue."

For *On Your Toes* (1936) Rodgers and Hart wrote their own book with director George Abbott. In pitting popular music and dance against classical, *On Your Toes* is the first time a Broadway musical used dance for dramatic purposes; the choreography was by George Balanchine (1904–83). Songs from *On Your Toes* include "There's a Small Hotel" and Richard Rodgers' ballet *Slaughter on Tenth Avenue*.

Babes in Arms (1937) was a cast without a star, whose youthful energy made up for the lack of star power. Without the encumbrance of star salaries, the 289-performance run was highly profitable.

I'd Rather Be Right, from 1937, had a book by George Kaufman and Moss Hart, and starred George M. Cohan as Franklin Roosevelt. Although *I'd Rather Be Right* was deeply satirical during its pre-Broadway tryouts, by opening the bite had been removed from whatever political humor remained, and it was simply a rousing good time starring a beloved old star making a return to the stage at age fifty-nine.

I Married an Angel opened in 1938 to rave reviews. Critics and audiences were enchanted by the story of a wealthy banker, bored with mortal girls who marries an angel but realizes that perfection can be inconvenient. This show ran for 338 performances at the Shubert Theatre.

Six months later *The Boys From Syracuse,* an adaptation of Shakespeare's *The Comedy of Errors* with a book and direction by George Abbott, opened at the Alvin Theatre where it ran for 235 performances. An off-Broadway revival in 1963 ran for 500 performances. Songs included "Falling in Love with Love," "This Can't Be Love" and "Sing for Your Supper."

Too Many Girls, their final show of the 1930s, featured a young Cuban conga player named Desi Arnaz. In some ways *Too Many Girls* was a throwback to the college musicals of the 1920s, with true love helping to win the big football game for Pottawatomie College. But Rodgers' music was hip and swingy; Hart's lyrics were full of witty rhymes and clever ideas; and most importantly George Abbott's staging kept the evening moving at a bright and breezy pace.

> **George Abbott (1887–1995)** appeared in his first Broadway play in 1914. As a writer he had his first play produced on Broadway in 1925, and wrote and directed his first Broadway play in 1926. He directed his first musical in 1935 and quickly became the most important and influential director of musicals well into the 1960s.

George Abbott, born in western New York State, raised there and in Wyoming, wrote his first play at the University of Rochester, and continued his studies at Harvard University. Abbott began his Broadway career in 1913 as an actor and worked in the theatre continuously until his death in 1995, eighty-two years later, at the age of 107. He directed twenty-three plays, most of which he also wrote, before he ever directed a musical. In the 1930s Abbott directed the Rodgers and Hart shows *Jumbo*, *On Your Toes*, *The Boys From Syracuse* and *Too Many Girls*. Later, in the 1940s and 1950s, Abbott became one of the most prolific book writers and directors of musicals on Broadway. He created a massive string of hits, and was frequently brought in as a show doctor to fix other directors' shows before they opened. As important as his credits, Abbott was a mentor to the entire generation of writers, directors, choreographers and other theatre artists who came into their own in the 1960s and 1970s. Abbott gave a chance to young unknowns like: Helen Hayes, Gene Kelly, Eddie Albert, Shirley MacLaine, Carol Burnett, Harold Prince, Leonard Bernstein, Bob Fosse and Jerome Robbins.

In the 1930s he was beginning to develop his style with musicals, known as "the Abbott touch." He insisted that his shows move quickly and that his actors speak loudly and clearly. It was Abbott, as much as Rodgers and Hart, who pushed the musicals of the later 1930s to a more integrated style in which everything kept the story moving forward – it was all a part of the pacing, which to Abbott was everything. In the 1930s alone, Abbott directed twenty-eight plays and musicals on Broadway, produced twenty others, wrote eight and appeared in two.

Friedrich Nietzsche said "whatever doesn't kill me makes me stronger." Neither the Depression nor talking pictures were able to kill the musical theatre, and ultimately, with the further integration of the musical and its politicalization, the musical grew up throughout the decade. It paved the way for the maturity that was to come early in the next decade.

Chapter summary

- The Great Depression.
- Talking movies.
- Stars of the 1930s.
- Revues and vaudeville in the 1930s.
- Hassard Short.
- Dietz and Schwartz.
- African-American revues.
- Revues become political.
- Book musicals of the 1930s.
- Cole Porter.
- Noël Coward.
- The Gershwins' 1930s musicals.
- The WPA and *The Cradle Will Rock*.

- Rodgers and Hart musicals of the 1930s.
- George Abbott.

Notes

1 Brooks Atkinson, "The Play: Smiling at the Ziegfeld," *The New York Times*, November 19, 1930. Web, accessed June 16, 2012, http://query.nytimes.com/mem/archive/pdf?res=F7061EFD395A11738DDDA00994D9415B808FF1D3
2 Brooks Atkinson, "The Play: Follies for 1931," *The New York Times*, July 2, 1931. Web, accessed June 16, 2012, http://query.nytimes.com/mem/archive/pdf?res=F00A1 7FE395E10728DDDAB0894DF405B818FF1D3
3 Brooks Atkinson, "The Play: Murder to Music in the New Version of Earl Carroll's 'Vanities'," *The New York Times*, September 13, 1933. Web, accessed June 16, 2012, http://query.nytimes.com/mem/archive/pdf? res=F00F11FC3D5516738DDDAA0994D1405B838FF1D3
4 J. Brooks Atkinson, "Reviewing the Revue: 'The Band Wagon' as Harbinger of a New Music Show Form – Beatrice Lillie, the Chaplin of the Middle Class," *The New York Times*, June 14, 1931. Web, accessed June 16, 2012, http://query.nytimes.com/mem/archive/pdf?res=F60F12F63D5F1B728DDDAD0994DE405B818FF1D3
5 J. Brooks Atkinson, "'The Play': Design and Dance in an 'American Revue' That Represents Modern Taste in Artistry," *The New York Times*, October 6, 1932. Web, accessed June 21, 2012, http://query.nytimes.com/mem/archive/pdf?res=F00D17F6385 513738DDDAF0894D8415B828FF1D3
6 Brooks Atkinson, "The Play: Emancipation of the Musical Drama in 'Music in the Air' by Kern and Hammerstein," *The New York Times*, November 8, 1932. Web, accessed June 21, 2012, http://query.nytimes.com/mem/archive/pdf?res=F40614FA3 55516738DDDA00894D9415B828FF1D3
7 J.X. Bell, Cole World Wide: Cole Porter Biography. Web, accessed June 21, 2012, http://www.coleporter.org/bio.html
8 Cole Porter, cited in William McBrien, *Cole Porter*, New York: Vintage Books, 2000, p. 200.
9 J. Brooks Atkinson, "'Of Thee I Sing': Stinging Satire of National Politics in a Hilarous and Original Musical Comedy," *The New York Times*, January 3, 1932. Web, accessed June 23, 2012, http://query.nytimes.com/mem/archive/pdf?res= FA0B1FFC355B13738DDDAA0894D9405B828FF1D3

Further reading

Cole Porter

Citron, Stephen. *Noel and Cole: The Sophisticates*. Montclair, NJ: Hal Leonard, 2005.
McBrien, William. *Cole Porter*. New York, NY: Vintage, 2000.

Rodgers and Hart

Marx, Samuel. *Rodgers and Hart: Bewitched, Bothered and Bedeviled: an Anecdotal Account*. New York, NY: G.P. Putnam and Sons, 1976.

The second act

8 A bright golden haze, 1939–45

The American musical comes of age

The opening of Rodgers and Hammerstein's *Oklahoma!* on March 31, 1943 was the pivotal event in the American musical theatre of the 1940s. *Oklahoma!* completed the development of the integrated musical, and established a new structural model in which every element was driven by story or plot.

Development towards the integrated musical had started with Kern, Bolton and Wodehouse's Princess musicals, advanced through *Show Boat* and the Gershwins' satirical trilogy in the 1930s. But prior to *Oklahoma!*, musicals included gratuitous entertainment elements as respite from relentless plots. The final element to be integrated was choreography. Songs had been plot- and character-driven by the mid-1910s, and scenic spectacle had fallen away in the budget-strapped 1930s. But "bringing on the dancing girls" was a well-worn tradition in musicals in the first forty years of the twentieth century – it was a sure way to perk up an audience and keep them attentive.

Agnes de Mille's choreography for *Oklahoma!* kept the story moving forward in ways that choreography never had before. Into classical theatrical ballet, she integrated folk dance forms to tell story ("The Farmer and the Cowman"), she used dance to reveal character and relationships ("All Er Nuthin'") and she dug deep into the recesses of Laurie's psyche and id in the "Dream Ballet." Laurie, conflicted by her feelings towards two men, takes a whiff of the Peddler's "Elixir of Egypt," meant to reveal the "truth" of her heart, and falls into a dream in which Laurie's conflict is acted out in ballet. All of the choreography in *Oklahoma!* was created to advance the story.

But before we get to *Oklahoma!* …

The wind-up

The work that Hammerstein did with Kern on *Show Boat* bears directly on the work he did with Rodgers in *Oklahoma!*, even though there was a fifteen-year gap between them. The satirical musicals of the 1930s prepared audiences to deal with serious issues in a musical. *Porgy and Bess* is another progenitor of *Oklahoma!* By the early 1940s, the musical theatre was rife with experimentation. Three musicals in particular paved the way for *Oklahoma!*: *Cabin in the Sky* (1940), *Pal Joey* (1940) and *Lady in the Dark* (1941).

Cabin in the Sky, "a Negro fantasy in two acts and nine scenes," was written by Vernon Duke, John La Touche and Lynn Root. It told the story of "Little Joe" Jackson who dies and should end up in hell, but thanks to the love of a good woman and faithful wife, Petunia, is given a second chance to get into heaven. Despite the show's rave reviews, it only ran for 156 performances, and never received a major revival or tour. Brooks Atkinson's review states, "Perhaps *Cabin in the Sky* could be better than it is, but this correspondent cannot image how. For the musical fantasy, which opened at the Martin Beck last evening, is original and joyous in an imaginative vein that suits the theatre's special genius. [...] Ethel Waters has been essential to happiness in the theatre for some time. But she has never given a performance as rich as this before."[1] The brilliant cast also included Todd Duncan, Dooley Wilson and Rex Ingram; but the real star of the evening was director and choreographer George Balanchine (1904–83).

Originally from St. Petersburg, Russia, Balanchine, an international ballet star, had founded and was ballet-master of New York City Ballet. By 1940, in addition to his work in the ballet, Balanchine had choreographed twelve Broadway musicals, including *On Your Toes, Babes in Arms* and *The Boys From Syracuse*. Balanchine both staged and choreographed *Cabin in the Sky* in order to get a fluidity of movement from scene to song and between scenes. Balanchine begins the emergence of the director/choreographer. Much of *Cabin in the Sky*'s success is attributed to Balanchine's visionary approach. A fantasy, *Cabin in the Sky* lent itself to fantastical staging. Balanchine employed the Katherine Dunham Dancers,[2] allowing him access to the physical vocabulary of traditional and contemporary Black American dance, which he incorporated with ballet. Integrating these different styles, Balanchine choreographed the entire show, including scene changes performed in view of the audience, to create a seamless evening that flowed from beginning to end, in an effort to create the cinematic flow so much desired beginning in the 1940s. Brooks Atkinson further points out, "Musical shows seldom acquire dancing such as [Balanchine] has directed here – motion in many lines set on fire with excitement. If the rules of Equity permitted, probably the dancers in *Cabin in the Sky* would be glad to pay Mr. Balanchine something for the privilege of appearing under his direction, for he has released them from the bondage of hack dancing and ugliness."[3]

Creating a physical vocabulary from folk, ethnic and ballet, Balanchine used dance to drive the play forward as never before. Other choreographers later developed this further; Agnes de Mille would be credited with this innovation with her work on *Oklahoma!* Although Balanchine continued to choreograph for the musical theatre, most of the rest of his career was in ballet. The only other original Broadway musical Balanchine directed and choreographed was *What's Up*, the first Lerner and Lowe musical. *Cabin in the Sky* is an important step along the path to the integrated musical and towards the rise of the director/choreographer.

Rodgers and Hart, throughout their collaboration, never became formulaic; they always strove to push the musical theatre forward. Their second to last musical, *Pal Joey*, was an important step on the path towards the integrated musical, most importantly in the nature of its lead character and its subject matter. *Pal Joey*, based on a series of short pieces by magazine columnist John O'Hara, tells the story of Joey Evans, "a guy who is master of ceremonies in cheap night clubs, and the pieces are in the form of letters from him to a successful band leader."[4] Joey, a second-rate entertainer scrapping and struggling to get ahead, accepts the patronage of a wealthy older married woman, Vera Simpson, in exchange for providing her sexual favors. He is the first "anti-hero" in a Broadway musical – he is a user and a manipulator of people, and ultimately a loser, as he winds up at the end of the show exactly where he started. The idea of such a repellant person as the central character in a musical was unheard of. The original production starred an unknown Gene Kelly, who went on to become one of the greatest stars of movie musicals of the 1940s and 1950s. Audiences at the time were also not used to encountering female characters who were older and sexually predatory, particularly married ones who sought prey outside their marriage. Brooks Atkinson wrote, "If it is possible to make an entertaining musical comedy out of an odious story, *Pal Joey* is it. The situation is put tentatively here because the ugly topic that is up for discussion stands between this theatregoer and real enjoyment of a well-staged show. ... John O'Hara has written a joyless book about a sulky assignation. ... Can you draw sweet water from a foul well?"[5]

Pal Joey featured a first-act finale called "Pal Joey/Joey Looks to the Future Ballet," which is a precursor to the "Dream Ballet" in *Oklahoma! Pal Joey* ran for 374 performances, followed by a three-month tour. By 1952, and its first revival, the musical theatre audience was ready for characters like Joey and Vera and it ran for 540 performances. This time Brooks Atkinson wrote, "In 1940 *Pal Joey* was regarded by its satellites as the musical that broke the old formula and brought the musical stage to maturity. There was a minority, including this column, that was not enchanted. But no one is likely now to be impervious to the tight organization of the production, the terseness of the writing, the liveliness and versatility of the score and the easy perfection of the lyrics. [...] *Pal Joey* was a pioneer in the moving back of musical frontiers, for it tells an integrated story with a knowing point of view."[6] While it did retain vestiges of the dance-as-entertainment model, Robert Alton's choreography for *Pal Joey* integrated dance into the telling of the story more than any other musical until *Oklahoma!* Because several of the numbers are set in the seedy nightclub Joey works in, those numbers burlesque the typically tacky numbers that would have been performed in those venues – "The Flower Garden of My Heart" (in which the girls wore little more than flower petals) and "That Terrific Rainbow" (similarly clad in swathes of colored fabric) set the place and characters while simultaneously being simply entertaining. Of these numbers Atkinson wrote, "the dance routines, satiric in accent, are pretty much in the old patterns, but there is something refreshing about the return of the musical comedy."[7]

The third important show leading up to *Oklahoma!* is Moss Hart, Kurt Weill and Ira Gershwin's *Lady in the Dark,* about Liza Elliott, a magazine publisher who is unable to make decisions; she must choose between two covers for the upcoming edition, and between two suitors, Kendall Nesbit and Randy Curtis. *Lady in the Dark* is a play, in which all the musical sequences are dream sequences, trips into Liza's psyche. These sequences are supposed to have reflected Hart's own experiences with psychoanalyst Gregory Zilboorg. In-depth exploration of the psyche of the central character was the same path that de Mille would take with *Oklahoma!'s* "Dream Ballet."

The *New York Times* review of *Lady in the Dark* read:

> What Mr. Hart is doing is not precisely new. It was the ideal of Wagner's music drama. [...] It differs chiefly in degree from *Cabin in the Sky* and *Pal Joey*, which this year have been striving after a more adult conception of the musical stage [...]. The American musical stage is a sound basis for a new, centrifugal dramatic form, and *Lady in the Dark* takes a long step forward in that direction.[8]

In these three shows we see a musical theatre that is more substantial, more mature than the musical comedies that came earlier. The ultimate result of this urge opened at the St. James Theatre on March 31, 1943, produced by the Theatre Guild, the first collaboration between Richard Rodgers and Oscar Hammerstein II, *Oklahoma!*

A beautiful mornin'

Prior to *Oklahoma!'s* opening, the 1942–43 season looked fairly dismal. It was comprised of vaguely patriotic musical revues like *Star and Garter,* a burlesque revue with songs by Irving Berlin, Harold Arlen and Harold Rome and starring Gypsy Rose Lee; *This is the Army,* the Irving Berlin hit from World War I, retooled to stir up patriotic fervor for World War II, and *New Priorities of 1943*, starring Harry Richman, Bert Wheeler, Henny Youngman and Carol Bruce. Cole Porter's *Something for the Boys,* starring Ethel Merman, opened in 1943, also with a patriotic theme.

Composer **Richard Rodgers** (1902–79) and lyricist/book writer **Oscar Hammerstein** (1895–1960) had each had wildly successful careers before they became the collaborative team that redefined the American musical with *Oklahoma!*

The Theatre Guild was committed to producing non-commercial plays. The Guild's fundraiser, *The Garrick Gaieties,* had launched the careers of Rodgers and Hart in 1925. Guild director Theresa Helpburn asked Rodgers to read Lynn Riggs' script for a play The Guild had produced in 1931 called *Green Grow the Lilacs*. Rodgers claims that he was enchanted with the piece and agreed to musicalize it immediately. Lorenz Hart's health was at the end of a long spiral down. When Rodgers met with him to talk about the property, it was clear that Hart was in no condition to work. Rodgers told Hart that he needed to go into a sanitarium to dry out and offered to go in with Hart so that they could work on the show there; but Hart declined, and went to Mexico instead. Rodgers recalls, "When he returned a month later he had to be carried off the train on a stretcher."[9] Rodgers had already spoken with Hammerstein, and they had agreed that if Hart was not able to write, that Rodgers and Hammerstein would write together.

Had Rodgers and Hammerstein never written together, each of them would be remembered today as one of the great writers of the musical theatre. There was not much in their earlier careers that made them seem natural collaborators. Hammerstein's greatest successes had been in operetta, and all more than ten years earlier, and Rodgers was the king of the jazzy, swingy popular tune-infused musical that had reigned for the last ten years. But these unlikely collaborators were both attracted to *Green Grow the Lilacs* and both respected each other's artistry and craft. This collaboration brought out sides of them heretofore unexplored – the sum of the collaboration was somehow greater than even its considerable parts.

Oklahoma! broke all box-office records and ran for 2,212 performances, almost five years, holding the record for longest-running musical for fifteen years. It sold more tickets, made more money, sold more merchandise, and the film rights were reported to have sold for over $1,000,000, although Rodgers and Hammerstein insisted that any planning for a movie version had to be held off until the Broadway production had closed.

It broke new ground in a lot of ways. The traditional opening of a musical in 1943 was a large and energetic ensemble number that introduced the audience to the setting and the local color and a few of the principal characters. *Oklahoma!* opened with an old woman sitting alone onstage churning butter, sounds of the prairie morning are heard in the introduction and from offstage a lone cowboy sings about the beautiful morning. In the opening scene: Aunt Eller and Curly banter, Curly probing for information about her niece, Laurey; Laurey comes out of the house and pretends to want Curly to go; Curly promises Laurey a great evening if she will go with him to the box social in "The Surrey with the Fringe on Top." Will Parker enters, just back from a rodeo in Kansas City, which he sings about. Curly leaves, Ado Annie comes in with Ali Hakim, with whom she has been "ridin' a piece;" Ado Annie explains her conflicted feelings about boys to Laurey in "I Cain't Say No;" Ali Hakim sells Laurey a magic potion meant to make all things clear; Will Parker flirts with Ado Annie; and finally the ensemble enters fully halfway through the first act.

Before *Oklahoma!*, common wisdom was that theater tickets were bought overwhelmingly by tired businessmen who wanted to see pretty young girls cavorting around the stage in attractive or scanty costumes. In *Oklahoma!* the female ensemble doesn't come onstage until halfway through the first act, and when they do they are wearing long skirts, petticoats and full blouses. There is a great deal of humor in *Oklahoma!,* but it is all character and situational humor rather than the gags and bits that audiences were used to. Although it has been attributed to various sources, it was likely Broadway producer Mike Todd who reported on *Oklahoma!* during its pre-Broadway tour, "No girls, no gags, no chance."

Rodgers and Hammerstein's writing established a whole model of structural and writing norms beginning with *Oklahoma!,* becoming the predominant form of American musical theatre for more than twenty years. These innovations include:

- The lyrics are written before the music.
- All elements are now integrated and driven by the telling of the story.
- Scene structure – dialog builds into song, and the climax of the song is the climax of the scene.
- Play structure – the play simultaneously follows a plot and a sub-plot, featuring two parallel couples, one serious and one comic, both illuminating the central issue of the play.

Prior to *Oklahoma!,* Rodgers would write a melody and have Hart set lyrics to it. It infuriated Rodgers that he would spend days struggling over a melody only to have Hart write a lyric to it in minutes. But *Oklahoma!* was more story-driven, and more text-driven than musical theatre had been to that point; this necessitated that the lyrics be written first. Hammerstein was one of the few lyricists who also wrote the book, and so he was able to write from scene into song seamlessly. *Oklahoma!* established a new precedent in the structure of scenes. In *Oklahoma!* and musicals that came after, a scene had a rising line of dramatic tension; when the emotion and dramatic tension became too heightened for ordinary speech to suffice, characters were lifted into song, and the climax of the song would usually be the climax of the scene. In *Oklahoma!,* there is a primary plot and a sub-plot that reflect each other. In the primary plot, the primary couple, Laurey and Curly, deal with the issues keeping them apart until they are joined by the end of the show; in the secondary plot, the secondary couple, Ado Annie and Will Parker, play out a comic version of Curly and Laurey's dilemma. This became the standard structure for a musical starting with *Oklahoma!*

The Theatre Guild, having fallen on hard times, had given control of the project to Rodgers and Hammerstein, who resisted efforts to bring in a star (Shirley Temple had been suggested), insisting instead on a cast unknown to audiences. Alfred Drake created the role of Curly and went on to become one of Broadway's great leading men. Character actors Joseph Buloff and Howard da Silva created the roles of Ali Hakim and Jud Fry and both went on to long successful acting careers. Celeste Holm, the original Ado Annie, went on to star in Broadway plays, musicals and Hollywood films. To direct *Oklahoma!,* the Theatre Guild hired Russian director Rouben Mamoulian, whose only previous Broadway musical had been the Theatre Guild's *Porgy and Bess.* As a serious director of drama, Mamoulian was an apt choice for this musical play. To create the dances they hired a young choreographer with almost no musical theatre experience, Agnes de Mille.

Agnes de Mille (1905–93), choreographer and director, changed the face of musical theatre choreography with her work on *Oklahoma!* and went on to become a major force in the evolution of the director/choreographer.

Born in New York, Agnes was daughter of a successful playwright and niece of famous movie mogul, Cecil B. de Mille. She was raised in Hollywood and graduated from UCLA at nineteen magna cum laude. Moving back to New York after college, she attempted a career as a dancer, but lacking strong enough technique and a dancer's body, she was not castable. Agnes continued to study and to create projects for herself to perform in, for which she also choreographed, arranged her own music and designed her own costumes. By 1940 she was one of the founding members of Ballet Theatre (now American Ballet Theatre), where she continued work as a dancer and choreographer. In 1942 she was commissioned to create the choreography for *Rodeo*, with a score by Aaron Copland. *Rodeo* brought her to the attention of Theresa Helpburn, who brought Rodgers and Hammerstein to see the ballet, who in turn hired her to choreograph *Oklahoma!*

Up until *Oklahoma!*, producers, directors, writers and important backers were able to fill dancing choruses with girls they were, or would like to be, romantically involved with; the level of skill suffered, but the dances were created accordingly and it was good enough. De Mille insisted that all of her dancers be thoroughly trained ballet dancers, and she maintained casting approval for all dancers and replacements – unheard of at the time. She created specific, fully fleshed characters for each dancer, using their technical strengths to her advantage. Each dancer had a story and a through-line in every piece. While the idea of subtext was not new to acting, applying the concept to individual dancers in a musical was innovative. In de Mille's choreography, every gesture or movement had a meaning, and all was used to drive the story forward.

Audiences had seen dream sequences before, in shows like *Pal Joey* and *Lady In The Dark*; but such a thorough examination of a character's psyche expressed through dance was a revelation. Freudian analysis and dream therapy had become popular in New York in the late 1930s and early 1940s and the kind of deep probing exploration of Laurey's subconscious, the confused pull between the nice guy and the animalistic bad man, would have been very accessible to the 1940s audience. The choreography of *Oklahoma!* extends way beyond the "Dream Ballet." De Mille's other contributions include: the story of a girl trying to put on a brave public face despite public humiliation in front of her gossip-happy friends in "Many a New Day," the battle of the sexes played out in "All Er Nothin'," the barn dance that almost becomes a melee in "The Farmer and the Cowman" and more.

Documenting musicals also changed as *Oklahoma!* was the first Broadway musical to make an original cast recording. Before this, songs from American musicals were often recorded, but rarely with the actors from the shows and never in the original contexts nor with the original choruses, orchestra, arrangements or orchestrations; songs were recorded by popular singers in whatever style might sell a record. In 1943 Decca made the original cast recording of *Oklahoma!,* which featured the songs as they were performed in the show, in the same order, sung by the original actors who sang those songs in the theater recreating their stage performances for the recording, supported by the production's original chorus, and orchestra, conducted by the show's conductor. So much of our familiarity with musicals today comes from the original cast recording. The original set of six 78-rpm records of *Oklahoma!* sold over a million copies; those ten-inch vinyl records, with only room for one song per side, featured: the "Overture," "Oh What a Beautiful Mornin'," "The Surrey with the Fringe on Top," "Kansas City," "I Cain't Say No," "Many A New Day," "People Will Say We're in Love," "Pore Jud is Daid," "Out of My Dreams," "All Er Nuthin'," "Oklahoma!," "Finale." Cast recordings had been made in London since the late 1920s, but most were of very limited release or interest. *Oklahoma!* offered the first Broadway cast recording.

Changing tides

Oklahoma! broke box-office records in New York, on the road around the world. When the original New York production closed, it had run over five years, an astounding record at the time. It would be the longest-running musical until it was overtaken by *My Fair Lady*. *Oklahoma!* had imitators almost as soon as it opened, and those musicals that didn't follow the new model that Rodgers and Hammerstein had stumbled across found themselves not running terribly long.

Chapter summary

- *Cabin in the Sky.*
- *Pal Joey.*
- *Lady in the Dark.*
- *Oklahoma!*
- Agnes de Mille.

Notes

1 Brooks Atkinson, "'The Play': Ethel Waters Heads Players of 'Cabin in the Sky,' a Musical Fantasy With a Negro Cast," *The New York Times*, October 26, 1940. Web, accessed July 27, 2012, http://query.nytimes.com/mem/archive/pdf?res=F50C11FF3A5A11728DDDAF0A94D8415B8088F1D3
2 Katherine Dunham was known as "the matriarch and queen mother of black dance," according to Joyce Aschenbrenner, *Katherine Dunham: Dancing a Life*, Urbana: University of Illinois Press, 2002.

3 Brooks Atkinson, "'The Play': Ethel Waters Heads Players of 'Cabin in the Sky,' a Musical Fantasy With a Negro Cast," *The New York Times*, October 26, 1940. Web, accessed July 28, 2012, http://query.nytimes.com/mem/archive/pdf?res=F50C11FF 3A5A11728DDDAF0A94D8 415B8088F1D3

4 Letter from John O'Hara to Richard Rodgers, cited in Richard Rodgers, *Musical Stages: An Autobiography*, New York: Random House, 1975. p. 198.

5 Brooks Atkinson, "The Play: Christmas Night Adds 'Pal Joey' and 'Meet the People' to the Musical Stage," *The New York Times*, December 26, 1940. Web, accessed July 30, 2012, http://query.nytimes.com/mem/archive/pdf?res=F20F14F63458127A93C 4AB1789D95F448485F9

6 Brooks Atkinson, "At the Theatre," *The New York Times*, January 4, 1952. Web, accessed July 30, 2012, http://query.nytimes.com/mem/archive/pdf?res=F70C1EFD 3E5F177B93C6A9178AD85F468585F9

7 Brooks Atkinson, "At the Theatre," *The New York Times*, January 4, 1952. Web, accessed May 5, 2014, http://query.nytimes.com/mem/archive/pdf?res=F70C1EFD3E 5F177B93C6A9178AD85F468585F9

8 Brooks Atkinson, "Lady in the Dark," *The New York Times*, February 2, 1941. Web, accessed July 30, 2012, http://query.nytimes.com/mem/archive/pdf? res=F20A1FFA3D5F167B93C0A91789D85F458485F9

9 Richard Rodgers, *Musical Stages: An Autobiography*, New York: Random House, 1975, p. 217.

Further reading

One of the best places to start further research is with the biographies or autobiographies of the composers, lyricists, book writers, directors, choreographers and stars of the period. That being said, here are some very good resources.

Pal Joey

Marmorstein, Gary. *A Ship Without A Sail: The Life of Lorenz Hart*. New York, NY: Simon and Schuster, 2012.

Oklahoma!

Carter, Tim. *Oklahoma!: The Making of an American Musical*. New Haven, CT: Yale University Press, 2007.

Easton, Carole. *No Intermissions: The Life of Agnes de Mille*. New York, NY: Da Capo Press, 2000.

Nolan, Frederick. *The Sound of Their Music: The Story of Rodgers and Hammerstein*. London: Everyman Ltd., 1978.

9　The Golden Age, 1945–64

An era of great musical dramatists

In the 1920s and 1930s the American musical theatre was driven by great songwriters, writing great songs that transcended the musical theatre stage to become the American songbook. The American musical theatre of the 1940s was driven by a generation of brilliant musical theatre dramatists. No longer are a few good songs enough to justify a musical; this is the age of the musical theatre as great literature. The songs of the musical theatre still become popular music, but first and foremost they function dramatically.

America in 1945

The end of World War II brought social, political and cultural change. Millions of American soldiers returned home and procreated, resulting in the baby-boomer generation, born between 1946 and 1964. The boomers' parents were the driving economic and cultural force during this time. As America's entrance into World War I, the Great Depression and World War II had defined their generations, this almost twenty-year period of upward mobility defined this generation. Americans saved the world (for the second time) and were ready to move up the social and economic ladders – and popular culture reflected this.

Thanks to popular music and television, Americans of the 1950s were more attuned to musical theatre than ever before or since. Contemporary popular music was predominantly the songs of the musical theatre, covered by popular artists. And television, new to American homes, broadcast full-length musicals and excerpts into the living rooms of Americans across the country, leaving them wanting more.

The Rodgers and Hammerstein era

Oklahoma! set the bar. Hammerstein had broken new ground in 1929 with *Show Boat*, but this time no market crash interrupted the wholesale adoption of this new paradigm. Rodgers and Hammerstein's *Oklahoma!* provided the model for the American book musical, and opened the Golden Age of the American musical theatre.

In their nine Broadway musicals, Rodgers and Hammerstein continually pushed the boundaries of form and content. *Carousel* opened not with an overture, but with an extended instrumental piece, "The Carousel Waltz," which established the important exposition points in mimed and choreographed movement. *Carousel* deals with an abusive relationship and social bias based on class. The Theatre Guild produced *Carousel*, Rouben Mamoulian directed and Agnes de Mille choreographed the show. Again they cast unknowns, John Raitt and Jan Clayton, rather than stars. Factory worker Julie Jordan loses her job for dating the roustabout, Billy Bigelow, who marries Julie, then loses his job and treats Julie abusively in anger. Billy, learning that Julie is pregnant, attempts robbery, but when it goes badly, he takes his own life. At the entrance to heaven, Billy is given a chance by the Starkeeper to return to earth and perform a good deed. Billy convinces his now teenaged daughter to rise above the taunting of classmates. Billy is an abusive spouse, a cheat, a petty criminal and a suicide ... and yet Rodgers and Hammerstein create a satisfying ending, in which Billy offers contrition and finds redemption.

Some musical theatre historians consider *Allegro* (1947) the first step towards the concept musicals of the 1970s. Agnes de Mille directed and choreographed this highly experimental piece, but was unable to focus the story. *Allegro* was one of Rodgers and Hammerstein's least successful efforts. It tells of Dr. Joseph Taylor who becomes a successful big city doctor, but loses touch with his small-town roots and his sense of self because of his success. Hammerstein was painstaking in writing the sprawling story, but without source material Hammerstein had no roadmap to follow. Stephen Sondheim, who at seventeen years old was working as a go-fer on the production, has said, "Years later, in talking over the show with Oscar [...] I realized he was trying to tell the story of his life ... Oscar meant it as a metaphor for what had happened to him. He had become so successful with *Oklahoma!* and *Carousel* that he was suddenly in demand all over the place. What he was talking about was the trappings, not so much of success, but of losing sight of what your goal is."[1]

Rodgers and Hammerstein's *South Pacific* (1949) won ten Tony Awards and the Pulitzer Prize. *South Pacific*'s wartime setting appealed to a nation recently home from World War II. The central issues are Nellie Forbush's acceptance of Emile De Becque's multiracial children, and Lieutenant Cable's inability to reconcile his old-money, racially biased family with the native Tonkinese girl with whom he falls in love, which leads to his acceptance of a suicide mission. Nellie learns to accept and lives; Cable fails to reconcile and dies. Racial and social acceptance becomes one of the major issues of the musicals of the 1950s and 1960s. *The King and I* (1951) also dealt head-on with the questions of cultural bias and acceptance of people who are different.

Even their less successful shows, *Me and Juliet* (1953) and *Pipe Dream* (1955) turned profits. Their final two collaborations were *Flower Drum Song* (1958), which took place in San Francisco's Chinatown, and *The Sound of Music* (1959), perhaps their most beloved show based on the international success of the 1965 film version.

In addition to their writing, Rodgers and Hammerstein were also producers, including the long-running play *I Remember Mama* (1944) and the Irving Berlin musical *Annie Get Your Gun* (1946). Today the Rodgers and Hammerstein Organization is one of the largest theatrical licensing organizations in North America, holding the North American rights to hundreds of the world's most popular musicals, including those of Rodgers and Hammerstein, Rodgers and Hart, Andrew Lloyd Webber and many others.

Preserving musical theatre history

The 1940s musicals are so much more familiar to us than those from before, partly because these musicals were written in a form that we are more familiar with today; but also because these shows produced original cast recordings that documented both the shows and the productions. *Oklahoma!* was the first musical to release an original cast recording, recorded by the original artists, meant to simulate the experience of seeing the show in the theater. The *Oklahoma!* original cast recording was a smash hit, selling over a million copies in 1943. After the success of the recording of *Oklahoma!*, Decca, Columbia and later RCA were eager to release original cast recordings. Recording companies even occasionally invested in musicals in exchange for the rights to record them.

The Golden Age

Rodgers and Hammerstein could never have created *Oklahoma!* without Agnes de Mille. De Mille integrated dance in *Oklahoma!*, initiating a new era in musical theatre dance. Just as characters move from dialog to song, characters moved from naturalistic movement to dance when their need or their emotion became too intense. On the heels of *Oklahoma!*, a ballet expressing the main character's inner psychology become *de rigueur*. Prior to *Oklahoma!*, dancers were hired by the producers, frequently without regard to their dancing ability; after *Oklahoma!*, musical theatre dancers were highly trained, the most appropriate for their roles or ensembles and were hired by the choreographer.

De Mille had struggled in the early years of her career, but found her niche in musical theatre. Between 1944 and 1964 she choreographed over twenty productions on Broadway, including *Bloomer Girl* (1944 and 1947), *Carousel* (1945, 1949, 1954 and 1957), *Brigadoon* (1947, 1950, 1957 and 1961), *Allegro* (1947), which she directed in addition to choreographing, *Gentlemen Prefer Blondes* (1949), *Paint Your Wagon* (1951) and *110 in the Shade* (1963). De Mille created unique physical vocabularies to define characters and relationships. In addition to her choreography, she wrote extensively about dance and dance in theatre.

It follows that since the Rodgers and Hammerstein model took narrative thrust as its driving mechanism, their success initiated a period of great musical theatre dramatists. Young musical theatre writers had to approach their work as musical dramatists, rather than simply songwriters, and the old pros from an earlier period were forced to reinvent themselves.

On the Town (1944)

The first important new musical appeared roughly a year and a half after *Oklahoma!* Jerome Robbins, Leonard Bernstein, Betty Comden and Adolph Green, and designer/producer Oliver Smith all had their first Broadway success with *On the Town*, helmed by veteran director George Abbott. *On the Town*, based on Robbins and Bernstein's ballet *Fancy Free*, is about three sailors on leave for one day in New York. The ballet's set designer, Oliver Smith, had introduced twenty-five-year-old Robbins to twenty-five-year-old Bernstein, and when Smith suggested a musical based on the ballet, Bernstein brought in friends, Adolph Green and Betty Comden, to write the book and lyrics.

Choreographer and director **Jerome Robbins (1918–98)** spent his career balancing popular culture and high culture – living simultaneously in the worlds of musical theatre and ballet. He began his career at the start of the Golden Age, and directed, choreographed and conceived some of the most pivotal musicals at the end of the Golden Age, celebrating its pinnacle and helping to move it to the next stage.

Jerome Robbins was one of the most important choreographers and directors from 1944 to 1964. Robbins' most important contributions were *West Side Story* (1957), *Gypsy* (1959) and *Fiddler on the Roof* (1964), but he also choreographed shows like *Call Me Madam* (1950) and *The King and I* (1951) and co-directed *The Pajama Game* (1954). In all, he choreographed and/or directed twenty-two Broadway musicals. Robbins spent his career straddling the worlds of musical theatre and ballet – his classical work informed his musical theatre work and vice versa. Robbins' shows were grounded in unique physical vocabularies that defined the world of the play and the characters within it. In *West Side Story* he combined classical ballet with jazz dance as an expression of the youthful energies of the rival gangs; in *Fiddler on the Roof* he borrowed from the world of Jewish folk dance to develop the physical vocabulary of the residents of Anatevka; *The King and I* juxtaposed the European polka against Asian dance traditions and techniques. Although Robbins' brilliance was unquestionable, his cruelty to those who worked for him was legendary. "Jerome Robbins was cruel, controlling, given to sudden, childish temper tantrums, willing to do anything to get what he wanted out of his dancers and actors."[2]

The only *On the Town* creative team member with experience was director George Abbott. A Broadway director since 1926, Abbott became one of the most prolific directors of the Golden Age, with credits including: *Billion Dollar Baby* (1945), *High Button Shoes* (1947), *Where's Charley?* (1948), *Call Me Madam* (1950), *Wonderful Town* (1953), *The Pajama Game* (1954), *Damn Yankees* (1955), *Once Upon a Mattress* (1959), *Fiorello!* (1959) and *A Funny Thing Happened … Forum* (1962). Abbott directed, and frequently wrote the books for, twenty-six musicals between 1944 and 1976. As legendary as Robbins' cruelty, was Abbott's respectful and gentlemanly demeanor. He always wore a suit and tie and was deferentially addressed "Mr. Abbott." Many of the important creative artists of the Golden Age and beyond started their careers working for Abbott.

Composer **Leonard Bernstein (1918–90)** had one foot in the musical theatre and the other in the world of classical music. He elevated popular culture and stripped away the austerity from high culture, making it immediately accessible.

Bernstein, like Robbins, spent his life balancing classical music and the musical theatre. His score for *On the Town* combined classical music, swing and jazz. In juggling the two worlds, Bernstein created fewer musicals than many of his contemporaries, but his work was spectacular. Bernstein's score for *Wonderful Town* (1953) was informed by a wide range of contemporary styles and drew great acclaim from critics. *Candide* (1956), an operetta based on Voltaire's comic novella, was not successful, closing after seventy-three performances; but the score was hailed by the critics and became a favorite. Brooks Atkinson wrote, "[Bernstein] has used 'Candide' for a musician's holiday. The score is a brilliant one. […] Working in a jubilant mood, Mr. Bernstein has written a score that skips gaily over the Voltaire theme, now poking fun at the characters or at traditional musical forms, but again taking the side of the characters in melodies or dances that are more simpatico than Voltaire could be."[3] *West Side Story* (1957) had originally been titled *East Side Story*, and turned Romeo and Juliet into an Italian-Catholic boy and a Jewish girl in New York's lower East Side during the Easter/Passover season. An article in the *New York Times* about Puerto Rican gangs refocused Bernstein, Robbins and book writer Arthur Laurents on the gang turf-wars in New York's West Side. Bernstein also wrote the jazz opera, *Trouble in Tahiti* (1952), for a cast of two principals and a scat-singing trio ensemble; its sequel *A Quiet Place*, written thirty-one years later in 1983; and his *Mass*, whose subtitle is "A Theatre Piece for Singers, Players, and Dancers," which was commissioned by Jacqueline Kennedy for the inaugural production of the John F. Kennedy Center for the Performing Arts in Washington, DC. His final musical *1600 Pennsylvania Avenue* failed, closing after seven performances. After Bernstein's death, his estate authorized a choral version of this musical, retitled *A White House Cantata*.

Betty Comden (1917–2006) and Adolph Green (1914–2002) were the longest-lasting collaborative writing team ever. They wrote lyrics, books and screenplays for some of the greatest film and stage musicals.

Betty Comden and Adolph Green were lifelong writing partners whose work was funny, literate and touchingly human. They went on to write books and/or lyrics for eighteen Broadway musicals, including: *Wonderful Town* (1953), *Peter Pan* (1954), *Bells Are Ringing* (1956), *Do Re Mi* (1960), *Applause* (1970), *On the Twentieth Century* (1978) and *The Will Rogers Follies* (1991). They also wrote the screenplays for some of the greatest movie musicals, including *Singing in the Rain* and *The Bandwagon*.

Born in Wisconsin, **Oliver Smith (1918–94)**, scenic designer and producer, was the most prolific designer of Golden Age musicals. In addition to production work, Smith was devoted to training the upcoming generation of designers.

Oliver Smith began his fifty-year Broadway career as a designer and producer in 1944. In addition to *On the Town*, he designed scenery and lighting and produced plays, musicals and ballets. Notable designs include: *My Fair Lady* (1957), *West Side Story* (1958), *The Sound of Music* (1950), *Camelot* (1961), *Hello Dolly* (1964) and *I Do! I Do!* (1967). With 138 Broadway productions to his credit, Smith received twenty-five Tony Award nominations and ten Tony Awards, more than any other designer.

Irving Berlin redux

The biggest success of 1946, *Annie Get Your Gun*, ran for almost three years. Producers Rodgers and Hammerstein planned for *Annie Get Your Gun* to have a score by Jerome Kern. When Kern passed away, Rodgers and Hammerstein asked Berlin to write the show; but he declined, claiming that he couldn't write "hillbilly" music. Berlin feared he would be unable to write character- and plot-driven songs, which had become the standard since his last Broadway musical. However, Berlin took the script home and came back to Rodgers and Hammerstein's office several days later with completed versions of "Doin' What Comes Naturally," "You Can't Get a Man with a Gun" and "There's No Business Like Show Business" (see Figure 9.1). *Annie Get Your Gun* starred Ethel Merman. Although reviews for *Annie Get Your Gun* were lukewarm, the public took the show to its heart, keeping it running for 1,147 performances on Broadway and longer in London. It was the biggest hit of Berlin's career. Why – what was this show's appeal?

The story of a strong independent woman who ultimately chooses to take a submissive role to assure the success of her marriage would be played out in many Golden Age musicals. By 1945 World War II was over and millions of

Figure 9.1 Richard Rodgers, Irving Berlin, Oscar Hammerstein II (left to right), and Helen Tamiris (back), watching hopefuls who are being auditioned on stage at the St. James Theatre

troops were returning home to the U.S. During the war, many men had gone overseas to fight the war, and their work had been taken up by the women left behind. When the war ended, many women had to leave the workplace and return to the home so that the returning veterans could return to work. Not surprisingly, then, this story played out, in various forms, throughout this era.

Berlin never lost his bent towards patriotism. Having made the transition from songwriter to musical dramatist, he went on to write *Miss Liberty* (1949), about the creation of the Statue of Liberty, and *Call Me Madam* (1950), which starred Ethel Merman as Mrs. Sally Adams, based on a real-life Washington DC Democratic fundraiser, Perle Mesta. His final Broadway musical was *Mr. President* (1962) about a fictitious U.S. President. Berlin, who had been born Israel Baline in Tyumen, Siberia, in 1888, died one of the most beloved songwriters and most successful theatre writers at age 101, in 1989.

Brigadoon and *Finian's Rainbow* (1947)

Lyricist and book writer **Alan Jay Lerner (1918–86)** and composer **Frederick Loewe (1901–88)** wrote three of the biggest hits of the Golden Age: *Brigadoon*, *My Fair Lady* and *Camelot*.

Finian's Rainbow and *Brigadoon* were the two big hits of the 1946–47 season. This first year of the Tony Awards, the best choreography award was split between Agnes de Mille's *Brigadoon* and Michael Kidd's *Finian's Rainbow*. *Finian's Rainbow* was a satire of racial prejudice and class-based economic injustice in the American South. It ran for 725 performances. Despite its initial success, revivals have not succeeded, due to the topical nature of the material.

Brigadoon, on the other hand, which initially ran for fewer performances, has become a standard part of the repertoire. *Brigadoon* was the first successful Broadway musical by Alan Jay Lerner and Frederick Loewe. Few lyricists wrote their own books; Lerner and Hammerstein were the two most prominent.

In *Brigadoon*, two Americans hunting in the Scottish Highlands stumble across an enchanted town that only appears for one day every hundred years; Tommy, one of the Americans, falls in love with local Fiona, and his love allows him to stay forever. John Bush Jones reads *Brigadoon* as an isolationist utopia, representing America's desire to retreat from international conflict into Brigadoon's highland mist. As Agnes de Mille had joined classical ballet to American folk dances in *Oklahoma!*, she joined classical ballet to Scottish folk dance in *Brigadoon*. *New York Times* critic Brooks Atkinson said, "For once the modest label 'musical play' has a precise meaning. For it is impossible to say where the music and dancing leave off and the story begins in their beautifully orchestrated Scottish idyll."[4]

After writing *Paint Your Wagon* in 1951, Lerner and Loewe's *My Fair Lady* opened in 1956. Many writers had attempted musicalizing George Bernard Shaw's *Pygmalion*, but Lerner, in realizing the need to retain as much of Shaw's original play as possible, found the answer. With a more than six-year run, winning seven Tony Awards out of eleven nominations, *My Fair Lady* was the biggest hit ever. William Paley, the head of CBS, had put up the bulk of the money in exchange for the rights to the original cast album, through Columbia Records. In 1962 Warner Brother bought the film rights for the unimaginable price of $5,000,000 and the stipulation that the rights to the film would transfer to CBS seven years after the movie's release. Between ticket sales, the original cast record, movie tickets, tours and productions all over the world, *My Fair Lady* produced more revenue than any prior theatrical property to date. Broadway musicals had been running longer, creating bigger profit (or losses) and expanding ancillary markets; but *My Fair Lady* set a new standard, and started producers looking at the industry from a very different financial perspective.

Camelot followed *My Fair Lady*, in 1960. The idealistic utopian society Arthur seeks in *Camelot* was a clear metaphor for the idealism of America's new, energetic, idealistic President, John F. Kennedy. Shortly after Kennedy's assassination, Theodore White quoted Kennedy's widow in an interview in Life Magazine:

"When Jack quoted something, it was usually classical," she said, "but […] at night, before we'd go to sleep, Jack liked to play some records; and the song he loved most came at the end of this record. The lines he loved to hear were: 'Don't let it be forgot, that once there was a spot, for one brief shining moment that was known as Camelot'."[5]

The lyric appeared as the banner headline on that day's *Journal-American* newspaper. Lerner described the performance of the tour of *Camelot* in Chicago the night that the article appeared:

The theatre was packed. The verse quoted above is sung in the last scene. Louis Hayward was playing King Arthur. When he came to those lines, there was a sudden wail from the audience. It was not a muffled sob; it was a loud, almost primitive cry of pain. The play stopped, and for almost five minutes everyone in the theatre – on the stage, in the wings, in the pit, and in the audience – wept without restraint. Then the play continued.[6]

Loewe retired to Palm Springs, but was coaxed out of retirement by Lerner to write the movie musical *The Little Prince* (1974) and to adapt their 1958 movie musical *Gigi* for the stage in 1973. Lerner was one of the great book writer/ lyricists, despite a tempestuous personal life, which included amphetamine addiction and eight marriages.

High Button Shoes (1947)

Composer **Jule Styne** (1905–94) was a child prodigy as a classical pianist by age ten. After a career as a dance band leader and popular Hollywood songwriter, he moved to Broadway. Styne wrote over 5,000 songs.

In 1947, George Abbott, Jerome Robbins and Oliver Smith collaborated on *High Button Shoes*, with score by Jule Styne and Sammy Cahn. The story involved a phony scheme by two con men in New Jersey in 1913. The highlight of the show was Robbins' second act opening, the "Bathing Beauty Ballet," which took the tone of a Mack Sennett silent comedy. "The actors careen across the stage, in and out of a row of boardwalk bath houses, slamming doors, falling, rolling, leaping to their feet, colliding with one another, in a master-piece of intricately plotted chaos that bears all the marks of the developing Robbins style, wit, character, drama and precision."[7]

Gypsy (1959) is considered by many to be the greatest musical of the Golden Age. With music by Styne, lyrics by Stephen Sondheim, book by Arthur Laurents, produced by David Merrick and direction and choreography by Jerome Robbins it couldn't have a better pedigree. In reviewing the 1989 Broadway revival, Frank Rich wrote, "Gypsy is nothing if not Broadway's own brassy, unlikely answer to King Lear."[8] *Gypsy* is based on the autobiography of the famous striptease artist, Gypsy Rose Lee and focuses on Lee's mother, Rose. The story of the ferocious stage mother provided material for a bravura performance by Ethel Merman.

One of the last great musicals of the Golden Age was Styne's *Funny Girl,* with lyrics by Bob Merrill and production supervision by Jerome Robbins. *Funny Girl* ran for over three years, even though it was overshadowed at the Tony Awards by *Hello, Dolly!* Styne had twenty-one musicals produced on Broadway between 1947 and 1993.

Where's Charley? (1948)

Composer, lyricist and book writer **Frank Loesser (1910–69)** was born into a German-Jewish family in New York. Loesser wrote two of the era's greatest musicals, *Guys and Dolls* and *How to Succeed in Business Without Really Trying.* Each of Loesser's musicals and characters has a unique musical and lyric vocabulary.

Where's Charley?, based on Brandon Thomas's 1892 farce *Charley's Aunt,* featured a book and direction by George Abbott, choreography by George Balanchine and a first theatre score by Hollywood songwriter, Frank Loesser. The show starred song and dance man Ray Bolger, whose Tony-winning performance charmed audiences and kept the show running for just shy of two years. Loesser was one of the most successful and one of the most stylistically versatile Broadway composers.

Loesser's *Guys and Dolls* (1950) is one of the greatest musicals of all time. A perennial favorite in regional, stock and amateur productions, the score contains beautiful ballads, "More I Cannot Wish You" and "I've Never Been in Love Before," specialty numbers, "Adelaide's Lament," "Sit Down You're Rocking The Boat," and "Luck Be A Lady." Abe Burrows' book features a unique structure; while there are two couples, the two primary characters, Miss Adelaide and Sky Masterson, are parts of different couples. The two stories are balanced, neither is a sub-plot, both are primary plots, so the pace of the show never slows. *Guys and Dolls* ran for three years and has had five Broadway revivals.

Loesser wrote music, book and lyrics for his American musical/opera *The Most Happy Fella* (1956) and for *Greenwillow* (1960). In 1961, with book writer/director Abe Burrows, Loesser wrote *How to Succeed in Business Without Really Trying* (1961), based on a book by the same name. *How to Succeed* satirically tweaked the conformist, button-down world of business; and in so doing it won seven Tony Awards, the New York Drama Critics Circle Award and the 1962 Pulitzer Prize in Drama. *How to Succeed* ... ran for almost three and a half years.

Loesser's scores all take place in vastly different worlds and have vastly different vocabularies and sounds: an Edwardian farce, the frantic, comic New York of Damon Runyon, a Napa Valley winery, a rural American fable, the offices of corporate New York in 1961. And yet, in every score Loesser sounds comfortable in all of his characters and the worlds in which they live.

Loesser's last produced show, *Pleasures and Palaces*, directed and choreographed by Bob Fosse, closed before reaching Broadway in 1965. One final musical was discovered after Loesser's death. *Senor Discretion Himself* was based on a short story by Budd Schulberg. Although never completed, it received a workshop production in 1985 and a regional production at Arena Stage in 2004.

Loesser not only wrote, but he formed his own publication company, Frank Music, which he used to help and encourage young writers. Among others, Richard Adler and Jerry Ross, writers of *The Pajama Game* and *Damn Yankees*, received early encouragement and support from Loesser. Jerry Herman's mother arranged for Loesser to hear her son's songs and meet with him; Loesser provided great encouragement.

Kiss Me Kate (1948): Cole Porter's reprise

Kiss Me Kate tells the backstage story of a theatrical troupe putting on Shakespeare's *The Taming of the Shrew*. Like Irving Berlin, Cole Porter had achieved tremendous success writing music and lyrics for shows in the day of the great songwriter. Although Porter feared that he would not be able to write a score in which the songs came from plot and character and drove the story forward, *Kiss Me Kate* was Porter's greatest success, sweeping the awards and running over two and a half years. It is one of the most often produced musicals of the 1940s. Having achieved success in the new integrated style, Porter continued writing Broadway musicals; including: *Out of This World* (1950), *Can-Can* (1953), and *Silk Stocking* (1955).

The Pajama Game (1954) and *Damn Yankees* (1955)

> Composer and lyricist team, **Richard Adler** (1921–2012) and **Jerry Ross** (1926–55) found great success in their first two produced shows. Tragically Ross died at twenty-nine, and although Adler continued to work, he never found a partner to equal Ross.

Richard Adler and Jerry Ross, protégés of Frank Loesser, had had some success writing popular songs and had contributed songs to a Broadway musical revue in 1953. In 1954, their first full musical, *The Pajama Game,* told the story of labor negotiations and the pursuit of love between labor and management in the Sleep-Tite Pajama Factory. Running for over 1,000 performances, *The Pajama*

Game was the first show produced by Harold Prince, who had been a stage manager for George Abbott. Prince and Robert Griffith, another Abbott stage manager, brought their old boss onboard to write the book and co-direct with Jerome Robbins, and hired first-time choreographer, Bob Fosse. Adler, Ross, Abbott, Robbins and Fosse kept the story moving and the characters engaging. *The Pajama Game* won Tony Awards for Best Musical, Best Choreography and Best Featured Actress in a Musical.

Just short of a year later, the same creative team, minus Robbins, opened *Damn Yankees*, based on the novel *The Year the Yankees Lost the Pennant*, a contemporary baseball retelling of the Faust story. Also breaking the magical 1,000 performance mark, *Damn Yankees* won awards for seven of its nine Tony nominees, including Best Musical, Best Actor and Actress in a Musical and Best Choreography.

When Ross died six months after *Damn Yankees* opened, Adler kept working as a composer, lyricist and producer, but never found the degree of success that he had with Ross. Although Adler and Ross only produced two musicals, these are both produced with great regularity by theaters around the world.

Fanny (1954)

In 1954 *Fanny* opened, based on a trilogy of plays by French dramatist Marcel Pagnol. The score by Harold Rome was soaring and romantic, evocative of the Marseilles port setting. Praise was lavished on stars Ezio Pinza, Walter Slezak and Florence Henderson, on Joshua Logan's book and direction and on Jo Mielziner's designs. *Fanny* ran just over two years.

> **David Merrick (1911–2000)** was the most prolific Broadway producer during the Golden Age of the American musical. Merrick produced eighty-eight shows on Broadway in fifty-four years. He was powerful, sometimes ruthless and there was no publicity stunt he was not willing to try to keep a show of his open.

Fanny was the first musical produced by David Merrick. Merrick would be the biggest and most important producer of musicals through the 1970s. Merrick's methods were anything but gentlemanly – tantrums and outbursts intimidated his creative team, as Howard Kissel chronicles in his biography of Merrick, *The Abominable Showman*. At a time when Broadway musicals were advertised almost exclusively locally in New York, he placed ads in major national magazines. "He also spent an unheard of $4,400 to place ads in Sunday papers in Atlanta, Baltimore, Chicago, Cincinnati, Detroit, Houston, Memphis, Minneapolis and even St. Louis. He placed ads in the *Paris Herald-Tribune* on the principle that the bulk of transatlantic passengers still traveled by boat and passed through New York on their way home. The one musical they were likely to know about before they docked was *Fanny*."[9]

There were no lengths that Merrick would not go to in publicizing his shows; he was without scruples when it came to business. One of Merrick's most infamous stunts happened to promote the musical *Subways Are For Sleeping*. The reviews for the show were uniformly bad, so Merrick found people in the New York area with the same names as the seven major critics. He hired limousines to bring them into Manhattan, took them out to expensive dinners, gave them the best seats in the house and then out for drinks before returning them home. During the post-show cocktails he asked his guests how they liked his show and they gushed their praises. Merrick then took out a newspaper ad quoting all seven of his "critics," with the headline "7 Out of 7 Are Ecstatically Unanimous About *Subways Are For Sleeping*," offering direct quotes and attributing them to people with the same names as the critics. One edition of the newspapers hit the streets before the hoax was discovered, but the accompanying buzz about the stunt helped keep the show open for 205 performances. *42nd Street*'s director/choreographer Gower Champion passed away late on the afternoon the show opened. David Merrick made sure that nobody knew, and came onstage at the curtain call to inform the cheering audience and glowing cast; Merrick's announcement made the front page of every New York paper, and assured the success of the show. Merrick had postponed the opening several times and then released the following cryptic statement on August 9 to the press:

> The Great Man way up there has said that this show is very important for people all around the world to see in these gloomy times. He wants to be sure that the show is ready, that it can be a memorable musical. He will give the word when He feels the show is ready. I am waiting for the courier to arrive. When he arrives and gives the word, I will place an ad for the show and promptly open it.[10]

There was speculation that Merrick alone knew how ill Champion was and postponed the opening to make the most of Champion's passing; these speculations were never substantiated.

Born and raised in Mason City, Iowa, **Meredith Willson (1902–84)** only had three musicals produced, but he is one of the very few to have written music, lyrics and book without collaborators and to have done so successfully.

The Music Man (1957)

In 1957 *West Side Story* lost the Best Musical Tony Award to Meredith Willson's *The Music Man*, which has become one of the best-loved musicals in the canon of the musical theatre. Willson was born and raised in Mason City, Iowa. He attended Frank Damrosch's Institute of Musical Art, which later became The Juilliard School, was a flute and piccolo player in John Philip

Sousa's band, played in the New York Philharmonic under Arturo Toscanini and then moved to Hollywood where he was a film composer. *The Music Man* celebrates small-town America and the charming con artist who gives up the con to settle down with Marion, the librarian; it played over 1,300 performances.

His second show, a more modest success, *The Unsinkable Molly Brown* tells the story of a spunky young girl from the wrong side of the tracks who grows up to be a survivor of everything, including the *Titanic*. His third and final show to reach the stage was *Here's Love*, an adaptation of the holiday film *Miracle on 34th Street*. His other musical, *1491*, about Columbus' attempts to finance his expedition only ever saw one production, at the Los Angeles Civic Light Opera Association in 1969.

Fiorello! (1959)

Composer **Jerry Bock (1928–2010)** and lyricist **Sheldon Harnick (b. 1924)** contributed several musicals to the Golden Age, most importantly Pulitzer Prize-winning *Fiorello!* and paradigm-shifting *Fiddler on the Roof.*

Jerry Bock and Sheldon Harnick began working together in 1957. Within the year they had their first musical on Broadway. *The Body Beautiful* was an unsuccessful musical about a Dartmouth graduate who aspires to be a prize-winning boxer, but it earned them an offer to write their second musical, *Fiorello!* Harnick recalls meeting Harold Prince at *The Body Beautiful*'s opening night party at Sardi's. Looking for a songwriting team for a musical about New York mayor Fiorello LaGuardia, he asked Bock and Harnick. *Fiorello!*, directed by George Abbott, was only the third musical to win a Pulitzer Prize for drama. The reviews were glowing and the show ran just shy of two years, a healthy run for the time.

They had two moderate successes in *Tenderloin* and *She Loves Me*. In *Tenderloin*, which ran for 216 performances, Reverend Brock, a social reformer in Manhattan in the 1890s, tries to clean up the red-light district. In the end it is shut down and Brock loses his church, but heads off to Detroit to spread the word there. The critics could not tell whether *Tenderloin* was meant to be serious or mocking.

She Loves Me marked the second directorial effort of producer Harold Prince, who had produced *Fiorello!* and *Tenderloin*, among others. *She Loves Me* is based on a Hungarian play, which is also the basis for the movie *You've Got Mail*. *She Loves Me* was hailed as a romantic confection by the critics, and it ran for 301 performances.

Their biggest hit was one of the most successful musicals ever, *Fiddler on the Roof*. Produced by Harold Prince and directed and choreographed by Jerome Robbins, this production ran for well over 3,000 performances, becoming the longest-running musical.

Historically, many of the major creative artists in the musical theatre have been Jewish – many first- or second-generation Americans of European descent. Consciously or not, many of them sought to create a version of the American dream on the stage that they could partake of themselves. While their religion was no secret, neither was it explicit. After World War II, and the founding of Israel as a Jewish state, dealing more explicitly with their Judaism became more common. Being able to tell this Jewish story in Jewish terms allowed the creative team to bring specificity to *Fiddler on the Roof*. Because of *Fiddler*'s specificity people around the world were able to connect to the material. The details allowed for a fullness of the life onstage, and ultimately made the heart of the drama, the dissolution of tradition, more poignant to the audience. *Fiddler* was not only the biggest hit up to that point, but would be pivotal in the transition to the concept musicals in the next period.

Bock and Harnick wrote two more shows together, *The Apple Tree* (1966), a series of three one-acts directed by Mike Nichols, and *The Rothschilds* (1970), chronicling the rise of the famous European-Jewish banking family. Both were only marginally successful.

Rock and roll comes to Broadway

Composer **Charles Strouse (b. 1928)**, born in New York, graduated from high school at fifteen, and from the Eastman School of Music at eighteen. After studying composition with some of the leading teachers of the day, including Nadia Boulanger and Aaron Copland, Strouse began pursuing a career in the musical theatre.

Since the beginning of the century, the popular songs of America came from the American musical. In the late 1950s America's tastes began to change; rock and roll began to appeal to America's youth. At the turn of the century ragtime had been scandalous and was thought to be dangerous to America's youth. In the 1920s the same was said of jazz, and in the 1940s of swing. Rock and roll was the new "devil music." By the 1960s the idea of using rock music onstage as the native idiom in which characters expressed themselves was not too farfetched.

Despite Charles Strouse's classical training, he and Lee Adams brought rock and roll to Broadway in *Bye Bye Birdie* (1960), although Monty Norman, Julian Moore and David Heneker had beaten them to it on the West End with the show *Expresso Bongo*. Both shows center on the manager of a rock and roll star of questionable talent who makes teenage girls go crazy, Bongo Herbert in *Expresso Bongo* and Conrad Birdie in *Bye Bye Birdie*. The London show was grittier and took a more satiric look at the sleaziness of the music industry, while *Birdie* was a sweet expression of teenaged energy and enthusiasm.

Director and choreographer **Gower Champion (1919–80)** began as a dancer, finding success as a dance team with his wife, Marge. He had begun choreographing for Broadway in 1948, but hit his stride with *Bye Bye Birdie* (1960).

Bye Bye Birdie firmly established Strouse and director/choreographer Gower Champion – they both contributed substantially to the final years of the Golden Age and to the transitionary period which followed. Strouse has written scores for fifteen Broadway shows and Champion has directed and/or choreographed seventeen, and performed both jobs on nine.

Experimental works – off-Broadway

While Broadway represented the mainstream in 1960, off-Broadway was a place for experimentation. In 1960 a small show opened written by two young men who had met in Texas and were now pursuing the musical theatre in New York. Tom Jones and Harvey Schmidt's *The Fantasticks* ran for forty-two years and 17,162 performances. Generations of audiences were introduced to *The Fantasticks* at the tiny Sullivan Street Playhouse in Greenwich Village. Having achieved such success, Jones and Schmidt never felt the need to create marketable hits, but have spent their careers in experimentation.

Their next show is very much a part of the Golden Age; *110 in the Shade* was produced by David Merrick and choreographed by Agnes de Mille. It ran for ten months. Jones and Schmidt's oeuvre will be discussed in detail in the next chapter.

Milk and Honey (1961)

Composer and lyricist **Jerry Herman (b. 1931)** was born to middle-class Jewish parents in New Jersey. Although his career began at the end of the Golden Age, his musicals, even the later ones, partake strongly of the Golden Age paradigm.

The last new voice to emerge in the Golden Age was Jerry Herman. Raised in Jersey City, at seventeen years old Herman played his songs for Frank Loesser, who urged him to continue writing. Upon graduation from the University of Miami, where he wrote and directed a college musical, *Sketchbook*, Herman moved to New York where he put together several different off-Broadway revues of material that he had already written: *I Feel Wonderful* (1954), *Nightcap* (1958) and *Parade* (1960).

In 1961 producer Gerard Oestreicher asked Herman to compose the score for a show about the founding of Israel, a sort of musical celebration of Israel.

Herman and book writer Don Appel traveled to Israel to research and wound up writing *Milk and Honey*, a musical with more of a plot. The show was very successful, running well over a year.

Herman was next hired by producer David Merrick to write the score for *Hello, Dolly!* (1964), and teamed with book writer Michael Stewart and director/choreographer Gower Champion. Working on *Hello, Dolly!* was not a happy experience for Herman. At one point when the show was trying out in Detroit, he ran into Charles Strouse and Lee Adams in the hotel lobby. Merrick had secretly invited Strouse and Adams to see the show and asked them to write a new first act closing number for it, without ever telling Herman. Although Strouse and Adams offered the title "Before the Parade Passes By," they did not write the song; Herman remained the sole composer/lyricist. *Dolly* was an international success, setting a record for long runs, and winning ten Tony Awards, a record held until *The Producers* won twelve in 2001.

The musical dramatist

From form and structure comes creativity; the form was so clearly defined for the musical theatre by Rodgers and Hammerstein that 1945–64 represented a period of tremendous creativity, of great writing. This period boasted great and creative producers, designers, directors and choreographers. Composers and lyricists who had, in earlier times, turned out great tunes were now great musical dramatists. This is the reason that so many of the shows from this period, some almost seventy years old, are still revived in major productions and constantly remounted in productions the world over.

The producers

Mention has been made of David Merrick and of Harold Prince and Robert Griffith. A small cadre of producers inhabited often non-descript offices around Times Square. Some of the top writers of the time also produced; it was an effective way to maintain control. They produced not only their work, but other plays and musicals as well: Jule Styne produced plays and musicals; Frank Loesser also produced plays and musicals, including *The Music Man*. Other producers of this time include the Shuberts, Cy Feuer and Ernest Martin, Kermit Bloomgarden, Joseph Kipness and Alexander Cohen. Most producers' offices produced between one and five plays or musicals in a season, and would be busy lining up scripts, scores, directors, choreographers, actors and theaters sometimes up to a year or more prior to opening. They ran production shops that worked efficiently on the synergy created by constantly producing multiple productions. There were allegiances and alliances that sometimes changed or shifted, but being able to call on the same artists and vendors time after time made it all possible and continued to keep New York the center of the musical theatre world in America. You could design an extraordinary set or costume anywhere, but you might only be able to execute it, on time and on budget, in one of the major New York scene shops. The business fed the art, and the art fed the business; and it truly was a Golden Age.

Chapter summary

- The cultural zeitgeist of the 1940s.
- The musicals of Rodgers and Hammerstein.
- The idea of documenting musical theatre through recordings.
- *On The Town* and Leonard Bernstein, Betty Comden and Adolph Green, Jerome Robbins and Oliver Smith.
- Irving Berlin's *Annie Get Your Gun*.
- *Finian's Rainbow* and *Brigadoon*.
- Lerner and Loewe.
- *High Button Shoes* and Jule Styne.
- *Where's Charley?* and Frank Loesser.
- *Kiss Me Kate* and Cole Porter.
- Adler and Ross, and *The Pajama Game* and *Damn Yankees*.
- David Merrick.
- Meredith Willson.
- Bock and Harnick.
- Charles Strouse and the introduction of rock and roll.
- Gower Champion.
- Jerry Herman.

Notes

1 Frederick Nolan, *The Sound of Their Music: The Story of Rodgers and Hammerstein* (reprint ed.), Cambridge, MA: Applause Theatre and Cinema Books, 2002 [1979], pp. 171–72.
2 Jack Helbig, "Booklist, Editorial Review," American Library Association. Web, accessed February 17, 2013, http://www.junglee.com/Dance-Demons-Life-Jerome-Robbins/dp/0399146520
3 Brooks Atkinson, "Musical 'Candide'," *The New York Times,* December 9, 1956. Web, accessed February 18, 2013, http://query.nytimes.com/mem/archive/pdf?res=FB0D13FE3B5A137A93CBA91789D95F428585F9
4 Brooks Atkinson, "The New Play," *The New York Times*, March 14, 1947. Web, accessed February 15, 2013, http://query.nytimes.com/mem/archive/pdf?res=F10713FB395510718EDDAD0994DB405B8788F1D3
5 Theodore H. White, "For President Kennedy: An Epilogue," *Life Magazine*, 1963, quoted in Alan Jay Lerner, *The Street Where I Live*, New York: W. W. Norton and Company, 1978, p. 250.
6 Alan Jay Lerner, *The Street Where I Live,* New York: W. W. Norton and Company, 1978, p. 252.
7 Amanda Vaill, *Somewhere: The Life of Jerome Robbins*, New York: Random House, Inc. 2008, p. 143.
8 Frank Rich, "Review, Theatre; 'Gypsy' is Back on Broadway With a Vengance," *The New York Times*, November 17, 1989. Web, accessed February 20, 2013, http://www.nytimes.com/books/98/07/19/specials/sondheim-gypsy3.html

9 Howard Kissel, *David Merrick: The Abominable Showman,* New York, NY: Applause Books, 1993, p. 95.
10 David Merrick, cited in "Postponed '42nd Street' to Play Special Preview," *New York Times,* August 9, 1980. Web, accessed February 18, 2013, http://query.nytimes.com/mem/archive/pdf?res=F40C17FC3A5F12728DDDA00894D0405B8084F1D3

Further reading

In this chapter we have dealt more with individuals than overarching trends. Almost all of these people have biographies or autobiographies. Here is a condensed list of one for each artist we have discussed; many more are available.

Richard Rodgers

Secrest, Meryle. *Somewhere for Me – A Biography of Richard Rodgers.* New York, NY: Applause Books, 2002.

Oscar Hammerstein

Fordin, Hugh. *Getting to Know Him: A Biography of Oscar Hammerstein, II.* New York, NY: Da Capo Press, 1995.

Agnes de Mille

Easton, Carol. *No Intermissions: The Life of Agnes De Mille.* New York, NY: Da Capo Press, 2000.
De Mille has also published extensively about dance, her work and her life.

Leonard Bernstein

Secrest, Meryle. *Leonard Bernstein: A Life.* New York, NY: Knopf Publications, 1994.

Betty Comden

Comden, Betty. *Off Stage.* Milwaukee, WI: Limelight Editions, 2004.

Adolph Green

Robinson, Alice. *Betty Comden and Adolph Green: A Bio-Bibliography (Bio-Bibliographies in the Performing Arts).* Santa Barbara, CA: Greenwood, 1993.

Oliver Smith

Mikotowicz, Thomas. *Oliver Smith: A Bio-Bibliography (Bio-Bibliographies in the Performing Arts).* Santa Barbara, CA: Greenwood, 1993.

Jerome Robbins

Vaill, Amanda. *Somewhere: The Life of Jerome Robbins.* New York, NY: Broadway, 2008.

George Abbott

Abbott, George. *Mister Abbott*. New York, NY: Random House, 1963.

Alan Jay Lerner

Jablonski, Edward. *Alan Jay Lerner: A Biography*. New York, NY: Henry Holt & Co., 1996.

Frank Loesser

Riis, Thomas L. *Frank Loesser (Yale Broadway Masters Series)*. New Haven, CT: Yale University Press, 2008.

Richard Adler and Jerry Ross

Adler, Richard, Lee Davis and George Abbott. *You Gotta Have Heart*. New York, NY: Dutton, Adult, 1990.

David Merrick

Kissel, Howard. *David Merrick – The Abominable Showman: The Unauthorized Biography (Applause Books)*. New York, NY: Applause Theatre & Cinema Books, 2000.

Gower Champion

Gilvey, John Anthony. *Before the Parade Passes By: Gower Champion and the Glorious American Musical*. New York, NY: St. Martin's Press, 2005.

Jerry Herman

Citron, Stephen. *Jerry Herman: Poet of the Showtune*. New Haven, CT: Yale University Press, 2004.

Charles Strouse

Strouse, Charles. *Put on a Happy Face: A Broadway Memoir*. New York, NY: Union Square Press, 2008.

Second intermission

10 The search for relevancy, 1964–70

A cultural and social shift

From the end of World War II through the early 1960s America prospered; the buttoned-down conformity of the Eisenhower years extended into the hope and possibility of the Kennedy era. By 1964, however, backlash against the status quo was being heard.

After the War, most women returned to the home, or to traditionally pro-scribed jobs like secretary, schoolteacher or nurse. Dissatisfaction with the status quo became vocal by 1961, when women's rights advocates sought President Kennedy as a potential ally in passing the Equal Rights Amendment. In 1963 Betty Friedan published *The Feminine Mystique*, a pivotal text for second-wave feminism in America, and around the world. The National Organization for Women was founded in 1966.

The Civil Rights Movement in America began in the mid 1950s with the Brown vs. the Board of Education ruling, declaring segregation of schools unconstitutional. Martin Luther King's strategy of non-violent civil disobedience led to the adoption of the Civil Rights Act of 1964, but there was a chasm between the passing of the act and its acceptance and implementation.

Sexual mores underwent a major upheaval at this time, with the legalization of "the pill." The availability of oral contraceptives suddenly made unwanted pregnancy affordably avoidable, putting a woman's reproductive system in her own control. Previously contraception had been substantially less reliable. Freed from unwanted pregnancy, in this pre-Aids time, the age of free love was born. The sexual revolution of the 1960s was also an outgrowth of the empowerment of women by various branches of the women's liberation movement.

The War in Viet Nam had begun, and in 1964 young men were burning their draft cards. The flames of the counter-culture movement, which had begun with the beat generation, and various movements to empower disenfranchised groups (women, African Americans, youths), were fanned by the youth of America in a backlash against the Viet Nam War.

All of this social change was accompanied by a great shift in popular culture. In popular music, 1964 was the year of "The British Invasion," with the intro-duction of The Beatles to American audiences. For the first time, substantial disposable income lay in the hands of teenagers, making their music, rock and roll, the most profitable sector of the music industry. In the art world, Andy Warhol and Roy Lichtenstein were establishing the rising ironic tone of the pop-art movement.

Just as the Golden Age of the American musical reached its peak, the times were changing out from under it. Although many musicals were created in the Golden Age model for years to come, they were increasingly less successful. Fewer musical theatre songs were being recorded by popular artists; the popular artists had become mostly singer/songwriters, singing their own songs. The show tune, which had defined the popular American song, was no longer relevant. *Hello, Dolly!* and *Funny Girl* had highly successful and profitable runs, but they were among the last of the musicals of the Golden Age.

Popular entertainment does not stand outside the times. Musicals achieve success and popularity, if they touch on people's lives, if they address the zeitgeist. The Rodgers and Hammerstein model had proven itself. It had given the Golden Age writers a framework on which to paint their masterworks and provided the basis for the successes of the last twenty years. But the world changed. The great writers of the Golden Age did not suddenly lose their artistry or their craft by 1965; what they lost – almost all at once – was their relevancy. The world had shifted suddenly and completely; and Rodgers, Lerner, Styne, and the rest found themselves substantially less relevant. The Golden Age of the musical theatre came to an end, as quickly as it had begun.

New traditions: *Fiddler on the Roof* (1964), *Golden Boy* (1964)

In January and March of 1964 *Hello, Dolly!* and *Funny Girl* opened. Dolly Levi and Fanny Brice each want to wind up married to the man of her dreams, an essential trope in the musical theatre of the Golden Age – a woman out in the world, in the workplace, being re-integrated into the home. Dolly succeeds, Fanny fails, but the goal is the same, the restoration of the traditional family and home structure. By September 1964, the Broadway musical was very different, as evidenced by the opening of *Fiddler on the Roof*.

Fiddler on the Roof is about the breakdown of tradition. Sheldon Harnick recalled, "[Jerome Robbins] kept asking that same question, 'What's it about?' I don't know which one of us finally said it. [...] But somebody said, [...] It's about the dissolution of a way of life.' Robbins got very excited. 'If that's what it's about,' he said, 'then we have to show our audience more of the way of life that is about to dissolve. We have to have an opening number about the traditions that are going to change. [...] And that was the beginning of 'Tradition.'"[1]

From our contemporary perspective, how could *Fiddler on the Roof* not have spoken to an audience whose world was breaking down and being restructured around them? Changing relationships between races, genders, generations – the 1960s and 1970s were defined by change. Visually *Fiddler on the Roof* was non-traditional, it was expressionistic; Boris Aronson's scene design took its inspiration from the paintings of Russian Jewish painter Marc Chagall, whose imagery had inspired the title. The physical production was not a literal representation of a place. All of this gave *Fiddler on the Roof* its universality, its appeal to audiences around the world.

The other successful musical of 1964 was *Golden Boy*, based on Clifford Odets' 1937 play. Producer Hillard Elkins hired Odets to adapt his play, about an Italian-American boxer, for a musical starring African-American entertainer, Sammy Davis, Jr. Charles Strouse and Lee Adams were hired to write the music and lyrics fresh off their successes with *Bye Bye Birdie* and *All American*. Odets died during the previews in Detroit, and his disciple, playwright William Gibson, came in to finish the rewrites.

During one of the tensest times in the history of U.S. race relations, turning Odets' play into a musical about an African-American boxer who falls in love with a white woman made it immensely relevant. During the pre-Broadway tour, Davis received death threats because of his onstage kiss with his co-star. *Golden Boy* ran for a very respectable 568 performances at the Majestic Theatre, followed by a successful run at the Palladium in London.

Man of La Mancha (1965), *Sweet Charity* (1966)

The 1964–65 season was predominantly made up of old-fashioned musicals that failed to find an audience: *Ben Franklin in Paris, I Had a Ball, Kelly, Do I Hear a Waltz?* and *Flora, The Red Menace* – none of which really resonated. The following season several shows achieved successful runs: Mitch Leigh's *Man of La Mancha*, Bob Fosse's *Sweet Charity* and Jerry Herman's *Mame*.

Man of La Mancha tells the story of Spanish writer Cervantes in prison, awaiting trial by the Spanish Inquisition. He is brought up before a kangaroo court of his fellow prisoners and must defend himself. This trope, the lone visionary standing up to the system, up to "the man," runs through the popular culture of the 1960s and 1970s. *Man of La Mancha* ends as Cervantes is taken off to face the Inquisitor, his integrity intact. Everyone, it seemed, in the 1960s/1970s was on a quest, in search of his or her impossible dream. The show began its run off-Broadway at the ANTA Washington Square Theatre in November 1965 and moved to Broadway in March 1968, where it ran for another three and a half years. The original production ran for 2,328 performances, winning Tony Awards for Best Musical, Best Composer and Lyricist, Best Actor in a Musical, Best Scenic Design and Best Direction.

Choreographer and director **Bob Fosse** (1927–87) was born in Chicago. His career as a young dancer took him to all manner of theaters and clubs, where he developed an affection for the seediness of the darker side of show business that informed his work for the rest of his life. Fosse was the first person to win a Tony, an Oscar and an Emmy Award all in the same year.

Sweet Charity, book by Neil Simon, music by Cy Coleman and lyrics by Carolyn Leigh, was conceived, directed and choreographed by Bob Fosse. Based on the Fellini film *The Nights of Cabiria*, *Sweet Charity* tells the story of a taxi dancer who keeps giving her heart to the wrong men, the "prostitute with a heart of gold." Fosse had been a successful choreographer in the Golden Age, but *Charity* was different. While the plot was driven by the story of Charity and her three suitors, Charlie, Vittorio Vidal and Oscar Lindquist, the show was driven by Fosse's highly theatrical vision and unique physical vocabulary. Fosse's vocabulary was rooted in the work of choreographer Jack Cole, the father of Broadway jazz dance. *Sweet Charity* star, and Fosse's wife and muse, Gwen Verdon had been Jack Cole's assistant for seven years. Fosse's physicality focused on movement in isolation. The choreography and Fosse's sense of showmanship kept *Sweet Charity* running for a year and a half. The *New York Times* said, "It is Bob Fosse's evening at the Palace. [...] The show's chief attractions are the staging and the dances by Mr. Fosse, which have style and theatrical viability."[2]

George Balanchine had been the first director/choreographer, followed by Agnes de Mille, Jerome Robbins and Gower Champion; but starting with Fosse's *Sweet Charity* there arose a small group of director/choreographer auteurs, which included Fosse, Michael Bennett and Tommy Tune.

Also that season, Jerry Herman's *Mame* (1966) was one of the last of the Golden Age musicals to find an audience and a substantial run. The story had already been a successful book, play and movie, *Auntie Mame*. Angela Lansbury proved that she was not just a gifted actress, but a star. Critics raved about Lansbury and audiences adored her as Mame. *Mame*'s appeal in the 1960s may have been the title character's embrace of her flamboyant individuality – she was no Dolly or Fanny, and never subjugated herself for anyone.

Cabaret (1966)

Producer and director **Harold Prince (b. 1928)** began his career as an assistant stage manager for George Abbott in 1950. He started producing musicals in 1954 with *The Pajama Game*, and he began doing double duty as producer and director in 1963 with *She Loves Me*. Prince is responsible for the development of the "concept" musical – the next advance after the integrated musicals.

Producer Harold Prince began directing in addition to producing in 1963 with shows like *She Loves Me* and *It's a Bird, ... It's a Plane, ... It's Superman*. During that time he had been developing a musical based on the play *I Am a Camera*. Having produced *Fiddler on the Roof*, and watched Robbins' developmental process, Prince began forging a process of his own.

When work began on *Cabaret* in the summer of 1963, Prince vividly recalled a nightclub in Stuttgart near where he had been stationed in 1951. "There was a dwarf MC, hair parted in the middle, and lacquered down with brilliantine, his mouth made into a bright red cupid's bow, who wore heavy false eyelashes and sang, danced, goosed, tickled and pawed four lumpen Valkyries waving diaphanous butterfly wings."[3] This inspired the Emcee and the Kit Kat Klub.

Composer **John Kander (b. 1927)** and lyricist **Fred Ebb (1928–2004)** were introduced in 1962 by music publisher Tommy Valando. Their collaboration lasted for forty-two years, and yielded some of the best scores produced during that time. Their first produced musical was *Flora the Red Menace*, starring nineteen-year-old Liza Minnelli, who remained a muse for Kander and Ebb throughout their careers.

Prince approached John Kander and Fred Ebb about writing the score for *Cabaret* while they were in Boston with *Flora the Red Menace*. They agreed to begin work on the score for *Cabaret* the day after *Flora* opened. Through the lengthy development process, Kander and Ebb ultimately wrote forty-seven songs for *Cabaret*, of which they used fifteen.

Structurally, *Cabaret* was like no musical that came before it. The primary plot revolves around Cliff and Sally and the secondary plot revolves around Herr Schultz and Fräulein Schneider. Ever since *Oklahoma!*, plot was the musical theatre's driving mechanism; but *Cabaret* continually interrupts the plots to present musical numbers at the Kit Kat Klub that comment on the action. This is a Brechtian device; in order to evoke Berlin before the war, Prince wanted the score of *Cabaret* to suggest the essence of Kurt Weill (Brecht's old collaborator). Lotte Lenya, Weill's widow, was the original Fräulein Schneider in *Cabaret*. There are two different kinds of musical numbers in *Cabaret*, traditional book songs (like "Perfectly Marvelous" and "It Couldn't Please Me More") and the songs commenting on the action (like "Two Ladies" and "Cabaret"). The show was visually non-traditional as well. Prince and set designer Boris Aronson wanted the audience to feel themselves in the situation, and to that end, as the audience entered the theater there was no front curtain and a large distorted mirror hung over the onstage bandstand, reflecting the audience back at themselves from onstage.

Prince's concept in creating *Cabaret* was "It could happen here." Times of political, social and economic unrest are unstable and ripe for a tyrant to arise; that this could happen in America of the 1960s was never stated explicitly, but it was the reason for doing the show, the concept behind the creation of *Cabaret*. Hammerstein had flirted with this kind of conceptual approach in *Allegro*, and Robbins in *Fiddler*, but in *Cabaret* we finally see the first fully articulated concept musical, a musical driven not by plot or story, but rather by an idea or concept.

Prince and others will refine the concept musical. The next major step forward happened in 1970. From 1966 to 1970 the musical theatre stalled and floundered, as audiences had lost interest in the old forms and artists and producers did not know where to go next. It was a fairly lean four years.

Rock and roll on Broadway: *Hair* (1968), *Promises, Promises* (1968)

The 1968–69 Broadway season saw three exceptional new musicals that captured the public's imagination and earned substantial runs.

Hair (1968), the American, tribal love rock musical, was a series of songs and sketches depicting the hippie lifestyle. Hippies combined the free-love movement with various Eastern religions and philosophies and the use of psychedelic drugs as a means to finding a deeper spiritual state. The hippie movement caught the public attention fresh on the heels of the "summer of love" and the human be-in in Golden Gate Park in San Francisco in 1967. Timothy Leary's mantra for the counterculture movement was, "turn on, tune it, drop out."

Joseph Papp, the producer of the New York Shakespeare Festival, originally produced *Hair* off-Broadway at his Public Theatre. The demand was so great that he immediately remounted the show in a discotheque and finally opened the show on Broadway in 1968, where it ran for 1,750 performances, and put out multiple national and international companies. *Hair* has remained immensely popular with audiences throughout the world.

Hair used a small rock band and introduced a rock and roll sound system, not heard in the musical theatre before. It also took a strong stance against the Viet Nam War in a very public venue; it was revolution gone commercial. Written by Gerome Ragni, James Rado and Galt MacDermot, *Hair* introduced Broadway audiences to many great young actors and singers: Diane Keaton, Melba Moore, Keith Carradine, Ted Lange, Meat Loaf and Ben Vereen all began their careers in *Hair*.

Late in 1968, David Merrick opened his musical adaptation of the Billy Wilder movie, *The Apartment*. *Promises, Promises* had a book by Neil Simon and score by Burt Bacharach and Hal David, one of the hottest popular songwriting teams, although they had never written a musical before. The choreography was by up-and-comer, Michael Bennett. *Promises, Promises* made its way into the heart of critics and audiences alike, and ran more than three years.

Burt Bacharach and Hal David had come from the world of pop music and were used to having control over the sound of their songs in the recording studio; they insisted on creating this environment in the theater and allowing the sound engineer similar control. For the first time in a musical, all principal actors wore microphones; the four-voice backup vocal group was written into the orchestration, as were a great number of electronic instruments. Orchestrator Ralph Burns had introduced the Cordovox to Broadway in *Sweet Charity*, but composer Burt Bacharach and orchestrator Jonathan Tunick combined electronic and acoustic to such a degree that it was necessary to mike every musician in order to blend and balance the sound. The control of what the audience heard was not in the hands of the actors or conductor, but in the hands of the sound engineer for the first time in Broadway history. It was a heavily produced electronic musical sound, even including pre-recorded passages. Today this is the norm, but at the time no audience had ever heard such a sound. *Promises, Promises* paved the way for every rock musical that was to come. Critics and scholars have decried the advent of the sound system as a loss of connection between the stage and with the actors, but it is an irrevocable fact today, and it started with *Promises, Promises*.

A hit to end the decade: *1776* (1969)

Sherman Edwards, an ex-high school history teacher and popular songwriter, approached producer Stuart Ostrow with his musical about the signing of the Declaration of Independence. Ostrow liked the idea and the songs, and suggested that Edwards approach book writer Peter Stone about improving Edwards' book. The result, *1776*, focused on John Adams' struggles to lead the Continental Congress to declare independence from England, and the writing and ratification of the Declaration of Independence. It was a smash, running for more than 1,200 performances and winning multiple awards.

In 1969, 250,000 people marched on Washington, DC in protest of the Viet Nam War, Richard Nixon was elected President of the United States, the Charles Manson cult killed five innocent people, the trial of the "Chicago Seven" began, a massive rock concert was held in Woodstock, New York, the Stonewall riots marked the beginning of the gay rights movement, police cracked down on student protests and the U.S. bombed North Koreans in Laos and Cambodia. In the midst of all the fervor that gripped the country, how could such an unabashedly patriotic musical, without an ounce of irony, be so successful? Stone wanted to emphasize both the patriotic nature of the movement for independence, and its revolutionary nature. "The events of July 4, 1776 mean more to us during these troubled times than most of us could ever imagine."[4] The country was in crisis in 1776 and was in crisis again in 1969. Stone implied in *1776* that people with the strength of their convictions needed to rise up once again and come to the aid of their country. The *1776* musical was not simply a retelling of historical events; it was an allegory that resonated deeply in 1969.

Sadly, a new irrelevancy

Between 1964 and 1970, plenty of other musicals opened, musicals that might have been successful a few years earlier. But with the vast cultural changes they no longer seemed relevant. These seasons were filled with shows like: *What Makes Sammy Run* (1964), *Drat, The Cat* (1965), *The Yearling*, *Hot September*, *Breakfast At Tiffany's*, *A Joyful Noise*, *Walking Happy* (1966), *Henry, Sweet Henry*, *How Now, Dow Jones* (1967), *Golden Rainbow*, *Darling of the*

Day (1968), Jerry Herman's *Dear World* (1969), Kander and Ebb's *The Happy Time* (1968), *Coco* (1969), and many more that were just not relevant any more. Charles Strouse and Lee Adams' *It's a Bird, ... It's a Plane, ... It's Superman* (1966), directed by Harold Prince, attempted to catch the kitschy, pop-art zeitgeist, but failed, eking out 192 performances.

An erotic revue and off-Broadway: *Oh, Calcutta!* (1969)

In 1969, producer Hillard Elkins opened a revue, *Oh, Calcutta!*, which rode in on the coat-tails of the sexual revolution and stayed. The show opened at the Eden Theatre off-Broadway; but it was reclassified as a Broadway show and later moved uptown. The show's creator, Kenneth Tynan, compiled sketches and songs by: Samuel Beckett, John Lennon, Sam Shepard, Jules Feiffer, David Newman and Robert Benton, Sherman Yellen, Peter Schickele (known as P.D.Q. Bach) and others. All of the sketches and songs were on sex-related topics, and *Oh, Calcutta!* featured a great deal of total nudity. *The New York Times* review began, "Voyeurs of the city unite, you have nothing to lose but your brains. [...] There is no show in town as witless as this silly little diversion. [...] The nude scenes, while derivative, are attractive enough. The best effects [...] the grope-in after the intermission. [...] In sum, Oh Calcutta! is likely to disappoint different people in different ways, but disappointment is the order of the night."[5]

By rights, *Oh, Calcutta!* should have closed quickly. However, after the curious voyeurs had bought their tickets, it became one of the hottest tickets for foreign tourists since it didn't require following a plot, dialog or lyrics – they were there mostly to see the beautiful naked bodies and sexually charged behavior. *Oh, Calcutta!* ran for 1,314 performances in its original run, 3,900 performances in London and the 1976 Broadway revival ran for just shy of 6,000 performances, making it the seventh longest running Broadway show ever.

For the most part, off-Broadway musicals of the 1960s were fairly innocuous, frequently gentle satires of beloved old forms. *Dames at Sea* satirized movie musicals of the 1930s. *Dames at Sea* opened in 1966 at the Caffe Cino, home of the off-off-Broadway movement starring first-timer Bernadette Peters, and moved in 1968 to the off-Broadway Lucille Lortel Theatre where it ran for over a year. *Curley McDimple*, also featuring Peters, opened in 1967, gently satirizing Shirley Temple films.

A revue of the songs of Belgian songwriter Jacques Brel, *Jacques Brel is Alive and Well and Living in Paris,* opened at the Village Gate in 1968. Four singer/actors and a small band gave voice to Brel's plaintive and personal songs. Despite generally poor reviews, audiences crowded into the Village Gate for over 1,800 performances.

Clark Gesner's gentle *You're a Good Man, Charlie Brown* brought Charles Schultz's *Peanuts* characters to life on stage, running at Theatre 80 St. Marks in the Village for 1,591 performances, and became a staple of high schools and community groups around the world.

By the end of the decade, rock and roll had begun to make inroads in the off-Broadway musicals. The biggest rock hit was a musical based on Shakespeare's *Twelfth Night*, Hal Hester, Danny Apolinar and Donald Driver's *Your Own Thing* (1968). *Your Own Thing* sustained a 933-performance run at the Orpheum Theatre, a national tour and London and Australian productions based on its light, good fun.

Chapter summary

The world changed in the 1960s and the musical theatre changed along with it. By the mid-1960s the Rodgers and Hammerstein model no longer worked.

- *Fiddler on the Roof.*
- *Golden Boy.*
- *Man of La Mancha.*
- *Sweet Charity.*
- Bob Fosse.
- *Cabaret.*
- Harold Prince.
- John Kander and Fred Ebb.
- *Hair.*
- *Promises, Promises.*
- *1776.*
- Off-Broadway.

Notes

1 "Landmark Symposium: *Fiddler on the Roof*," *Dramatists Guild Quarterly* 20, Spring 1983, p. 17.
2 Stanley Kauffman, "Theatre – Show That Wants to Be Loved – 'Sweet Charity' Opens at Refurbished Palace," *New York Times*, January 31, 1966. Web, accessed February 23, 2013, http://query.nytimes.com/mem/archive/pdf?res=F00811FD3E5 F16738DDDA80B94D9405B868AF1D3
3 Harold Prince, *Contradictions: Notes on Twenty-Six Years in the Theatre*, New York, NY: Dodd Mead Co., 1974, p. 126.
4 Peter Stone, *1776*, New York: Penguin Books, 1976, p. 172.
5 Clive Barnes, "Theatre: 'Oh, Calcutta!' a Most Innocent Dirty Show," *The New York Times,* June 18, 1969. Web, accessed February 23, 2013, http://query.nytimes.com/mem/archive/pdf?res=F00811FE3D5D1A7B93CAA8178DD85F4D8685F9

Further reading

Golden Boy

Strouse, Charles. *Put on a Happy Face: A Broadway Memoir*. New York, NY: Union Square Press, 2008.

Man of La Mancha

Wasserman, Dale. *The Impossible Musical: The "Man of La Mancha" Story*. New York, NY: Applause Theatre and Cinema Books, 2003.

Cabaret

Kander, John, Fred Ebb and Greg Lawrence. *Colored Lights: Forty Years of Words and Music, Show Biz, Collaboration and All That Jazz*. London: Faber and Faber Books, 2004.

Hair

Grode, Eric. *Hair: The Story of the Show that Defined a Generation*. Philadelphia, PA: Running Press, 2010.

Promises, Promises

Bacharach, Burt. *Anyone Who Had a Heart: My Life and Music*. East Hampton, NY: Harper, 2013.

Off-Broadway

Hischak, Thomas S. *Off-Broadway Musicals Since 1919: From Greenwich Village Follies to The Toxic Avenger*. New York, NY: Scarecrow Press, 2011.

The third act

The third face

11 New directions, 1970–82

A time of upheaval

Throughout the 1960s American culture was in a state of transition as was the American musical. Many musicals that might have been hits, had they opened earlier in the 1960s, failed to resonate with audiences. Some of the successes portended the musicals of the 1970s, but to artists and audiences alike, the future was anything but clear.

A shift at the top

> **Gerald Schoenfeld (1924–2008)** and **Bernard Jacobs (1916–96)** began their careers in theatre as lawyers for the Shubert organization, and after Lawrence Shubert, Jr.'s death in 1972 they took over the organization as Chairman of the Board and President. They became the most powerful men in the theatre of their time in terms of what was produced, who was involved and where and how long it ran.

Gerald Schoenfeld had been the Shubert Organization's primary lawyer since 1957, and had brought in Bernard Jacobs in 1958. In 1972 Lawrence Shubert Lawrence, Jr., grand-nephew of the original Shubert Brothers, died and Schoenfeld and Jacobs took over as Chairman of the Board and President. Under Schoenfeld and Jacobs, the Shubert Organization became more than landlords, insisting on financial participation in any show that played in their theaters. The Shubert Organization owned and operated sixteen theaters in New York, and others in Philadelphia, Washington, Boston and Los Angeles.

In 1974 Jacobs declared, "Last year was terrible. Two years ago was disasterville. Qualitatively and quantitatively, this season is the best in years."[1] That season Shubert Theatres housed *Equus*, *Pippin*, *Grease* and *Sherlock Holmes*. The following season they opened *A Chorus Line*, the biggest hit of the decade and one of the biggest of all time. Jacobs and Schoenfeld wielded immense power, and in using it they were directly responsible for the smaller number of new productions as well as for the smaller number of independent producers.

At the same time, the theatrical unions were demanding higher wages and greater benefits for their members. Throughout the decade, the cost of mounting a new musical on Broadway rose from an average of $250,000 to well over a million dollars. The effects on the ability to take daring risks, to engender creativity, were stifling. Given this, however, the 1970s saw some positive developments and some negative.

Contemporary pop music becomes the vocabulary for musicals

Hair and *Promises, Promises* had initiated the trend of the rock musicals. After some reluctance on the part of Broadway audiences, during the 1970s rock musicals became more prevalent. Rock musicals of the 1970s include some glorious hits and some infamous failures.

Some early rock hits

Pop songwriters Gary Geld and Peter Udell's *Purlie* (1970), based on Ossie Davis' play *Purlie Victorious*, tells the story of a traveling preacher, who returns to his small Georgia hometown to help African-American workers oppressed on Ol' Cap'n's cotton plantation; along the way he wins the heart of Lutiebelle Jenkins. The production's two stars, Cleavon Little and Melba Moore, both won Tony and Drama Desk Awards. *Purlie*, which ran for over a year and a half, and returned to Broadway after a national tour, signaled a shift in demographic, attracting a middle-class African-American audience for the first time. Reviewing the cast recording, John Wilson wrote, "*Purlie* is a musical […] that is built on the most pervasive sound in today's music, the mixture of gospel and blues that comes out as soul. […]The last original cast album that I can think of that can stand up to repeated listening as well as *Purlie* was *My Fair Lady*."[2]

Gary William Friedman and Will Holt adapted *The Me Nobody Knows* (1970) from the writings of inner city children. This revue, which told stories of poverty, racism, drug abuse, and ultimately hope, opened off-Broadway at the Orpheum Theatre, and after 208 performances transferred to Broadway, where it ran for an additional 376 performances.

Released as an album in 1970, Andrew Lloyd Webber and Tim Rice's *Jesus Christ Superstar* was one of the most successful and incendiary rock albums of all time. Applying the term "superstar" to Jesus Christ inflamed church leaders and devout Christians around the world. Pop artist Andy Warhol had coined the term "superstar" to describe the glamorous, if grungy, hangers-on who surrounded him, and applying such a glib term to Jesus Christ deeply offended many Christians. British producer Robert Stigwood and *Hair* director Tom O'Horgan's Broadway version of *Jesus Christ Superstar* became one of the longest running rock musicals of the 1970s. *Time Magazine* featured a cover photo of Jeff Fenholt as

Jesus with the headline *Jesus Christ Superstar Rocks Broadway*. Picketers who had neither heard the music nor seen the show marched in front of the theater, proving only that controversy sells tickets; people flocked to the box office to see what was so sacrilegious.

Two months after *Superstar* opened, Galt MacDermot's multi-racial rock adaptation of Shakespeare's *Two Gentlemen of Verona* opened. After playing outdoors in Central Park for the prior summer, *Two Gentlemen of Verona* moved to the St. James Theatre, where it won the Tony Award for Best Musical and ran for a year and a half.

In 1972, with two of the biggest rock musicals to his credit, MacDermot's career stalled with *Dude*, a rock allegory about good and evil which ran under two weeks, and *Via Galactica*, a science fiction rock musical, which ran under one week, and was the first musical to lose over $1,000,000. MacDermot's final musical, *The Human Comedy* (1984), based on the William Saroyan novel, closed after thirteen performances.

Early rock smash hits: *Godspell* (1971) and *Grease* (1972)

As a thesis project at Carnegie Mellon University, director John-Michael Tebelak created a theatre piece in which a tribe of hippie/clowns act out the stories of the Gospel of Matthew. Producer Edgar Lansbury optioned Tebelak's piece and asked Carnegie Mellon alum Stephen Schwartz to write songs to round out the evening. *Godspell* was a smash hit, running for over five years off-Broadway, followed by more than an additional year on Broadway. Each parable and song was a separate section unto itself; the integrated musical structure was put aside in favor of a revue-like structure. Like *Hair*, in *Godspell* dramatic thrust and narrative were done away with.

> Composer/lyricist **Stephen Schwartz (b. 1948)** saw tremendous success writing rock musicals for Broadway in the 1970s, and animated movies in the 1990s, long before he had his greatest success with the musical *Wicked*.

The most successful rock musical of the 1970s was *Grease*, which ran for more than eight years. Written by Jim Jacobs and Warren Casey, for a production in Chicago, *Grease* transferred to Broadway in 1972. It was "a raunchy, raw, aggressive, vulgar show. Subsequent productions sanitized it and tamed it down."[3] A musical about teenage hormones run rampant, and rock and roll, *Grease* spoke to the 1970s. It was the smash rock musical that proved that there was a substantial rock and roll theatre audience.

The songs in *Grease* were imitations of popular rock songs of the 1950s and 1960s. While many earlier rock musicals struggled with how to make rock and roll music come naturally out of the mouths of characters in situations in musicals, *Grease* simply stopped the plot to have moments of pure musical performance; in songs like "Greased Lightnin'," "Magic Changes" and "Freddy My Love," the characters could indulge in rock and roll fantasies. The integrated musical, after all those years of development, suddenly seemed outdated.

By 1972, the oldest of the baby-boomers were twenty-six years old. The powerful disposable income was shifting to the boomers, who had grown up on rock and roll and wanted to hear *their* music in musicals. Just as ragtime and later swing were, at first, inserted into musicals, and only slowly became their natural musical vocabulary, *Grease* (and *Hair*, *Promises, Promises*, *Purlie* and *Two Gentlemen of Verona*) put the music of this generation onto the musical theatre stage; it would take a while for that idiom to feel comfortable in the musical theatre. As audiences age, producers go in search of new, untapped markets, and the younger audiences, the baby-boomers, were ripe for tapping.

Rock and roll is here to stay – a step forward or back?

Micki Grant's 1972 *Don't Bother Me, I Can't Cope* was a revue exploring inner-city African-American life. Musical numbers about ghetto life, black power and women's rights spoke to a newly emerging market of hip, young ticket buyers. Clive Barnes wrote in *The New York Times*, "Miss Grant has produced what is almost the black equivalent of a flamenco show and it seems to be a mixture of block party and a revival meeting. Her music leans heavily on traditional black sources, such as the blues, calypsos, and spirituals, but from these sources she has written a charming and lively score and her lyrics whether they be about love or the ghetto have sweetness and wit."[4] Opening in Washington, DC in 1971, *Don't Bother Me, I Can't Cope* played Philadelphia, and reached Broadway in 1972, where it ran for 1,065 performances.

Stephen Schwartz, whose *Godspell* was running off-Broadway, wrote 1972's *Pippin*. *Pippin*'s almost five-year run was attributed to director/choreographer Bob Fosse, discussed later in this chapter.

Stephen Schwartz's next show, *The Magic Show*, was transferred to Broadway from the Toronto show starring new-age magician Doug Henning. Realizing the show needed an overhaul for New York, producer Edgar Lansbury asked Schwartz if he could supply a score in a matter of mere weeks. The result was a series of fun rock-based numbers having very little to do with what minimal plot there was, all of which barely served as an excuse for the magic tricks. Based on Henning's magic, the show ran for almost 2,000 performances, but had no tours, revivals or subsequent productions. The fun of the score aside, the evening was all Henning's.

The Wiz (1975), an African-American version of *The Wizard of Oz,* captured seven Tony Awards, and a four-year run. Using the story of Dorothy's journey to Oz and her attempt to get home, *The Wiz* stopped the story in its tracks for the musical numbers. The numbers were star turns by a talented group of performers including: Hinton Battle, Tiger Haynes, Stephanie Mills, Ted Ross, Dee Dee Bridgewater, André De Shields and Mabel King.

Two sexual musicals: *Let My People Come* (1974) and *Oh, Calcutta!* (1976)

In 1976, *Oh, Calcutta!*, discussed in the previous chapter, began a thirteen-year revival. Coming, as it did, at the height of the sexual revolution, and offering a show that didn't require a great command of the English language, it was perfect to sell to foreign tourists.

Two years earlier, Earl Wilson Jr.'s *Let My People Come* had offered even more graphic and titillating material, featuring numbers like: "I'm Gay," "Give It To Me" and others more graphically titled. It featured full nudity, and simulated sexual acts, live onstage. *Let My People Come* ran for two and a half years off-Broadway at the Village Gate, before transferring to Broadway, where it ran for just over a hundred performances. It also had a ten-year run in Philadelphia, eight years in Toronto, two national tours, companies in Los Angeles, San Francisco, New Orleans, Washington, DC, Boston, Seattle, Chicago, Madrid, London, Paris, Sydney, New Zealand and more.

Jarrett, Palmer and Wheatley learned with *The Black Crook*, in the 1860s, that sex sells, and it was still true more than a hundred years later. As with so many of the other rock musicals of the 1970s, *Oh, Calcutta!* and *Let My People Come*, the rules of the integrated musical had little or no bearing.

From the profane to the sacred

In 1976, director Vinnette Carroll and composer Micki Grant created the gospel musical, *Your Arm's Too Short to Box With God*, which ran for over two years on Broadway after a successful national tour. A *New York Times* article titled "Coast to Coast, [...] the Black Theatre Audience Grows"[5] stated that black musicals had successfully transitioned from crying out in anger to crying out in exaltation. Early in the decade a spate of African-American musicals spoke out in anger about racial and economic conditions, musicals like Melvin Van Peebles' *Ain't Supposed to Die a Natural Death* (1971). These angry musicals were able to attract relatively small African-American audiences. Van Peebles marketed his shows by urging ministers up and down the East Coast to bring busloads of their congregants. By 1976, however, shows that celebrated African-American life found much wider audiences and made a place for themselves on Broadway. Shows like *Bubbling Brown Sugar*, *Your Arm's Too Short to Box With God*, and an African-American Broadway revival of *Guys and Dolls* allowed African Americans to celebrate and exult their lives, attracting audiences of all races and backgrounds.

A new model for production: *The Robber Bridegroom* (1975/1976)

In 1973 producer Stuart Ostrow established the Stuart Ostrow Foundation's Musical Theatre Lab, a non-profit organization to sponsor workshops of original musicals. Until then, new musicals would try out in out-of-town previews. Popular tryout cities included New Haven, Detroit, Boston and Philadelphia. Ostrow's Lab provided a workshop where a musical could be developed bypassing the expensive pre-Broadway tour that traditionally preceded the New York opening.

In 1975 *The Robber Bridegroom*, which had gone through workshop, was produced by John Houseman's Acting Company. It played at the Saratoga Performing Arts Center, the Ravinia Festival and then to Broadway for two weeks, prior to a one-year national tour. This short Broadway appearance ran under a special contract outside the Producers League, while Broadway theaters were closed for three weeks by a musicians' strike. After the national tour, *The Robber Bridegroom* re-opened on Broadway, for an open run.

In addition to revivals of both *Hair* and *Jesus Christ Superstar*, 1978 saw the opening of *Runaways,* by composer/writer/musician/director, Elizabeth Swados. *Runaways* was a revue of the experiences of runaway youths. Originally intended for a short run at the Public Theatre, *Runaways* transferred to Broadway, where it ran for over seven months. Swados' other theatre pieces, also non-linear, non-plot driven, include: *Nightclub Cantata* (1977), *Dispatches, a Rock and Roll War* (1979), *The Haggadah, a Passover Cantata* (1980) and *Enter Life* (1982).

In 1979 *They're Playing Our Song* opened at the Imperial Theatre, where it had a successful run, despite the critical response. *They're Playing Our Song* is a comedy about a composer/lyricist team who juggle a romance along with their professional lives, by Neil Simon, with disco-influenced pop songs by real-life songwriting couple Marvin Hamlisch and Carole Bayer Sager. The play stops so that Sonja and Vernon can each reflect on the current state of their affair, each with three "inner voices" who acted as back-up singers, but none of the musical numbers drive the story forward. Engaging, entertaining, and inexpensive to run, with a cast of nine, *They're Playing Our Song* ran for a little over two and a half years.

New musical trends – style over substance

By the end of the 1970s any popular musical trend could provide the excuse for a musical; 1979's *Got Tu Go Disco* exploited the disco craze for eight performances. The road to the $2 million production included, "an inexperienced staff, two unknown stars, the real-life doorman and bartender of Studio 54, two directors, three scriptwriters, three choreographers, eleven composers, a cast of 36, and a $500,000 set with a dance floor that fills with 3,000 gallons of water and jackknifes toward the audience. On the first night of previews for *Got Tu Go Disco*, the band missed every one of the 32 musical cues."[6] The entire $2 million investment was lost. Nine months later, the musical *Reggae* opened with a score of reggae music. *Reggae* ran for twenty-one performances.

British composer **Andrew Lloyd Webber (b. 1948)** and lyricist/book writer **Tim Rice (b. 1944)**, who had rocked the world with *Jesus Christ Superstar*, repeated their success with *Evita* and *Joseph and the Amazing Technicolor Dreamcoat* before going on to separate careers. Webber is the most financially successful musical theatre composer of all time.

The big hit of the 1979–80 season was Andrew Lloyd Webber and Tim Rice's *Evita,* a muddled piece of writing saved by director Harold Prince and a stellar cast of newcomers, including Mandy Patinkin, Bob Gunton, and Patti LuPone, who became a star playing Eva Peron. Like *Jesus Christ Superstar, Evita* began its life as a concept rock musical released in 1976. The West End production was mounted in 1978, followed by the New York production in 1979. *Evita* won six Drama Desk Awards, and seven Tony Awards.

Webber and Rice's score combined elements of rock and symphonic music in a theatrical context. The lyrics were not always set with the emphasis on the correct syllable, and the music was peppered with dissonances and extra beats, but there is a self-important quality to the score that becomes a prevailing trend into the 1980s and 1990s. Dramaturgically, *Evita* is weighted more towards reportage of dramatic events than enactment of those events. Prince's success in *Evita* lay in taking an interesting, if flawed, score and applying a narrative to it. *New York Times* critic Walter Kerr saw through Prince's stage tricks, writing, " … we almost never see any of [the story] happen dramatically onstage. We hear about them second-hand, mainly from the omnipresent Che […]. Whenever Che is briefly silent, we are getting the news from lyrics or recitative sung by top-hatted aristocrats, breathless messengers, almost anyone at hand. It is rather like reading endless footnotes from which the text has disappeared."[7] All of the theatricality of the production successfully masked the fact that the emperor had no clothes. The model of self-important, self-serious musical drama hiding behind theatricality proved immensely successful. It would become one of the reigning paradigms of the mega-musical imports in the decade that lay ahead.

Dreamgirls opened in 1982, and much like *Evita,* the driving force, the singular vision behind *Dreamgirls* was director/choreographer, Michael Bennett. As he had done with *A Chorus Line,* Bennett and his creative team used every bar of music to drive the story forward. Audiences got to see more of the drama on the stage than they had in *Evita.* Due to the cost, the national tour only played in three cities, and it was 1985 until a full national tour was out on the road.

Dreamgirls was to have been a star vehicle for Nell Carter, titled *One Night Only.* The title became *Project #9* when it was workshopped at Joseph Papp's Public Theatre, but when Carter chose a television sitcom over *Project #9* it was put aside until Michael Bennett, flush with the success of *A Chorus Line,* became interested. After two workshop productions, and much turmoil with the unknown star, Jennifer Holiday, *Dreamgirls* opened in 1981 at the Imperial Theatre, where it played over three and a half years. Although any connection between *Dreamgirls* and the story of Diana Ross and the Supremes was denied, the stories are remarkably similar. Bennett used every musical moment to help move the story forward as hadn't happened in a rock show yet. In a decade in which the integration of elements seemed to have been abandoned, Prince and Bennett had begun steering rock musicals back towards plot-driven musicals.

The concept musical

Composer/lyricist **Stephen Sondheim (b. 1930)** began his career writing the lyrics to *West Side Story* and wrote the lyrics to *Gypsy* for his sophomore outing – two of the greatest musicals ever written.

Stephen Sondheim was born in 1930 in New York. After his parents' divorce in 1940 he moved with his mother to Doylestown, Pennsylvania. Sondheim's home-life was far from traditional, defined by, "luxorious loneliness, [...] drunken parties, [...] violent rages and seductive come-ons [all from his mother]."[8] Seeking sanctuary outside his home, he became friendly with neighbor, James Hammerstein, whose father was Oscar Hammerstein, II. Hammerstein became a father figure and mentor to Sondheim, who has said that if Hammerstein had been a geologist, he would have been a geologist; Sondheim just wanted to emulate Oscar.

When Sondheim gave Hammerstein a copy of a musical he had written for his school, the George School, titled *By George,* Hammerstein told Sondheim that it was terrible, and then spent the rest of the day teaching the craft of writing for the musical theatre. "He started with the first stage direction and went all the way through the show for a whole afternoon, really treating it seriously. It was a seminar on the piece as though it were *Long Day's Journey Into Night*. Detail by detail, he told me how to structure songs, how to build them with a beginning and a development and an ending, according to his principles. I found out many years later there are other ways to write songs, but he taught me, according to his own principles, how to introduce character, what relates a song to character, etc., etc. It was four hours of the most *packed* information. I dare say, at the risk of hyperbole, that I learned in that afternoon more than most people learn about songwriting in a lifetime."[9]

Hammerstein would be a friend, mentor and advisor to Sondheim for the rest of his life. Through Hammerstein, Sondheim met his most important collaborator. In 1949, nineteen-year-old Stephen Sondheim met twenty-one-year-old Harold Prince, at the opening night of *South Pacific*.

The first step in the ever-evolving musical theatre started in 1915, with Jerome Kern and the Princess musicals. Kern furthered this work with Hammerstein in 1927 with *Show Boat*. Hammerstein moved the art form to the next level in 1943 with *Oklahoma!,* and then turned the mantle over to Sondheim to take the musical theatre to the next stage of its evolution.

In 1957 Prince produced *West Side Story*, for which Sondheim wrote the lyrics. While Sondheim was busy writing the lyrics to *Gypsy*, Prince was producing *Fiorello* and *Tenderloin*, and directed his first Broadway musical, *A Family Affair* (1962), featuring a score by John Kander. Prince produced the first musical to feature lyrics and music by Sondheim, *A Funny Thing Happened on the Way to the Forum*. Prince spent the rest of the 1960s producing and directing some of the most important and successful musicals of the decade, including: *She Loves Me*, *Fiddler on the Roof* and *Cabaret*. Sondheim had two failures. *Anyone Can Whistle* was an experimental musical, for which Sondheim had written lyrics and music and Arthur Laurents wrote the book. After *Whistle*, Sondheim wrote lyrics to Richard Rodgers' music for *Do I Hear a Waltz?* following Hammerstein's death.

Looking for a project to work on together, Sondheim mentioned *Threes*, by actor/playwright George Furth, as the basis for a musical. *Threes* had no story; it was eleven vignettes. The development of many of Prince's productions from the 1960s had started with an idea (or concept) that drove all production decisions, rather than the story itself. This conceptual approach (as opposed to a narrative-driven approach) can be seen in *Allegro*, *West Side Story*, *Fiddler on the Roof* and *Cabaret*. Prince took this approach to a deeper level on *Threes*, which became *Company*. As work on *Company* progressed, Prince brought in choreographer Michael Bennett and set designer Boris Aronson, who had helped Robbins find the visual metaphor for *Fiddler on the Roof*.

Company examined the idea of committed relationships. The central character is a bachelor, Bobby, and each of the scenes revolves around Bobby and his married friends or the three girls he dates. Many of the songs step out of the scenes so that characters can comment on what is happening. There are a series of events, but the story is non-linear; there is not a discernible story that connects one scene or song to the next. An interesting structural device is the three birthday parties that bookend the show at the beginning of each act and the end of the second act. Are the three parties the same party (Bobby's 35th birthday) as they might have happened differently, or sequential parties that followed the chronology of Bobby's growth? Were they parties out of chronological order? Even the collaborators were not in agreement on this; the parties were the structural device on which the scenes were hung, and provided a chance for Bobby's friends to be together.

Sondheim wrote, "In every show there should be a secret metaphor that nobody knows except the authors. [...] In *Company*, we were making a comparison between a contemporary marriage and the island of Manhattan [...] It justified my writing a song about Manhattan, *Another Hundred People*, which is the only song that doesn't deal with one-to-one relationships."[10] New York City, itself, became a character in the play, and a metaphor for the central concept of the show. "For *Company*, Harold Prince and Aronson had discussed at length a Francis Bacon painting of a figure in motion behind a steel-and-glass coffee table. They decided that it captured the 'frantic, anxious, driven' quality of urban life, and ... Aronson presented Prince with that famous chrome-and-glass backdrop. ... Aronson had made a study of how many buttons he pushed on an average day in New York City ... Prince ... was delighted to find that Aronson had given him two working elevators to play with."[11]

Company was confusing, confounding and challenging to its audience in a way that the American musical theatre had never been. So at a time when the musical theatre was a place for audiences to go and escape from the pressures, confusions and realities of the everyday world, Prince and Sondheim had begun working on what would be a series of the most intellectually and emotionally stimulating and challenging pieces that musical theatre audiences had ever encountered. "Broadway theatre had been for many years supported by upper-middle-class people with upper-middle-class problems. These people really wanted to escape that world when they go to the theatre, and then here we are with *Company* talking about how we're going to bring it right back in their faces."[12]

Prince and Sondheim brought about the next stage of evolution, creating the concept musical. Where in the integrated musical every production choice is driven by the telling of the story, in the concept musical every choice is driven by the idea, or concept, behind the production. *Company* was not the most successful musical of the 1970 season – *Applause* and *Oh, Calcutta!* both had longer runs – but *Company* shifted the way that people considered the musical theatre. Following *Company*, Prince and Sondheim developed a series of musicals through 1982 that set the artistic bar high.

Sondheim's *The Girls Upstairs* was to have been produced by David Merrick in 1967, was dropped and picked up by Stuart Ostrow, who also let the project lapse. Prince agreed to direct and produce if Sondheim would do *Company* first. At this point the show's title was changed to *Follies*. *Follies* took place at a reunion of Ziegfeld-like showgirls on the eve of the demolition of the theater in which they once performed. The show was peopled by the aged showgirls, their significant others and the ghosts of their former selves. The book, by James Goldman, had begun as a traditional realistic melodrama. Sondheim says, "I started to wonder about where the characters come from, ... I asked for young counterparts to the middle-aged couples. Hal told us to use the material in their heads on the stage, and to stop thinking in realistic terms and instead to consider the simultaneity of past and present. ... With Hal prodding us we began to think in surrealistic rather than naturalistic terms."[13] Instead of a traditional scene structure, the focus shifted from one conversation to another in a cinematic style until the characters broke down and entered a nightmare fantasy sequence towards the end of the musical, in which they relived their greatest mistakes and regrets. The dramatic structure was driven not by a linear narrative, but by a theatrical logic unique to the piece itself. The principal characters are two ex-showgirls, Sally and Phyllis, and their husbands Ben and Buddy; their lives, once so full of promise, now seem filled with wrong turns, and ultimately stalled.

While *Follies* was about the "Follies" show-people and the follies of youth, it was also about the collapse of the "American Dream" and the follies that kept

Americans from living up all of its promise. The middle-aged couples in the audience in 1971 would have been born in the 1920s, raised during the Depression, struggled through the war and believed that they had earned their good times during the Eisenhower 1950s and Kennedy 1960s. Then "the dream" eluded them as they lived through the Viet Nam War, the shooting of Kent State students by National Guardsmen, the assassinations of John and Robert Kennedy and Martin Luther King, the Nixon presidency and the publication of *The Pentagon Papers*. Prince, Sondheim and Goldman found a way to make the story of a Follies girls reunion touch on the zeitgeist. An expensive show to run at the time ($80,000 per week), *Follies* ran for more than a year although it still managed to lose its entire $800,000 investment. It lost the Tony Award for Best Musical to the rock version of *Two Gentlemen of Verona*, but it won seven other Tonys.

Looking for their next project, and hoping for a success at the box office, Sondheim and Prince wanted to do a "romantic chateau-weekend musical" and attempted, unsuccessfully, to get the rights to Jean Anouilh's *Ring Around the Moon*. They settled on adapting Ingmar Bergman's film *Smiles of a Summer Night*. Content defined form, and *A Little Night Music* had a traditional linear plot. The concept here was an examination of follies of the heart. Although play structure and scene structure in Hugh Wheeler's book were relatively traditional, Sondheim and Prince moved the action fluidly from scene to scene with the use of a quintet of singers who swirled in and out of the action, commenting on the proceedings. The swirl of the waltz was central as a shifting mating dance and Sondheim wrote the entire score in 3/4 time, or variations thereof. Critics praised the show, which took six of its twelve nominations for Tony Awards, including Best Musical. Sondheim has ascribed *A Little Night Music*'s success to its linear plot, but in fact, it only ran seventy-nine more performances than *Follies*. Its substantially lower weekly operating expenses made its run profitable.

The next Sondheim/Prince collaboration, *Pacific Overtures*, also lost money, playing for 193 performances at the Winter Garden Theatre. *Pacific Overtures* tells the story of Japan being opened to trade from the West using the style of Kabuki, a traditional Japanese dance/drama. Prince has said, "we began to realize as we got deeper into the material that there was something about Kabuki that was so powerful and so clearly connected to the subject matter. I began to see a trajectory that took you from Kabuki to Ginza, in the 1970's, which is as Western as you can get."[14] Much of the criticism against *Pacific Overtures* attacked the lack of a central narrative-drive plot, despite the fact that this had never been Prince and Sondheim's preferred model. There was also criticism leveled at Sondheim, not for the first time nor the last, that his work was coldly intellectual, lacking in emotion.

There followed a hiatus of a little over three years, before what some consider the apex of the Prince/Sondheim collaborations, *Sweeney Todd* (1979). Sondheim brought the idea of musicalizing the 1840s story to Prince after seeing Christopher Bond's version of it in London. Prince was not excited at first:

It seemed to me to be relentlessly about revenge, and ... as a director I needed to see a metaphor. When I began to think of Sweeney's revenge as being against the class system that Judge Turpin represents I began to find a way to get inside the material ... In a larger way, we could say that from the day the Industrial Revolution entered our lives, the conveyor belt pulled us further and further from harmony, from humanity, from nature. I told [Sondheim and book writer Hugh Wheeler] to go ahead with their own work and ignore my metaphor. "We don't have to explain everything," I said, "the metaphor will be submerged in the material."[15]

For Prince, *Sweeney Todd* was a sociological examination of the degradation of humanity in the wake of the Industrial Revolution. Sondheim has said that for him it was a chance to create a musical thriller and to pay homage to film composer Bernard Herrmann, particularly Herrmann's score for the 1945 film *Hangover Square*. Sondheim has described the show as a "musical thriller with romantic ballads and comic songs that tend toward a music-hall tradition."[16] As Prince and Sondheim had embraced a waltz-operetta for *A Little Night Music* and Kabuki style for *Pacific Overtures*, *Sweeney Todd* was written in the style of the Grand Guignol. The Théâtre du Grand-Guignol was a theater in Paris from 1897 to 1962 that specialized in graphic, horror-show entertainment.

The reviews were glowing; Richard Eder wrote, "The musical and dramatic achievements of Stephen Sondheim's ... *Sweeney Todd* are so numerous and so clamorous. ... There is more artistic energy, creative personality and plain excitement in *Sweeney Todd* ... than in a dozen average musicals."[17]

Sweeney Todd had been capitalized at $900,000; the largest single investor was RCA Records, who had invested $100,000 with the remaining $800,000 spread out among 270 other investors, at an average investment of roughly $3,000. Despite its wild success with the critics and having won eight Tony Awards (including Best Musical), it only managed a run of 557 performances, before the production closed on Broadway, retooled in a smaller physical production and went on tour. By the end of the tour *Sweeney Todd* was able to show a profit, and subsequent productions around the world in theaters and opera houses have added to those earnings. However, it was becoming clearer that the ever-increasing cost of mounting a Broadway musical was putting profits out of the reach of those musicals that appealed to a limited audience. Musicals that require the audience to engage, to think, have a much smaller audience than those that require little thought, or those that are action-driven and can be marketed to non-English-speaking audiences.

The final Prince/Sondheim collaboration of this period, *Merrily We Roll Along* (1982), was a show about financial versus artistic success. *Merrily* told the story of composer Franklin Shephard who loses sight of his ideals and becomes a wealthy and powerful Hollywood producer. The structural conceit is that the show moves backwards in times, tracing Shephard from his shallow success in Hollywood to the New York rooftop where he dreamed of success with his idealistic young friends. Sadly, the musical never worked. Prince has referred to it as "the most painful experience of my life," and blamed the fact that there was no out-of-town tryout; the costs for taking a show out of town prior to its Broadway opening had become prohibitive. The production took several wrong turns early on, but because the show was in previews in New York, their failings were exposed for all to see. *Merrily* was the first show that Prince went into rehearsals without a clear vision of what it would look like, and the vision never appeared. Some compared the show's characters and its creators, claiming that Sondheim and Prince were writing about their own experiences; but neither Prince nor Sondheim had turned their back on artistic aspirations for commercial success. Prince kept *Merrily* in previews for almost seven weeks, and when it finally opened, *Merrily* closed after sixteen performances. In revivals and regional productions, artists adore working on *Merrily* but it never quite works for audiences.

In their six shows together between 1970 and 1982 Prince and Sondheim redefined the American musical. The Rodgers and Hammerstein integrated musical had ceased functioning, leaving the musical looking for what came next; Prince and Sondheim offered a model in the concept musical. They were not the only practitioners of the concept musical, just the first and the most successful. Further development of concept musicals fell to artists who were able to offer a unique singularity of vision, the director/choreographers.

The director/choreographers

Choreographers began additionally taking on directors' responsibilities as early as the 1940s; Balanchine had directed and choreographed *What's Up* (1943) and de Mille directed and choreographed Rodgers and Hammerstein's *Allegro* in 1947. Jack Cole had done double duty on *Donnybrook!* in 1961. Michael Kidd performed both responsibilities on seven musicals, from *Li'l Abner* (1956) to a revival of *The Music Man* (1980). Jerome Robbins was one of the most successful in the six musicals he directed and choreographed, including: *West Side Story* (1957), *Gypsy* (1959) and *Fiddler on the Roof* (1964). Gower Champion was practically a house director/choreographer for David Merrick; he performed the double function on nine musicals for Merrick, including *Carnival* (1961), *Hello, Dolly!* (1964), *Mack & Mabel* (1975), and *42nd Street* (1980).

Bob Fosse (1927–87)

Bob Fosse, referred to in the previous chapter, began as a dancer in New York and Hollywood. His distinct choreographic style uses small isolated movements, overt sexuality and allusion to vaudeville and other early entertainment forms. Fosse's choreography includes the frequent use of hats (he left Hollywood because his baldness limited his casting opportunities) and gloves (he disliked his hands). Turned in knees, rolled shoulders, sideways shuffling are all integral to the Fosse style. Fosse's style built on the work of Jack Cole, the father of theatrical jazz dance. "Jack influenced all the choreographers in the theatre from Jerome Robbins, Michael Kidd, Bob Fosse, down to Michael Bennett and Ron Field today. When you see dancing on television, that's Jack Cole."[18] Gwen Verdon, Fosse's muse and third wife, had spent seven years as Cole's assistant, and Carol Haney, who won her Tony Award for Fosse's *The Pajama Game*, began dancing for Jack Cole.

In 1954 co-directors Jerome Robbins and George Abbott and producer Harold Prince gave Fosse his first opportunity to choreograph a Broadway show, *The Pajama Game*, earning him critical praise. Fosse also choreographed *Damn Yankees* (1954), *Bells Are Ringing* (1955), *New Girl in Town* (1956) and *How to Succeed in Business Without Really Trying* (1961). He also began taking on both directorial and choreographic duties on *Redhead* (1959), *Little Me* (1962) and *Sweet Charity* (1966). Fosse's style can be seen in the earlier shows, but his choreographic vocabulary starts to really take shape in *Sweet Charity*.

Fosse's greatest year was 1972, when he won two Tony Awards for Best Direction and Best Choreography of *Pippin*, an Academy Award for Best Director of the film version of *Cabaret*, and an Emmy Award for directing Liza Minnelli's special, *Liza With a Z*.

Pippin was an extraordinary production of a minor piece of writing, but in Fosse's hands, and with his uniquely singular and dark vision, it became magical. An episodic story of self-discovery, *Pippin* is a coming of age story. Having recently completed his education, Pippin, son of Charlemagne, has all the energy in the world, but no idea where to channel it. After a series of failed attempts at a life lived large, Pippin loses hope. Fosse took a relatively sweet story and found all of the darkness in it. His autocratic manner angered the writers and star; he even had composer Stephen Schwartz barred from rehearsals. But when the show opened critics agreed that Fosse had made a riveting musical out of a slight property. Fosse's production commented on the material at every turn. Although the show *had* a linear plot, the driving mechanism was directorial vision rather than plot. It was masterful and ran for more than four and a half years.

Directorially, Fosse pushed all limits as far as they could go. For a number in which Pippin explores the pleasures of sex, Fosse created a graphic orgy scene; for a musical number in which Pippin experiences war, Fosse created a dance sequence featuring his *Manson Trio*, in which three dancers danced the glories of war while upstage of them, behind a scrim, people were slaughtered, throats were slit, limbs were tossed and so forth. There was nothing subtle about *Pippin,* and no doubt as to who was the auteur of the musical.

Shortly after opening, ticket sales started dropping. At the time Broadway producers did not waste their valuable advertising money on television, on the philosophy that television-watchers likely wouldn't pay for a live theater ticket. But producer Ostrow, looking to generate buzz about the show, hired the Ash/LeDonne Agency to film a television commercial using *Pippin* star Ben Vereen and two of Fosse's dancers, Candy Brown and Pam Sousa, performing Fosse's

Manson Trio. A voice introduced the spot by saying "Here's a free minute from *Pippin*, Broadway's musical comedy sensation, directed by Bob Fosse." At the end of the commercial the voice says, "You can see the other 119 minutes of *Pippin*, live at the Imperial Theatre, without commercial interruption."[19] It worked, sales went through the roof and soon television advertising was a part of every production's budget.

In 1974, while Fosse was editing the film *Lenny* and simultaneously rehearsing the musical *Chicago*, he suffered a heart attack and underwent open-heart surgery. The experience became the storyline for his 1977 movie, *All That Jazz*. The major difference was the film's Joe Gideon died, while Fosse lived.

Back on his feet, *Chicago: A Musical Vaudeville* opened to critical acclaim and ran just over two years. Fosse, John Kander and Fred Ebb used vaudeville styles as a metaphor for the phoniness of American celebrity. Each character in *Chicago* was based on a famous vaudeville personality, and each song was based on that character's most famous musical number: Amos's *Mr. Cellophane* uses Bert Williams' *Nobody* as its blueprint; Roxie's *Funny Honey* uses Helen Morgan's *Bill*; *When You're Good To Mama* is a Sophie Tucker number and on and on. Fosse's brilliance was using the thin and dirty façade of show business as a meta-textual comment on the tawdriness of American celebrity. Sadly, *Chicago* was overshadowed by the season's other big hit, *A Chorus Line*, and would have faded away without a tremendously successful concert revival that has been running on Broadway since 1996. Slick and exciting, the revival lacks Fosse's sharp sardonic eye, replacing it with a series of show-stopping numbers that don't add up to as much as they did in the original production.

Fosse's next show, almost three years later in 1978, was *Dancin'*, an evening of just dance numbers. *Dancin'* took a beating from the critics for being merely a dance concert, but audiences adored the show, keeping it running for four years.

Eight years later, Fosse's final musical, *Big Deal*, based on the film *Big Deal on Madonna Street*, opened and closed after sixty-nine performances. Rather than working with a composer or lyricist, Fosse used pre-existing songs from the early days of swing music. Reviews cited the dull, cheerless book and tone of the evening and the show closed an ignominious failure.

One year later Fosse died of a heart attack while preparing a revival of *Sweet Charity* in Washington, DC. He left behind a unique, highly sexualized style of theatre dance.

Born in upstate New York, director/choreographer **Michael Bennett** (1943–87) began his Broadway career dancing in *Subways Are for Sleeping*. While Fosse's choreographic style is uniquely identifiable, Bennett displayed a wider range stylistically.

Michael Bennett had been performing on Broadway since 1962, and choreographing since *A Joyful Noise* in 1966. He had been itching to direct as well, but accepted the offer to choreograph *Company*, wanting to work on the show. When Prince asked Bennett to choreograph *Follies*, Bennett was reluctant and asked if Prince would consider co-directing, an offer that Prince accepted; Bennett's first credit as a director/choreographer was *Follies*.

The following season he directed, choreographed and wrote the book for *Seesaw*. Bennett had been brought into *Seesaw* while it was out of town, in Detroit. After watching a performance he agreed to take over direction if the producers would abandon the current book, by Michael Stewart, bring in designer Robin Wagner to redesign the sets, and fire the leading lady, Lainie Kazan. Bennett's co-choreographer was Grover Dale, and Bob Avian and Tommy Tune served as associate choreographers. Bennett turned the show around, garnering strong reviews and winning a Tony Award for Best Choreographer. Unfortunately, the financial reserves were drained by the changes Bennett required, leaving no money to advertise the show. Even the relatively successful runs of the show in Philadelphia and Boston after it closed on Broadway were unable to earn the show's investment back.

Bennett's next show would be the biggest hit of the decade and of Bennett's life. A group of "gypsies," professional dancers who move from show to show, had been attending meetings hosted by Michon Peacock and Tony Stevens with the idea of creating a professional dance company for Broadway dancers. When Bennett was invited to attend he decided to tape a series of informal discussions about the life of a Broadway gypsy. The tapes were ultimately used to create dialog and lyrics for *A Chorus Line*. James Kirkwood and Nicholas Dante wrote the book using the dancers' own words, and music and lyrics were by Marvin Hamlisch and Edward Kleban, but Bennett oversaw the cutting and pasting of all of that material to create a seamless flow.

A Chorus Line did not have out-of-town tryouts, but had a lengthy series of readings and workshops, mostly sponsored by the Public Theatre. It became quickly apparent that the format of the show should be an audition, but the concept was an exploration of people who live out their dreams and aspirations; and therein lay *A Chorus Line*'s appeal. In the workshop it was not predetermined which characters would be cast in the show that they are auditioning for; that happened spontaneously from evening to evening. Actress Marsha Mason told Bennett that he had to let the character of Cassie be cast; the audience was too invested in her. Many of the cast had been part of the original taped discussions and were playing their own lives onstage, which added immediacy and a reality to the production. Nine Tony Awards and a Pulitzer Prize later, *A Chorus Line* ran for fifteen years. *A Chorus Line* was a concept musical that *had* a clear plot, the audition.

Joseph Papp's Public Theatre initially had to borrow the $1.6 million to produce *A Chorus Line*, which ultimately generated $277 million from the Broadway company alone. Michael Bennett's royalties from the various companies were reported to be upward of $1 million per week at the height of the show's success. From 1975 to 1990 and beyond, *A Chorus Line* provided constant and massive infusions of funds to the Public Theatre and the Shubert Organization.

Bennett's next show, *Ballroom*, about an aging widow who finds romance in a ballroom, received only mediocre reviews and closed fairly quickly.

But Bennett's final Broadway production, *Dreamgirls*, was another hit. *Dreamgirls* was the kind of auteur work that defined the 1970s. Bennett never allowed the pace of *Dreamgirls* to flag for a second. A terrific rock/gospel/pop/disco score, and a cinematic fluidity of motion, kept the show moving non-stop. "The most thrilling breakthrough of the extraordinary show is that whereas in *A Chorus Line* Michael Bennett choreographed the cast, in *Dreamgirls* he has choreographed the set. ... Bennett's use of [the plexiglass towers that dominated the set] was revolutionary. The towers moved to create constantly changing perspectives and space, like an automated ballet. ... They energized the action, driving it forcefully along. It's why there were no set-piece dance routines in the show: Dance and movement were organic to the entire action. But Bennett had made the mechanical set his dancers."[20]

From 1980 to 1985 Bennett developed a new musical called *Scandal* through a series of workshops, but the project was ultimately considered too sexually daring for the conservative post-Aids 1980s. He began pre-production work on *Chess*, but withdrew in 1986 for health reasons, and died from Aids-related lymphoma at the age of forty-four in 1987.

Revivals and other more traditional standard musical theatre fare

In addition to new musicals, the 1970s saw a huge number of revivals. Several major revivals surfaced in every season. There were some new book musicals without concepts or rock scores, but they were moderately successful at best.

The lone mega-hit traditional book musical of the 1970s was Charles Strouse and Martin Charnin's *Annie* (1977). *Annie,* had started in a production at the Goodspeed Opera House; and ran on Broadway for 2,377 performances. *Annie* made a generation of little girls want to belt out high notes just like Andrea McArdle, and it taught producers of the 1980s that there were profits to be made in musicals that children could take their parents to. *Annie* was entertaining and engaging for all audiences, young and old. In addition to Broadway, it launched four national tours, a West End production and a U.K. tour before the 1970s were over. *Annie* has been produced around the world.

Chapter summary

- Gerald Schoenfeld.
- Bernard Jacobs.
- Early rock musicals.
- *Godspell.*
- *Grease.*
- Stephen Schwartz.

- *Let My People Come.*
- *Oh Calcutta!*
- *The Robber Bridegroom.*
- Andrew Lloyd Webber.
- Stephen Sondheim.
- The director/choreographer: Bob Fosse, Michael Bennett.

Notes

1 Mel Gussow, "Bernard P. Jacobs – A Pillar of American Theatre as Shubert Executive, Dies at 80," *New York Times,* August 29, 1996. Web, accessed March 1, 2013, http://www.nytimes.com/1996/08/28/theater/bernard-b-jacobs-a-pillar-of-american-theater-as-shubert-executive-dies-at-80.html?pagewanted=all&src=pm
2 John S. Wilson, "Musicals: 'Purlie' and 'Applause'," *The New York Times,* May 3, 1970. Web, accessed February 27, 2013, http://query.nytimes.com/mem/archive/pdf?res=F10F12F9385C107B93C1A9178ED85F448785F9
3 Scott Miller, "Inside Grease, New Line Theatre, 2006." Web, accessed February 27, 2013, http://www.newlinetheatre.com/greasechapter.html
4 Clive Barnes, "Stage: 'Don't Bother Me, I Can't Cope' – Micki Grant Presents Foot-Stomping Musical Militancy with Gentleness," *The New York Times,* April 20, 1972. Web, accessed February 27, 2013, http://query.nytimes.com/mem/archive/pdf?res=F60E17FE3F5F117B93C2AB178FD85F468785F9
5 Paul Delaney, "From Coast to Coast, The Black Audience Grows – The Black Theatre Audience Grows," *The New York Times,* October 10, 1976. Web, accessed February 28, 2013, http://query.nytimes.com/mem/archive/pdf?res=FA081EFA3C5A1A7493C2A8178BD95F428785F9
6 Steven Gaines, "Got Tu Go Hustle: Presenting the Grand Man," *New York Magazine,* June 25, 1979, p. 55.
7 Walter Kerr, "Stage: 'Evita,' A Musical Perón," *The New York Times,* September 26, 1979. Web, accessed May 5, 2014, http://query.nytimes.com/mem/archive/pdf?res=F40617FA3B5D12728DDDAF0A94D1405B898BF1D3
8 Benedict Nightingale, "Coming Up Roses: A Biography of the Man Who Changed the Broadway Musical Against All Odds," *The New York Times Online,* 1988. Web, accessed March 1, 2013, http://www.nytimes.com/books/98/07/19/reviews/980719.19nightit.html
9 Stephen Sondheim, quoted in Stephen Banfield's *Sondheim's Broadway Musicals,* Ann Arbor, MI: University of Michigan Press, 1995, pp. 13–14.
10 Stephen Sondheim, *The Musical Theatre – A Talk by Stephen Sondheim in 1978. – The Sondheim Review.* Published online October 1, 2010. Web, accessed March 1, 2013, http://www.readperiodicals.com/201010/2071782271.html
11 Sylviane Gold, "'You can't do French farce in a dungeon' – Harold Prince on Design," *Theatre Crafts* 18 (8), p. 58.
12 Stephen Sondheim, *Broadway: the American Musical,* episode 5: "Tradition (1957–79)," television program, Public Broadcasting Network, November 4, 2012.
13 Foster Hirsch, *Harold Prince and the American Musical Theatre,* Cambridge, UK: Cambridge University Press, 1989, p. 93.
14 Foster Hirsch, *Harold Prince and the American Musical Theatre,* Cambridge, UK: Cambridge University Press, 1989, p. 109.
15 Foster Hirsch, *Harold Prince and the American Musical Theatre,* Cambridge, UK: Cambridge University Press, 1989, p. 120.
16 Foster Hirsch, *Harold Prince and the American Musical Theatre,* Cambridge, UK: Cambridge University Press, 1989, p. 122.

17 Richard Eder, "Stage: Introducing 'Sweeney Todd'," *The New York Times,* March 2, 1979. Web, accessed March 1, 2013, http://www.nytimes.com/books/98/07/19/specials/sondheim-todd.html
18 Anna Kisselgoff, "Jack Cole is Dead; A Choreographer," *The New York Times,* February 20, 1974, p. 40, "Cole died Sunday in Los Angeles after a brief illness."
19 *Pippin*. Advertisement. Various local New York television stations, 1975.
20 John Heilpern, "Bennett's Breakthrough: *Dreamgirls* Remembered," *The New York Observer*, January 7, 2007. Web, accessed May 5, 2014, http://observer.com/2007/01/bennetts-breakthrough-idreamgirls-iremembered/

Further reading

Gerald Schoenfeld

Schoenfeld, Gerald. *Mr. Broadway: The Inside Story of the Shuberts, The Shows and The Stars*. New York, NY: Applause, 2012.

Stephen Sondheim

Banfield, Stephen. *Sondheim's Broadway Musicals*. Ann Arbor, MI: The University of Michigan Press, 1995.
Secrest, Meryle. *Stephen Sondheim: A Life*. New York, NY: Vintage, 2011.

Harold Prince

Hirsch, Foster. *Harold Prince and the American Musical Theatre*. New York, NY: Applause Theatre & Cinema Books, 2005.
Ilson, Carol. *Harold Prince: A Director's Journey*. New York, NY: Limelight Editions, 2004.

Bob Fosse

Gottfried, Martin. *All His Jazz: The Life and Death of Bob Fosse*. New York, NY: Da Capo Press, 2003.

Michael Bennett

Mandelbaum, Ken. *A Chorus Line and the Musicals of Michael Bennett*. New York, NY: St. Martin's Press, 1990.

12 Joint ventures and mega-musicals, 1982–93

British rule

An overwhelming tide

By the 1980s, the American musical was in a state of crisis. The marketplace was narrowing rapidly and squeezing out all but the safest productions. Factors contributing to the "demise" of the musical theatre included:

- the danger of the degenerating neighborhood of the theater district and the surrounding area;
- the Aids epidemic, which caused the untimely death of many of that generation's musical theatre artists;
- defection of theatre artists to television;
- loss of audience to expanding number of cable channels and the availability of pre-recorded programming on video-cassettes;
- spiraling costs of union labor;
- lack of a singular producer's vision, as costs forced out single producers in favor of joint-venture production entities;
- redevelopment of the Shubert Organization;
- the cost of theater tickets.

Times Square and the surrounding neighborhood including the theater district, 42nd Street and most of 8th Avenue had been in decline since the 1960s. By 1980 the area was overrun by junkies, porn shops, prostitutes, drug dealers and homeless people squeegeeing the windshields of tourists' cars with dirty rags, hoping for a handout. Theater patrons felt uncomfortable in the neighborhood and would hurry away after seeing a performance.

The Broadway community was ravaged through the 1980s by the Aids epidemic. The first cases of the unknown epidemic were reported in 1981 and by the end of the decade the disease had taken many of the best and brightest of the musical theatre.

As for competing media, when movies first became popular at the turn of the twentieth century, it was feared that the competition would kill the live theatre. The arrival of radio, sound films and television raised the same needless fear. In the late 1970s cable television, previously used to deliver the three available networks (ABC, CBS and NBC) to remote locations, was deregulated, starting a twenty-year period of expansion. In 1980 there were twenty-eight cable channels; by 1990 there were seventy-nine, and rising. All these additional channels, competing for viewership, needed programming. The vast amount of programming required and the money being offered to writers, directors and producers drained the talent pool of the musical theatre to a degree never experienced before.

Video-tape players were introduced to the U.S. in 1977; by the 1980s saturation of the market had begun, and video rental stores sprung up on every street corner. For the first time, people could watch what they wanted to when they wanted to, either by recording their favorite shows and watching them later or renting copies of their favorite movies. This drastic shift in television viewing habits did substantial damage to theater attendance.

Between cable television and video-cassettes, the expanded number of home-viewing options shifted the demographic of the Broadway musical audience. Through the 1970s, there was a substantial local audience who went to live theatre regularly. In the 1980s, the demographic shifted to tourists. The market for a tourist audience favored musicals with a wider appeal. The least common denominator could sell the most tickets; there was less and less room for riskier, more challenging shows.

Theatrical labor unions quadrupled labor costs throughout the 1970s. Actors, musicians, stagehands, directors, choreographers, designers, ushers – all theater employees covered by unions saw spiraling increased wages and benefits. In 1956, the weekly expenses of *My Fair Lady* were $46,000 a week; in 2012, weekly expenses of *Spider-Man: Turn Off the Dark* were $1,000,000 per week, an increase of roughly 2,174 percent. These increases had begun in the 1970s, and by the 1980s the effect of these costs was seen in how Broadway was financed. Musicals cost substantially more to mount and to run. The small, single investor, putting $2,000 into a Broadway musical for the thrill of getting to hob-nob at the opening night party, was a thing of the past. A new structure of financing was required.

In order to raise the substantial funds now needed to mount a Broadway musical, producers had to join forces, to create joint ventures, in order to get their projects mounted. The individual producer, who had a singular vision and a singular voice in all decision, was supplanted by a partnership. Joint ventures involving several lead producers, a theater owner, associate producers and sometimes even a regional theater became the order of the day. Many learned *A Chorus Line*'s lesson, and the workshop began to replace the pre-Broadway out-of-town tryout.

Of the important new musicals on Broadway between 1982 and 1993 most had more than one lead producer. While *Carnival!* and *Hello, Dolly!* were David Merrick shows, *Pippin* was produced by Stuart Ostrow and *Dear World* was produced by Alexander Cohen; by the 1980s there were strings of people and organizations as lead producers of almost every new Broadway musical. The exceptions were few. Cameron Mackintosh produced *Miss Saigon* as a single lead producer. But Mackintosh had seen such tremendous profits from mega-hit

The Phantom of the Opera that he was able to mount *Miss Saigon* less expensively in London and move it to Broadway, retaining the sole producer credit. Joseph Papp was the sole lead producer of *The Mystery of Edwin Drood*, originally workshopped at his Public Theatre, moved to the Delacorte Theatre in Central Park and then to Broadway; but Papp had money from *A Chorus Line*, which was still running at the Shubert Theatre. Only the money generated from *Phantom of the Opera* or *A Chorus Line* offered enough ready money to produce a new musical on Broadway without taking on partners.

The Shubert Organization, under Bernard Jacobs and Gerald Schoenfeld, had become not only landlords and sometimes producers, but active participants in the productions housed in their theaters. They owned and managed more Broadway theaters than any other organization and only shows deemed potentially successful, who gave the landlord participating shares, could play a Shubert theater. The personal tastes of Schoenfeld and Jacobs determined, in great part, what did or did not get produced. During this time the other major theater owners adopted the Shubert business practices and entered into partnership with their tenants. The Shubert Broadway theaters were:

- The Ambassador
- The Ethel Barrymore
- The Belasco
- The Booth
- The Broadhurst
- The Broadway
- The Cort
- The Golden
- The Imperial
- The Longacre
- The Lyceum
- The Majestic
- The Music Box
- The Plymouth (now the Gerald Schoenfeld)
- The Royale (now the Bernard B. Jacobs)
- The Shubert
- The Winter Garden.

The Nederlander Organization, in operation since 1912, was the second largest owner/manager of Broadway theaters. James Nederlander began participating in producing musicals as early as 1973's *Seesaw*, but by the 1980s it was the rule, rather than the exception. Nederlander Broadway theaters were:

- The Alvin (now the Neil Simon)
- The Brooks Atkinson
- The 46th Street (now The Richard Rodgers)
- The Lunt-Fontanne

- The Marquis
- The Minskoff
- The Nederlander
- The Palace
- The Uris (now The Gershwin).

The Nederlanders also owned theaters in Los Angeles, Chicago, Detroit, Durham, Charleston, San Diego, San Jose, Tucson, and London.

Jujamcyn Theatres was the third largest owner of theaters. In 1970 Virginia and James Binger bought the St. James Theatre and the Martin Beck from Virginia's father, and in the early 1980s they bought their three other theaters, calling themselves Jujamcyn for their children, JUdith, JAMes and CYNthia. In 1987 they hired Rocco Landesman to run the organization; Landesman initiated an aggressive policy of developing new shows. Jujamcyn Theatre were:

- The St. James
- The Martin Beck (now The Al Hirschfeld)
- The Eugene O'Neill
- The Ritz Theatre (now The Walter Kerr)
- The Virginia Theatre (now The August Wilson).

As economic realities impacted the financing of new musicals and recouping investment, ticket prices rose drastically, shifting audience demographics. Top ticket prices for orchestra seats in the early 1970s were $10.00. They rose 50 percent to $15.00 in 1974, when Richard Burton joined the cast of *Equus*; after his departure from the play the new top price remained. Three years later the top price skyrocketed to $25.00 for the top tickets to *The Act* starring Liza Minnelli (for which the price of a standing room ticket also rose by 50 percent from $5.00 to $7.50). While those prices seem inexpensive from today's perspective, that change represents an increase of 250 percent in seven years. By 1980 the average Broadway top ticket price was up to between $55 and $65, up 600 percent or more from ten years before.

Local audiences, who had been regular theatergoers, found themselves reducing their theatergoing to adjust to the steep ticket price. And in what became a vicious cycle, musicals were forced to be spectacular events in order to justify the expense of the tickets. The economic realities of the 1980s did not allow for much experimentation in material or production.

The very few hits

These problems contributed to the very small number of new musicals produced in each season. Historically roughly 70 percent of new Broadway musicals have failed. In a season when forty new musicals open, that means there might be twelve successful shows; in a season when twenty new musicals open, there might be six successful shows. In a season when only four or five new musicals open on Broadway, there might or might not be a single success. Few shows opened, most closed within a few days, a very few lasted for more than a few months. In those few instances where adventurous shows were produced during this period, they tended to be overshadowed by safer shows.

A shifting business model – the mega-musical

All of the above conditions forced a drastic shift in the business model of the Broadway musical. In the 1920s a musical could pay back its investors in four weeks or so; a longer run was pure profit. By the 1950s highly anticipated shows were selling huge amounts of tickets in advance of opening, so shows like *The King and I* paid back their investors on opening night. With these business models it was reasonable to spread production money around, open a large number of musicals and see what became profitable.

By the 1980s the costs of production had risen so high and the market had been so fractured that the only way to recoup and make a profit was to have a long run in New York with cloned companies of the show in major cities around the world and on tours, to strategically saturate the market. This spawned the mega-musical; instead of distributing investment across a range of musicals in a season, one massive hit was the only route to financial success.

Producer **Cameron Mackintosh (b. 1946)** began his career as a stagehand at London's Theatre Royal, Drury Lane, when he was still a teenager. He began producing in London in 1969 but his career exploded in 1981 with Andrew Lloyd Webber's *Cats*. In 2011 he was listed as the third wealthiest person in the British music industry.

As it was becoming more and more expensive to mount new musical works in New York, producers sought alternatives. The first mega-musical was *Cats*; and with its success, the idea of producing a new musical internationally, in a city where initial costs would be lower than New York, and transferring a complete show to Broadway took hold. In mounting a new show from scratch, musical numbers, scenes, costumes, orchestration can all come and go quickly, making costs skyrocket. The unions had seen to it that New York production was unaffordable. Out of this came a new international producer, Cameron Mackintosh.

The trend of the mega-musical mirrors that of the Hollywood blockbuster. At a time when there was very little room on movie screens for small, independent films, the only movies booked into theaters were the big hits. With mega-musicals, British producer Cameron Mackintosh made the production of Broadway musicals a truly international and global business. Mega-musicals leaned heavily on spectacle. Just as simple stories and car chases made action movies easily exportable to foreign markets, simple stories with heavy elements of stage spectacle made musicals easily exportable to foreign markets and highly attractive to foreign tourists with little command of English.

These musicals were all designed to be cloned, reproduced cookie-cutter like, so that the performances were identical whether you saw the show in New York, London, Berlin, Vienna, Sydney, Buenos Aires or any of a hundred different cities.

In "The Megamusical and Beyond: The Creation, Internationalization, and Impact of a Genre," Paul Prece and William A. Everett define the mega-musical as "thematically sentimental and romantic; most feature plots that 'merge aspects of social consciousness' and are thus designed to evoke strong emotional reactions from audiences. Megamusicals tend to feature set designs, choreography, and special effects that are 'at least as important as the music."[1] Additionally, the finances of mega-musicals are higher, the initial investments are higher, but so are the profit potentials, once the show is running worldwide. Mega-musicals tend to be through-composed, having little or no dialog; in this way they hark back to melodrama and operetta from the turn of the twentieth century. Mega-musicals are replicated throughout the world; their logos are immediately identifiable. These shows were marketed to within an inch of their lives. Long before *Cats* opened in New York, the logo (two dancers silhouetted in two yellow cat eyes) hung above the Winter Garden Theatre making passersby look up curiously; the same thing happened with the poor little waif girl who came to mean *Les Misérables* and the *Miss Saigon* helicopter.

The model worked; many of the mega-musicals became massive hits, but they started being *all* there was. The number of shows opening each season was shrinking rapidly, and the number of shows that could sustain a financially successful run was shrinking in proportion. By the 1980s, each season seemed to have one major show, which garnered the critical attention and took the awards amongst a few lesser shows. The one exception in the 1980s, the one genuinely good season, was 1983–84.

The 1983–84 season

The 1983–84 season included its share of flops, like *Marilyn*, the Marilyn Monroe musical that ran for seventeen performances, and *The Human Comedy*, Galt MacDermot's adaptation of Saroyan's play which ran for thirteen performances and finished MacDermot's theatre career. It also included a couple of near misses: Richard Maltby and David Shire's *Baby* ran for 241 performances; *The Tap Dance Kid* charmed audiences, if not critics; and John Kander and Fred Ebb's *The Rink* brought Broadway divas Chita Rivera and Liza Minnelli together to play mother and daughter. But the heavy hitters of the 1983–84 season were Stephen Sondheim and James Lupine's Pulitzer Prize-winning *Sunday in the Park with George*, and Jerry Herman and Harvey Fierstein's *La Cage aux Folles*.

La Cage, which swept the Tony Awards, beating *Sunday in the Park* in almost all categories, was a very simple, old-fashioned musical except that it featured a same-sex couple. George and Albin run a transvestite club in St. Tropez, where George produces and Albin is the star attraction. When their son gets engaged to the daughter of an ultra right-wing politician, Albin must go into hiding so that he doesn't upset the prospective in-laws. At the end all are loved and accepted. Structurally and dramaturgically *La Cage aux Folles* was traditional and safe; and was rewarded for being so, earning substantial profits from companies all over the world.

Sunday in the Park with George was like nothing anyone had ever seen before. Painter Georges Seurat was a pointillist; by placing colors next to each other on the canvas, he would create the desired color in the viewer's perception. Sondheim found a musical equivalent of Seurat's pointillism in using tones next to each other to create shifting tonalities. In the first act, Sondheim and Lupine speculated on the characters in Georges Seurat's 1884 painting *A Sunday on La Grande Jatte* and the creative process and motives of the painter. Using these speculations they created an exploration of the act of artistic creation. The second act explores the psyche and conflicts of a contemporary artist who is frustrated and blocked – and may or may not be Georges Seurat's great-grandson, but is certainly his spiritual offspring. Riveting, compelling, moving and the product of two of the musical theatre's greatest practitioners and intellects, *Sunday in the Park* not only failed to win the awards, but it failed to recoup its initial investment after 603 performances.

Aside from 1983–84, Rule Britannia

But after the 1983–84 season there was hardly a new American musical that was able to find an audience. Broadway was dominated by the mega-musicals, mostly English imports. This era was ruled by *Cats*, *Me and My Girl*, *Starlight Express* and *Les Misérables*.

One season earlier, the 1982–83 season, had only one success, Andrew Lloyd Webber's *Cats*, the first mega-musical, which ran for eighteen years in New York. Teaming up with composer Andrew Lloyd Webber to produce *Cats*, Cameron Mackintosh created an international theatrical product and established a new model for musical theatre production. With rising production costs in New York, *Cats* was produced first on the West End in London and later identical productions were strategically placed around the globe. There were productions in twenty-six countries, and 300 cities, worldwide, plus national and international tours. By the time *Cats* closed in New York and London it had become the most profitable theatrical venture in history, and had been seen by an estimated 35 million people in North America alone.

Cameron Mackintosh was not the sole producer on *Cats*; he shared the responsibilities (and risks) with Andrew Lloyd Webber's production organization, The Really Useful Group, Ltd. Essentially plot-less, *Cats* is a series of poems by T.S. Eliot, set to music. In the 1982–83 season, *Blues in the Night*, *Merlin* and *My One and Only* offered no competition for awards or audience. The season was so slim that T.S. Eliot won the Tony Award for Best Book of a musical for *Cats*, eighteen years after his death. The tag line used on the *Cats* advertising was, "now and forever," and they practically made it.

Two seasons past without a success on the order of *Cats*. *Big River*, which would have been considered a minor effort in an earlier era, swept the awards in 1985. Its competition was Harold Prince's ambitious but confused *Grind*; a revue of Ellie Greenwich's pop songs from the 1960s, *Leader of the Pack*; and *Quilters*, an evening of songs and stories about women who make quilts.

In 1986 *The Mystery of Edwin Drood* swept the season against Bob Fosse's final show *Big Deal*, Andrew Lloyd Webber's *Song and Dance*, and *Tango Argentino*, a dance revue of tango dances.

Cameron Mackintosh brought Claude-Michel Schönberg and Alain Boublil's *Les Misérables* to the West End, then to Broadway and the world. On Broadway it won eight of its twelve Tony nominations, raves from the critics and passionate fans who flocked to see the show over its sixteen-year-run on Broadway and at theaters around the world. *Les Misérables*, based on the sprawling Victor Hugo novel, is operatic: arias, duets, trios, ensemble numbers, and recitative. Like many of the mega-musicals, *Les Misérables*, while short on intellectual rigor, was long on deeply felt emotion. *Les Misérables* actually had some competition from two other British imports, both mega-musicals, *Me and My Girl* and *Starlight Express*.

The year 1988 saw the most successful mega-musical, in fact, the most successful musical of all, Andrew Lloyd Webber's *Phantom of the Opera*. Produced by Cameron Mackintosh and The Really Useful Company Ltd., *Phantom of the Opera* was the first successful show by director Harold Prince since his split with Stephen Sondheim six years earlier. *Phantom of the Opera* offered a compelling story, spectacle, a glorious score reminiscent of Puccini (the Puccini estate brought a plagiarism suit that was settled out of court). *The New York Times* review read, "Mr. Lloyd Webber has again written a score so generic that most of the songs could be reordered and redistributed among the characters (indeed, among other Lloyd Webber musicals) without altering the show's story or meaning."[2] But the score, although generic, was soaring and appropriate, and it almost didn't matter; *Phantom*'s marketing created an advance sale large enough to make it profitable on opening night, despite its tremendous expense. Productions have been sent around the world, and to date *Phantom* has grossed $5.6 billion dollars.[3]

Actors' Equity tried to deny Cameron Mackintosh the right to use Sarah Brightman as his female lead in the New York production of *Phantom of the Opera*. Ms. Brightman was Andrew Lloyd Webber's wife, and the woman for whom he had written the role. The ensuing negotiations were fodder for the tabloids, and ultimately offered Mackintosh a great deal of free publicity, by running almost daily. *Phantom of the Opera* swept the awards, and has been running across the world ever since.

In 1990 and 1991, when Mackintosh was preparing to open *Miss Saigon* on Broadway, Actors' Equity attempted to deny Mackintosh the right to bring Jonathan Pryce, star of the West End production of the show, to New York.

Again, the resulting scuffle was followed closely in the newspapers and offered Mackintosh almost daily exposure with enough controversy to make people want to see what all the fuss was about.

Toward the end of the 1980s a small number of American musicals were successful, although nowhere near as successful as the British imports. Stephen Sondheim and James Lupine's *Into the Woods* (1987) could not take the Best Musical Tony from *Phantom of the Opera*. Nor did *Grand Hotel* (1989) win the award, and although *City of Angels* (1989) did take the top prize, none of these three American hits came anywhere near the length of run or profit of *Cats* or *Les Misérables*. *Jerome Robbins' Broadway* won the Best Musical Tony (1989), as did *The Will Rogers Follies* (1991), but neither of them had runs to rival the British mega-musicals.

Unsuccessful mega-musicals

Not all mega-musicals were successful, and those that failed, failed big. What had been a sure-fire formula at the beginning of the decade, by the end was a little less sure.

Chess (1988), a cold war political musical by Tim Rice and two former members of the rock group ABBA, was to have been directed and choreo-graphed by Michael Bennett, but Bennett withdrew for health reasons. *Cats* and *Les Misérables* director Trevor Nunn took over the project. Nunn and his artistic team felt that the $12 million London production had missed the mark, although it did manage to run for almost three years, and so they reimagined the show for Broadway. After an overhaul of the material and the physical production, the first preview ran for four hours. Whittled down to three and a quarter hours, the show almost never met its $350,000 weekly running expenses. Although the show was playing to houses that were 80 percent full, the bulk of those were half-price tickets, and *Chess* closed after sixty-eight performances, losing almost all of its $6 million capitalization for the Broadway production.

Nunn also directed Andrew Lloyd Webber's *Aspects of Love* (produced by Lloyd Webber's The Really Useful Theatre Company). *The New York Times* review of *Aspects of Love* began, "Andrew Lloyd Webber, the composer who is second to none when writing musicals about cats, roller-skating trains and falling chandeliers, has made an earnest, but bizarre career decision in 'Aspects of Love,' his new show at the Broadhurst. He has written a musical about people. Whether 'Aspects of Love' is a musical for people is another matter."[4] Despite an eleven-month run, *Aspects of Love* closed having lost its entire $8 million investment.

Webber's next show, *Sunset Boulevard*, also directed by Nunn, is what critic Frank Rich termed a flop-hit. *Sunset Boulevard* found its audience; it ran for two and a half years, but because running expenses were so high it lost more than its initial cost. The show had cost $13 million to mount and it lost an estimated $20 million. Weekly advertising, budgeted at $40,000 per week, wound up costing $183,352 per week. Patti LuPone had been promised the starring role but was not ultimately contracted to play the role on Broadway; she sued the producers receiving a settlement of $1 million. The initial tour closed fairly quickly when it was discovered that the expense of transporting the elaborate set was substantially higher than had been calculated.

The production philosophy of "bigger is better" had reached an end. By 1993 it had run its course. During the reign of the mega-musical those who rode the gravy train got very wealthy, but the ride was over and it was time to find a new model for the ever-shifting musical theatre.

A look back at popular culture of the 1980s

Through the 1980s, wealth was glamorized and placed above everything else as a benchmark of success and achievement. In the 1987 movie *Wall Street*, Gordon Gekko proclaimed that "greed is good," and summed up the feeling of the times. In the 1960s and 1970s personal enlightenment and finding truth held sway; in the 1980s it was the bottom line. Of course this major component of the zeitgeist spilled over into the Broadway musical. Sadly, the more decisions were driven by the bottom line, the less deeply felt and personally expressive theatre became. The 1980s was a decade of exceptionally slick product that was eminently reproducible and even more marketable. The freewheeling experiments of the Princess musicals, *West Side Story* or *Cabaret* could never have happened in the 1980s. The avant-garde of the previous period sought to connect with their audience and leave them impacted, thinking about what they had seen; the mega-musicals of the 1980s sought to give their audiences non-stop spectacle that would numb them out for two and a half hours and then return them to their lives untouched. The year 1981 brought the blockbuster movie *Raiders of the Lost Ark* to screens in exactly the same manner; the movie displays extraordinary craftsmanship in every aspect of filmmaking, but it was designed to give its audience an experience analogous to a roller-coaster ride – thrills and chills at every turn, but delivered safely back to the platform unscathed at the end of the ride. Movies, musicals, and all other forms of popular culture followed this formula to success.

Although the 1980s saw some wonderfully entertaining shows, great writers, directors, actors all creating musicals at the highest level, the artistic creativity of the previous forty years or so was supplanted by business and marketing creativity in the 1980s. Hyping, packaging, merchandising and promoting a show before it was open, or even written, established musicals as product to be sold in international franchises. Once the audience was in the theater the product had to live up to the hype, but the hype was what defined the musical theatre of the 1980s.

The audience for the smaller shows, the shows that ran only in New York, was shrinking as the musical became less and less relevant to the lives of Middle-America. Musicals had to be content to be historical footnotes, like *The*

Rink, Jelly's Last Jam or *My One and Only* or come up with marketing strategies to make them the next *Cats* or *Les Misérables*.

Chapter summary

- A number of factors contributed to the declining number of new musicals produced every season. These forces include:
  - the degradation of Times Square and surrounding neighborhood
  - Aids
  - the loss of a generation of theatre artists who defected to Hollywood
  - the loss of audience to both cable television and video-recording
  - the spiraling costs of union labor
  - lack of singular producers
  - the redevelopment of the Shubert Organization
  - the cost of theater tickets.
- A look at theater owners and managers.
- The number of new musicals is way down, as economics require hits to have substantially bigger payoffs.
- The mega-musical.
- Cameron Mackintosh.
- The 1983–84 season.
- The mega-musical dominates through the 1980s and into the 1990s, until it becomes financially top-heavy and is no longer a useful business model.

Notes

1 Paul Prece and William A. Everett, "The Megamusical and Beyond: The Creation, Internationalization, and Impact of a Genre," *The Cambridge Companion to the Musical,* Cambridge, UK: Cambridge University Press 2008, p. 246.
2 Frank Rich, "Stage: Phantom of the Opera," *The New York Times,* January 28, 1988. Web, accessed March 3, 2013, http://www.nytimes.com/1988/01/27/theater/stage-phantom-of-the-opera.html?pagewanted=all&src=pmhttp://www.nytimes.com/1988/01/27/theater/stage-phantom-of-the-opera.html
3 Patrick Healy, "Dream Big, Girl," *The New York Times,* March, 24, 2013, Arts and Leisure, p. 1.
4 Frank Rich, "Review/Theatre; Lloyd Webber's 'Aspects of Love'," *New York Times,* April 9, 1990. Web, accessed March 7, 2013, http://www.nytimes.com/1990/04/09/theater/review-theater-lloyd-webber-s-aspects-of-love.html

Further reading

Cameron Mackintosh

The best source for information about Cameron Mackintosh are the plentiful articles and interviews available online.

13 The corporate musical, 1993–2001

Time for change

By 1993 the mega-musical had run its course; it had become top-heavy and financially unviable. *Sunset Boulevard* closed after a two and a half year run, having lost $20 million. As the financially unrestrained 1980s gave way to the fiscally responsible 1990s in the American economy, the American musical seemed unsure of itself. As more money was required to mount fewer shows, larger corporate entities necessarily evolved to produce shows. As the tide turned, regional theaters with government subsidies and preferential union contracts were where new musicals were mounted, replacing the traditional out-of-town pre-Broadway tryouts.

In New York, several theatre companies had been operating under LORT contracts (League of Resident Theatres) with the theatrical unions, allowing them to pay below Broadway wages. However, by the 1990s two of these theaters were regularly producing musicals, selling tickets at Broadway prices and being eligible for Tony Awards. This allowed Lincoln Center and The Roundabout Theatre Company to produce more artistically challenging musicals. Lincoln Center's larger theater, the Vivian Beaumont, was their "Broadway" space, and their smaller Mitzi Newhouse was their "off-Broadway" space.

In the 1990s some new and interesting voices in the American musical began to appear off-Broadway and beyond, in venues where expenses didn't demand massive audiences. By the 1990s, Broadway was home to massive entertainments that needed to replicate virally across continents, and sell tickets and merchandise internationally to earn a profit. But off-Broadway, smaller, more intimate musicals were targeted to smaller, more discerning audiences. Off-Broadway became the spawning ground for some of the most interesting new pieces of the decade.

The beginning of this period on Broadway

The 1992–93 season looked promising, including a spate of new musicals. The two most successful were Kander and Ebb's *Kiss of the Spider Woman* and director Des McAnuff's production of *The Who's "Tommy."*

After a 1990 workshop at SUNY Purchase, *Spider Woman* was produced by Toronto producer Garth Drabinsky, of Live Entertainment, Ltd. Kander and Ebb had been pushing the boundaries of musical theatre since *Cabaret*, and *Kiss of the Spider Woman* was no different. This musical tells the story of two prisoners who share a cell in deplorable conditions in an undisclosed South American country – one is imprisoned for his political activism and the other for being homosexual. Together they transcend their dank cell by escaping into lavish fantasy sequences involving a 1940s movie star; and in so doing they find they are not so different. *Spider Woman* played for six months in Toronto followed by six months in London before opening in New York. Despite mostly negative reviews, the show found a New York audience. But the reviews combined with the dark nature of the material forestalled the tours or international productions necessary to become financially successful.

McAnuff's *The Who's "Tommy"* began regionally at the La Jolla Playhouse in San Diego prior to Broadway. Regional theaters, with their subsidies and favorable union contracts, had been used to develop new musicals as far back as *A Chorus Line* and Joseph Papp's Public Theatre, and *Les Misérables*, originally co-produced by the Royal Shakespeare Company. Originally a 1969 album by British rock group, The Who, *Tommy* had already been a movie and appeared on various stages, including the Metropolitan Opera House, but the property was re-imagined by McAnuff and Pete Townshend for Broadway. The music was familiar to audiences, but McAnuff and his design team found a new visual palette for musical theatre in their use of video and flying sequences. "To say that the scenery is phenomenal is a bit like pointing out that the Grand Canyon is deep. [...] That the designers have been able to marry the surrealism of Magritte to the cool formalism of Robert Wilson to the explosiveness of Pop Art, without producing a hodgepodge, is only part of their triumph. [...] The scenery actually plays an integral role in the narrative, filling in blanks, getting us from point A to point C, telling us what is going on between songs when no one else is."[1] *Tommy* had an extensive life in tours, regional and international productions.

The 1992–93 season also included: Ahrens and Flaherty's *My Favorite Year* at Lincoln Center's Vivian Beaumont Theatre; Marvin Hamlisch, David Zippel and Neil Simon's adaptation of Simon's movie *The Goodbye Girl*; a biographical musical about producer Mike Todd, *Ain't Broadway Grand*; and Willy Russell's *Blood Brothers*, which had been running in England since 1983. *Blood Brothers* ran for 840 performances, but ran for more than 10,000 performances in London.

The 1992–93 season had been a good one, but the next season new musicals were few and far between, replaced with revivals: *She Loves Me*, *Camelot*, *Joseph and the Amazing Technicolor Dreamcoat*, *My Fair Lady*, *Damn Yankees*, *Carousel* and *Grease*. Of the few new musicals *The Red Shoes*, Jule Styne's final score, ran for five performances and *The Best Little Whorehouse Goes Public* was a sixteen-performance sequel to *The Best Little Whorehouse in Texas*. The two new musicals of interest were Stephen Sondheim's *Passion*, and

Disney's *Beauty and the Beast*. *Beauty and the Beast* changed the face of Broadway.

Mega-musicals had established a model in which musicals marketed globally proved extremely profitable. On April 14, 1994, *New York Times* columnist Alex Witchell wrote, "This season, the role of the Beast, usually played on Broadway by the Shubert Organization with its 16 theatres, will be played instead by the Walt Disney Company, which is almost single-handedly rejuvenating 42nd Street by renovating the New Amsterdam Theatre. It is also producing the most expensive Broadway musical in theatre history, opening tomorrow night at the Palace Theatre. What's that? Booing? Applause? Both."[2] During the 1970s and 1980s, 42nd Street had been taken over by drug addicts and prostitutes; Mayor David Dinkins had persuaded Disney to invest money in revitalizing 42nd Street. With Hollywood-sized money to invest in their theatrical ventures, and the Disney brand name, Disney Theatrical took the musical theatre by storm, bringing with them their way of doing business, which was highly corporate. The 1980s had been the time of the joint ventures; the 1990s were the time of the corporate musical.

Beauty and the Beast established Disney as a player on Broadway. Disney had learned a lesson from *Annie*, creating musicals that kids could bring their parents to. They brought their own brand of Disney magic in heightening merchandising to a degree Broadway had never seen and in further expanding the global market. As of 2007, "*Beauty and the Beast* has been seen by more than 26 million people, has grossed more than $1.4 billion worldwide and played in a total of 13 countries and 115 cities."[3] And that was in ticket sales alone; it did not include sale of coffee mugs, key chains, leather jackets, Christmas ornaments, posters, CDs, souvenir programs, zippered hoodies, T-shirts, purses, snowglobes, tote bags, magnets, charm bracelets, dolls, enchanted roses, tiaras, lapel charms, or any other products for sale at the souvenir kiosks Disney installed in all theaters where the show played or online. In 1994, instead of simply spending $300 for mezzanine tickets for a family of four, most patrons could add an additional $200 to $300 for various merchandise and memorabilia.

With *Beauty and the Beast*, Disney introduced a cadre of national and international supervisors of dance, music and acting. These new employees traveled the world maintaining the product, ensuring that, all over the planet, people saw identical performances. Since these supervisors needed to justify their large salaries to the front office, rehearsals and note sessions were called in each city. The Broadway musical was bigger business, but people complained about the "theme park" mentality.

> It's long been known as the fabulous invalid and the Great White Way, but we may have to start calling it Six Flags Over Broadway. While there has always been a raffish, thrill-seeking side to theatergoing, the distinction between Broadway and a theme park grew decidedly narrower during the 1993–94 season. [...] the Walt Disney Company came to town, commandeered the Palace Theatre with the stage version of one of its biggest

animated features, *Beauty and the Beast*, turned the lobby into a mammoth souvenir boutique and proclaimed its intentions of renovating a theatre of its very own on 42nd Street.[4]

Corporate producers

In the late 1980s several production entities came into being, corporations that produced or participated in the production of Broadway shows. Dodger Theatricals was one of the earliest of these corporations, formed in 1982 to produce *Pump Boys and Dinettes*. The Dodgers have participated in thirty-eight productions between 1982 and 2013.

Between 1989 and 2001 PACE Theatrical Group participated in twenty Broadway musicals. PACE entered a partnership with Jujamcyn Theaters in 1997 to create and distribute theatrical product. "The decision by Jujamcyn Theaters and the Pace Theatrical Group to form a partnership in the creation, production and, in a sense, distribution of Broadway shows is not only one of the most significant developments to occur in the industry in recent years, it also signals a change in the way Broadway makes theater. The revolution is in the growing number of entertainment companies that are seeking to create vertical theatrical empires, financing and supervising the production of multimillion-dollar plays and musicals from start to finish, running them in their own theaters and even taking them on the road."[5]

Clear Channel Entertainment, also known as SFX Theatrical Group, was even more prolific, with thirty-six productions between 1995 and 2005. Clear Channel was a subsidiary of a larger corporation, the largest owner of billboards, AM and FM radio stations, with major interests in XM radio, television stations and other media outlets.

Many entertainment corporations created subsidiaries to develop Broadway musical properties. Movie corporations, television networks, recording companies and publishing companies all opened subsidiaries to oversee participation in their theatrical interests.

Most Broadway musicals of this period were produced by multiple producers and corporate entities. *Victor/Victoria* listed seven lead producers, a co-producer and four associate producers. Broadway grew further removed from the single visionary producer mounting a production based on his or her personal aesthetic. The "David Merricks," "Joseph Papps" and "Stuart Ostrows" were replaced by boards of individuals and corporate representatives, each with their own interests to protect; it was substantially harder for creativity to thrive in this environment. And it got worse; although twelve producers were not uncommon on a single show in the 1990s, the number would escalate. *Hairspray* (2002) listed twenty producing partners; *Catch Me If You Can* (2011) listed thirty.

New voices in the 1990s

In the 1990s a new generation of musical theatre composer/lyricists emerged; many of these found a new model for success in shows with very short runs either off-Broadway or regionally. Their shows developed followings among musical theatre fans, thanks in great part to access to audio and video recordings distributed digitally online. Many of these shows have became the staple material of regional and educational theaters.

Michael John LaChiusa, Andrew Lippa, Adam Guettel and Jason Robert Brown were central to the musical theatre of the 1990s. Part of the appeal of their shows is their intellectual and artistic rigor, which is not for everyone, and not for the widest possible entertainment market. That most of their shows were created for smaller theaters with smaller budgets also makes them imminently more producible by regional and educational theaters – smaller casts, sets, costumes and musicians.

A fifth important new voice tragically passed away on the eve of his first success. Jonathan Larson died of aortic dissection after the final dress rehearsal of the off-Broadway production of his musical *Rent*. The sixth important new composer/lyricist found success, if not acclaim, in a series of traditional Broadway productions – Frank Wildhorn, who burst onto the scene with *Jekyll and Hyde*.

> Composer, lyricist and book writer **Michael John LaChiusa (b. 1962)** is one of the new generation of musical theatre writers – writing not only music and lyrics, but the book as well. In his twenties he worked as a musical director and accompanist.

Michael John LaChiusa's scores are widely eclectic. With influences including Arnold Schoenberg, John Cage, Philip Glass, George Gershwin, Richard Rodgers and Stephen Sondheim, LaChiusa references and evokes a range of eras and styles in his compositions. After participating in the BMI Lehman Engel Musical Theatre Writer's Workshop, his first produced work was the chamber opera *First Lady Suite* in 1993, at the Public Theatre. *First Lady Suite* connects Jacqueline Onassis, Mamie Eisenhower and Eleanor Roosevelt, women of the White House having been an interest of LaChiusa's since childhood. One month later, his first full-length musical, *Hello Again*, opened at Lincoln Center's Mitzi Newhouse Theatre. Based on Schnitzler's *La Ronde*, *Hello Again* is a series of scenes and songs depicting a daisy chain of sexual liaisons that ultimately leads back to the person with whom it began. In *Hello Again*, LaChiusa began a long-term relationship with director and choreographer Graciela Daniele.

After 1995's unsuccessful *The Petrified Prince*, LaChiusa's next full musical was *Marie Christine* in 1999 at Lincoln Center's Vivian Beaumont Theatre. LaChiusa found, in Audra McDonald, a great interpreter of his highly eclectic style. "Mr. LaChiusa is working from the disparate, clashing strands of American culture; Ms. McDonald, whose command of musical dialects here ranges from the operatic to gospel, turns that paradox into something intensely personal, finding conflicting impulses in a single breath."[6] Despite glowing reviews, the show only ran for the forty-two scheduled subscription performances.

The year 2000 saw the Broadway production of LaChiusa and director George Wolfe's *The Wild Party*, based on Joseph Moncure March's 1928 narrative poem. The story is about a Jazz-Age party hosted by a couple whose relationship is burning out; the party degenerates into an orgy, with the aid of cocaine and homemade gin, and ultimately ends in tragedy. Despite strong critical response, LaChiusa and Wolfe's expressionistic vaudeville only ran for sixty-eight performances.

Little Fish, in 2005, based on two short stories, *Days* and *Flotsam*, directed and choreographed by Daniele off-Broadway, closed in three weeks. Other recent musicals include 2005's *What I Wanna See* at the Public Theatre, *The House of Bernarda Alba* in 2006 at Lincoln Center's Mitzi Newhouse Theatre, *Queen of the Mist* in 2011 at the Gym at Judson, and *Giant* in 2012 at the Public Theatre. Despite their disappointing box-office performance, each of these shows has garnered praise for LaChiusa. In his review of *Giant*, Ben Brantley wrote, "Mr. LaChiusa has a wide musical vocabulary, and he deploys it deftly in numbers that subtly incorporate the styles of different eras and cultures, from the 1920s to the 1950s. He has the reputation of being a cerebral, even recondite, composer, but this is a tuneful and accessible score."[7]

Some consider LaChiusa one of the progeny of Stephen Sondheim, as an artist and an intellect. He has been accused of being cerebral to the point of being aloof. Despite relatively short initial New York runs, many of LaChiusa's shows have found success in subsequent productions regionally and in educational theater. LaChiusa writes for those audiences seeking intellectual fare more than the large-scale productions offering the thrills of cloned Broadway productions on tour around the world.

Composer, lyricist and librettist **Andrew Lippa (b. 1964)** was born in Leeds, England. His family emigrated to a Michigan suburb when he was three years old. Like LaChiusa, Lippa began his career as a pianist, accompanist and musical director.

Also, like LaChiusa, Andrew Lippa participated in the BMI Lehman Engel Musical Theatre Writer's Workshop in the late 1980s. Lippa considers his biggest influences to be Motown, 1970s popular music and Leonard Bernstein.

Lippa's 1995 *john & jen*, a two-actor musical, opened at the Goodspeed Opera House, and moved on to a six-month run off-Broadway. *john & jen* examines the relationships between a brother and sister, and the sister and her son – the same actor plays both men.

In 2000, Lippa's own version of *The Wild Party*, based on the same material as LaChiusa's, was produced off-Broadway. Neither production fared well, although both have their advocates and both are regularly produced in regional and educational theaters.

Lippa contributed three new songs to a short-lived Broadway revival of *You're A Good Man, Charlie Brown* in 1999, and wrote music for 2004 children's musical *A Little Princess*, which premiered in Palo Alto, California.

In 2010 *The Addams Family* brought the beloved television and film characters to the Broadway stage and brought Lippa a Tony nomination for best score. Despite mediocre reviews, the production sustained a run of 722 performances and produced a tour. Lippa's latest musical *Big Fish* opened and closed in fall of 2013. Many of Lippa's shows have proven popular in regional productions.

Composer and lyricist **Adam Guettel (b. 1964)**, the son of Mary Rodgers and grandson of Richard Rodgers, has been one of the most successful of the new breed of musical theatre writers, although his output has been somewhat limited.

The first produced musical theatre score by composer/lyricist Adam Guettel was the haunting *Floyd Collins*, based on the true story of a Kentucky man who dies when he becomes trapped in a cave. After premiering at Philadelphia's American Music Theater Festival in 1994, it ran off-Broadway for twenty-five performances at Playwrights Horizons in 1996. *Floyd Collins* dazzled critics, quickly becoming a staple of regional theaters. Guettel followed *Floyd Collins* with *Saturn Returns*, a song cycle, performed at the Public Theatre for sixteen performances; both shows were directed by Tina Landau. *Saturn Returns* was recorded and released in 1999 under the title *Myths and Hymns*. Guettel's music has been referred to as chromatic, complex and eclectic.

In 2005, Guettel's *The Light in the Piazza* opened at Lincoln Center, earning him two Tony Awards for best score and best orchestration. *Piazza* told an intimate and compelling story of mother and daughter Margaret and Clara Johnson, at a time when most Broadway musicals were full of spectacle, but low on humanity. Guettel explores depth of character in the chromatic and complex score by fusing components of popular music and traditional musical theatre sounds with the vocabulary of his influences: Igor Stravinsky, Maurice Ravel, Claude Debussy and Benjamin Britten. *Piazza* had a successful initial run of 504 performances, and produced a one-year tour. *Piazza* has also become a staple for regional and education theaters.

Composer, lyricist and librettist **Jason Robert Brown (b. 1970)** grew up in a New York suburb and, after two years of study at the Eastman School, began his career as a keyboardist, arranger and conductor in the early 1990s.

Jason Robert Brown began as a rehearsal pianist on Kander and Ebb's *Kiss of the Spider Woman* in 1993. He worked as an arranger, pianist and conductor on William Finn's *A New Brain*, LaChiusa's *The Petrified Prince*, and Lippa's *john & jen*, among others. As a writer, Brown's first show was the song cycle *Songs for a New World*, which ran at the WPA Theatre for twelve performances, directed by Daisy Prince, daughter of Harold Prince.

Harold Prince had suggested that Stephen Sondheim write a musical based on the 1913 trial of Leo Frank, a Jewish factory manager in Atlanta, Georgia, accused and convicted of raping and murdering a thirteen-year-old girl. Frank was given a reprieve from his death sentence, but was lynched by an angry mob. When Sondheim turned the show down, Prince asked Brown to write the music and lyrics. *Parade* opened at Lincoln Center, earning Brown a Tony Award for best score. *Parade* ran for eighty-five performances.

Brown's next musical, *The Last Five Years*, was inspired by his own failed marriage. Directed once again by Daisy Prince, *The Last Five Years* only has two characters. The male character's story begins at the beginning and goes forward chronologically; the female character's story starts at the dissolution of their relationship and journeys back to the beginning. Although the show received mediocre reviews and managed to run for just over two months, it has become a staple of smaller theaters across the world.

In 2008, Brown's *13* opened on Broadway, an original musical about the angst of being thirteen years old, played by a cast of thirteen teenagers. Brown wrote music and lyrics, orchestrated and arranged the music. Although Ben Brantley, in the *New York Times*, found the score "buoyant," he also found the show formulaic and wrote, "*13* ultimately feels as pre-processed and formulaic as that money-churning Disney franchise *High School Musical*."[8] Brown's latest show is *The Bridges of Madison County*, which opened January 2014 to strong critical response.

This new model

This new wave of musical theatre writers in the 1990s carried with them a wide range of influences. As these writers were coming into their own "repurposed culture," taking cultural artifacts and combining them in new ways to give them new meanings, was beginning to be seen across disciplines in popular culture. Certainly hip-hop and rap music took advantage of this by using sampling and sound clips to create new works. In a similar vein, these musical theatre composers were riffing on the techniques and feels of a diverse set of styles, a wealth of shared cultural artifacts. Referencing Schoenberg, Bernstein and Stevie Wonder within a single phrase was a whole new way of creating music for the musical theatre.

While most of these shows might be viewed as failures based on their short runs and failure to recoup investments, these musicals have proven tre-mendously popular and successful in subsequent productions worldwide. The business model has changed, and recoupment within the initial production is no longer the benchmark. This model favors the rights-holders, since not only investors, but the creators – writers, directors, choreographers – are paid royalties for their work.

Removing the need to recoup yielded musicals of a more challenging nature to audiences – a "higher end" product. A small independent film can be highly profitable within its niche market, even up against mainstream blockbuster movie hits, and so could these musicals. Many of these writers' musicals, song cycles and individual songs have achieved great popularity among musical theatre fans, inspiring performances at venues around the world.

Composer, lyricist and librettist **Jonathan Larson (1960–96)** was raised in suburban New York and tragically died of an aortic aneurism after the dress rehearsal of his great hit, *Rent*, at age thirty-six.

Jonathan Larson's *Rent* was the hit of the 1995–96 season. In 1989 Larson had put together a reading of a musical based on George Orwell's *1984*, but with no production, the Orwell estate refused him the rights to the novel. His next work was a "rock monologue" in which he expressed his anger about the Orwell musical. The "rock monologue" was originally called *30/90*, then *Boho Days*, and finally *Tick, Tick … Boom!* This piece brought Larson to Ira Weitzman's attention; Weitzman recommended him to playwright Billy Aronson, who was writing a contemporary adaptation of Puccini's *La Bohème*. Wanting to make the piece more about his own life experiences in Soho, Larson made an arrangement with Aronson to take over the project himself.

Larson transferred Puccini's story to New York's Lower East Side, and replaced consumption with Aids. In the same way that Gower Champion's death brought publicity and curiosity to *42nd Street*, *Rent*'s success was spurred on by Larson's untimely death after the final off-Broadway dress rehearsal. During the off-Broadway run, *Rent*'s move to Broadway was carefully planned.

A new generation of musical theatre fans rallied, referring to themselves as "rent-heads," some seeing more than 100 performances of the show, helping *Rent* run for more than twelve years, becoming the ninth longest running Broadway show and grossing over $280 million.[9] The producers of *Rent* wanted the appearance of a spontaneous hit, but it was carefully test-marketed and packaged. *Rent* featured a new generation of Broadway rock singers including Daphne Rubin-Vega, Anthony Rapp, Adam Pascal, Idina Menzel and Taye Diggs. Larson posthumously won Tony and Drama Desk Awards and a Pulitzer Prize.

In 2001 *Tick, Tick … Boom!* received a production at the Jane Street Theatre, where it ran for eight months.

Composer **Frank Wildhorn (b. 1958)** grew up in New York and Florida, and has had one of the most prolific careers of the composers of his generation.

Jekyll and Hyde in 1997 was composer Frank Wildhorn's first full Broadway score, although he had written the music for two songs in *Victor/Victoria* (1995). As a Broadway composer, Wildhorn was a wildly successful writer of pop songs and power ballads. *Jekyll and Hyde* was originally produced at the Alley Theatre in Houston in 1990 and again in 1995 and had been on the road during 1995 and 1996. Like *Rent*, *Jekyll and Hyde* developed a loyal following of fans who came back to see the show many times; they referred to themselves as "Jekkies" and conferred regularly in chat rooms. Although *Jekyll and Hyde* ran for almost four years on Broadway, it lost more than $1.5 million.

Wildhorn's *The Scarlet Pimpernel*, originally released as a concept album, opened on Broadway in November 1997, directed by Peter Hunt. As the production was winding down, a new executive producer joined the venture, bringing a new creative team with him. The production was completely revised in October 1998 and remained open with direction by Robert Longbottom. The production was revised again for a three-month tour, which then returned to Broadway. One Broadway run saw three completely different productions.

Alley Theatre artistic director, Gregory Boyd, and Wildhorn wrote *The Civil War*, which also began as a concept recording, followed by a première at the Alley Theatre. With *Civil War* on Broadway, while *Jekyll and Hyde* and *The Scarlet Pimpernel* were still running, Wildhorn had three shows on Broadway simultaneously. Although *Civil War* opened and closed on Broadway in 1999 after unanimous negative reviews, the tour was successful. That is the problem with most of Wildhorn's shows; the songs are good, but not theatrical. They do not move the story forward or reveal character. The shows stop to let audiences listen to a great song, and then the shows return to the story, which they had put aside for the sake of the song.

After *Civil War*, Wildhorn took a five-year hiatus, but came back strong. He wrote thirteen new musicals in ten years, across the world: *Camille Claudel* (2003, Goodspeed Opera House), *Dracula, the Musical* (2004, La Jolla Playhouse and Broadway), *Waiting for the Moon* (2005, Lenape Performing Arts Center), *Cyrano de Bergerac, The Musical* (2006, Japan), *Rudolph – The Last Kiss* (2006, Budapest), *Never Say Goodbye* (2006, Japan), *Carmen* (2008, Czech Republic), *The Count of Monte Cristo* (2009, Switzerland), *Bonnie and Clyde* (2009, La Jolla, and 2011 Broadway), *Wonderland* (2009 Florida, 2011 Broadway), *Tears of Heaven* (2011, South Korea), *Mitsuko* (2011, Japan), *Zelda* (2012, Flat Rock Playhouse). Planned are *Excalibur* (2014, Theatre St. Gallen) and *Havana* (Pasadena Playhouse). Despite negative reviews and productions that lose millions of dollars Wildhorn continued to write and get his material produced.

Jukebox musicals

Throughout the 1980s, the number of cable television channels rose; each channel needed programming to attract viewers. Many promising young musical theatre talents became television writers, directors and producers in the 1990s. Young musical theatre writers who had spent years developing a musical, only to see it close off-off-Broadway in a few weeks, could move to California and get a well-paying job in television. Given the choice between waiting on tables or earning a handsome wage doing the thing that they loved to do, it only made sense. It became harder for producers and directors to find writers to write their shows. One answer to this problem was the jukebox musical. Jukebox musicals use a previously existing catalog of songs as the score of a musical. Some jukebox musicals are revues, like *Smokey Joe's Café* (1995); others have plots, created so the previously existing songs can service the plots, like *Mamma Mia!* (1999).

There had been composer revues before this; *Ain't Misbehavin'* (the music of Fats Waller, 1978), *Eubie!* (the music of Eubie Blake, 1978), *Sophisticated Ladies* (the music of Duke Ellington, 1981) and others. By the 1990s jukebox musicals were becoming more and more prevalent, and those with plots were becoming more sophisticated.

Plot-less revues from 1992 to 2001 include:

- *Five Guys Named Moe*, songs of jazz artist Louis Jordan (1992);
- *A Grand Night for Singing*, the music of Rodgers and Hammerstein (1993);
- *Smokey Joe's Café*, the songs of Jerry Leiber and Mike Stoller (1995);
- *Swinging on a Star*, the songs of Johnny Burke (1995);
- *Dream*, the songs of Johnny Mercer (1997);
- *An Evening with Jerry Herman*, the songs of Jerry Herman, (1998);
- *Fosse*, choreography pieces by Bob Fosse from different shows and movies, all which had their own pre-existing music (1998); and
- *Swing!* (1999).

Some of the jukebox musicals of the 1990s that attached plots to pre-existing songs include:

- *Forever Plaid*, an off-Broadway musical about a guy group from the 1950s who are killed and given the chance to sing one last concert (1990);
- *Return to the Forbidden Planet*, combining Shakespeare's *The Tempest* and the 1956 science-fiction film *Forbidden Planet* using early rock and roll songs (1991);
- *Jelly's Last Jam*, the life of Jelly Roll Morton, using his music (1992);
- *Play On*, an adaptation of Shakespeare's *Twelfth Night*, set in Harlem in the 1940s using Duke Ellington songs (1997);
- *Putting It Together* – at a black tie party in Manhattan, an older disillusioned couple meet a younger less jaded couple and a narrator leads us through the evening using the songs of Stephen Sondheim (1993 off-Broadway at Manhattan Theatre Club, 1999 on Broadway);
- *Mamma Mia!*, the story of a young woman who is getting married and her mother who is not quite sure who her father is, provides an excuse for the characters to perform the music of 1970s Swedish rock group ABBA (2001).

Jukebox musicals also participate in the trend of reusing artifacts of popular culture to create new art. By the twenty-first century, jukebox musicals had become a staple of the American musical.

What else was happening in the Broadway musical?

The number of new musicals mounted from 1993–2001 dropped to an all-time low. Figure 13.1 compares the mid-decade season in each decade since the 1910s.

The 1914–15 season saw twenty-three new musicals open on Broadway including *Nobody Home*, the first of the Princess musicals. In the 1924–25 season forty new musicals opened on Broadway. Despite the ravages of the Depression the 1934–35 season saw twenty-eight new musicals on Broadway. Eighteen new musicals opened on Broadway in each of the 1944–45 and 1954–55 seasons. Nineteen new musicals opened in the 1964–65 season. The number dipped to thirteen in the 1974–75 season. Gerald Bordman wrote, "the 1984–85 season may well go down in history as Broadway's worst,"[10] at eight new musicals. The 1994–95 season saw the production of only two new musicals, *Sunset Boulevard* and *Smokey Joe's Café*.

Figure 13.2 shows the number of new musicals from 1993 to 2001. The best seasons were the 1997–98 and 1999–2000 seasons with eight new musicals each; the 1994–95 season was the worst of all, with only two new musicals. The statistic held; roughly 70 percent of new musicals failed and closed quickly. Smart producers with a marginal musical learned to wait until as late in the season as possible before bringing their show to Broadway, hoping for a few last-minute Tony nominations in a horrible season. During this decade it was occasionally hard for the Tony Award nominating committee to come up with enough nominees in some categories.

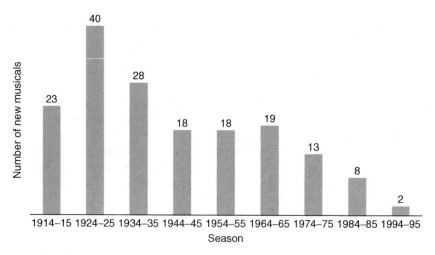

Figure 13.1 The number of new Broadway musicals in the mid-season of each decade

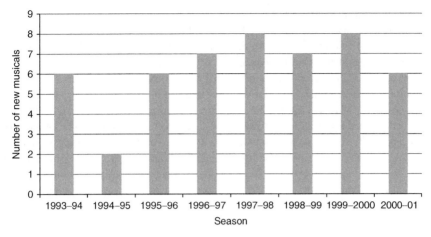

Figure 13.2 The number of new musicals per season 1993–2001

An overview of the 1993–2001 seasons

Kander and Ebb's *Kiss of the Spider Woman* swept the 1993 Tony Awards, except for Best Director and Best Choreographer, which went to Des McAnuff and Wayne Cilento for *The Who's "Tommy."*

Despite the fact that the 1994 Best Musical Tony Award went to Sondheim and Lapine's *Passion* over Disney's *Beauty and the Beast*, the Disney show ran almost twenty times as long as the Sondheim show. *Beauty and the Beast* established a new standard for merchandising and also represented a huge step towards branding musical theatre.

With only two new musicals in the 1994–95 season, *Sunset Boulevard* won Tony Awards for Best Book and Best Score and Best New Musical. Harold Prince's revival of *Show Boat* won five Tony Awards including Best Direction.

The hit of 1995–96 season was *Rent*, which won Tony Awards for Best Musical, Score, Book and Featured Actor, followed by *Bring in Da Noise/Bring in Da Funk*, which took awards for Best Director, Lighting Design, Choreography and Featured Actress. For the first time, the awards went overwhelmingly to rock shows created by artists new to Broadway and the musical theatre.

Julie Andrews was nominated for her performance in *Victor/Victoria*, but declined the nomination "in protest of what she viewed as the humiliation the musical had received in earning just a single Tony nomination."[11] Richard Maltby and David Shire's *Big* was nominated for five awards, and won none. *Big* had accepted a needed infusion of funds during their pre-Broadway tryout from toy store FAO Schwartz. Once FAO Schwartz became a partner, the emphasis shifted to getting more time onstage for the kids. The writers did substantial re-writes for a successful national tour that was launched shortly after the show closed on Broadway.

The smash of the 1996–97 season was the revival of Kander and Ebb's *Chicago*, which began as part of the *Encores!* series. *Encores!* had begun producing a series of concert mountings of rarely heard musicals in 1994. *A Chorus Line* had originally overshadowed *Chicago*, but in 1996 the musical about exploiting the celebrity of murderers for their entertainment careers came on the heels of the O.J. Simpson murder trial; the concept of celebrity criminals made *Chicago* a part of the zeitgeist. Producer Barry and Fran Weissler moved the concert directly to Broadway, where it has been playing ever since. The *Chicago* revival won seven Tony Awards. Maury Yeston's *Titanic* won five Tony Awards and ran on Broadway for just under two years followed by a successful national tour. The other new musicals of the season were: *Play On!*, an African-American adaptation of Shakespeare's *Twelfth Night* using the music of Duke Ellington; *Steel Pier*, the Kander and Ebb dance marathon musical; *The Life*, Cy Coleman's musical about the lives of the pimps, prostitutes, drug dealers, users and homeless people who lived in Times Square before Disney cleaned it up; and Frank Wildhorn's *Jekyll and Hyde*.

The two contenders for the 1997–98 Tony Awards were both massive productions based on visual spectacle, produced by large corporate entities. *Ragtime*, produced by Livent in Toronto, was a mega-musical. Producer Garth Drabinsky auditioned composer/lyricist teams before hiring Lynn Ahrens and Stephen Flaherty. Ahrens and Flaherty had met at the BMI Lehman Engel Musical Theatre Workshop in the early 1980s and had prior success with *Lucky Stiff* off-Broadway (1989) and *Once on This Island* on Broadway (1990), and *My Favorite Year* (1992). Playwright Terrence McNally wrote the book based on E.L. Doctorow's novel. Fresh off his success adapting and directing *The Grapes of Wrath* for Broadway, Frank Galati was brought in to direct and Graciela Daniele to choreograph. Drabinsky bought two older theaters on 42nd Street that had fallen into disrepair, the Lyric and the Apollo, and spent $22.5 million having them rebuilt into one theater, The Ford Center, for the opening of *Ragtime*.

Yet, despite all the credentials and all the money lavished on it, *Ragtime* did not receive critical praise. "*Ragtime* would seem to be the kind of musical that brings Broadway audiences to their knees in adoration. Then why does this $10 million show, [...] feel so utterly resistible? [...] There is much to admire in *Ragtime*, ... but there is finally little to fall in love with."[12] The appeal of the score and the visual spectacle of the production and Livent's tremendous publicity machine kept the show running for two years. However, the high weekly expenses kept the show from ever recouping its investment. Musicals of this size could no longer earn what was needed to meet the weekly expenses, and so there was almost no way for a show this big to show a profit in 1998.

The other heavy hitter of the season had an even larger and more aggressive single production entity behind it, Disney's *The Lion King*. *The Lion King* was adapted from the Disney movie. Having had great success putting its movie *Beauty and the Beast* onstage, Disney was determined to expand its market. Unlike *Beauty and the Beast*, *The Lion King* did not attempt to reproduce the visuals of the movie live and onstage. Instead, they brought in an avant-garde theatre artist from the downtown scene to develop a vocabulary of more poetic visual imagery. Director and puppet-designer Julie Taymor was known for a kind of ritualistic theatre that relied heavily on puppetry. While the production was visually stunning, critics felt that Taymor lacked the ability the tell a story well or to find sentiment in the characters or plot points of the story. While Taymor might indeed have had these shortcomings, she had a plot ready made for her in the movie, which itself was an adaptation of Shakespeare's *Hamlet*. *The Lion King* won multiple Tony Awards, and ultimately the powerful Disney machine has been able to keep *The Lion King* running as part of its flagship enterprise on Broadway; to date it has grossed over $5 billion from its companies worldwide, and is the first musical to have grossed over $1 billion from its Broadway company alone.[13]

1998–1999 was the season of dance on Broadway. The best musical of the season was a revue of choreographic pieces by Bob Fosse titled *Fosse*, produced by Livent. British choreographer Matthew Bourne created a contemporary dance piece based on the classical ballet *Swan Lake*. *Swan Lake* won three Tony Awards. The other musical of artistic interest in this season was the Jason Robert Brown musical *Parade*, directed by Harold Prince.

In addition to those shows Broadway also saw Frank Wildhorn's *Civil War*, *Footloose* (based on the 1984 movie), and the revue *It Ain't Nothin' But the Blues*. *It Ain't Nothin' But the Blues* had been running off-Broadway when the producers realized what a slow season it had been on Broadway. They decided to move the show and see if they could pick up any awards; they did not.

Dance also played heavily in the 1999–2000 season. Shows like *Swing!* and *Riverdance* (the Irish step-dancing extravaganza) were plotless, dance-driven evenings. Not nearly as successful as the previous season's *Footloose*, *Saturday Night Fever* made the transition from screen to stage. But the big hit was Susan Stroman's *Contact*, at Lincoln Center. *Contact* was a three-act dance concert. Each act told a different story. There was no dialog, no original score, and *Contact* was performed to prerecorded music. Despite public and industry concern over whether or not this show qualified as a musical, it swept the Tony Awards, winning awards for Best Choreography, Best Direction, Best Featured Actor and Actress in a Musical and Best Musical.

Also in the 1999–2000 season were Michael John LaChiusa's *Marie Christine*, starring Audra McDonald, two versions of *The Wild Party* (one on Broadway, the other off) and Elton John's *Aida*. *Aida* was produced by Hyperion Theatricals, one of whose primary organizational members was Disney Theatrical Productions. *Aida* had all of the marketing and cross-promotional wizardry one could expect from a Disney show and ran for four and a half years at the Palace Theatre.

The first season of the new millennium saw several interesting failures, one interesting new voice on Broadway, and the biggest hit Broadway had seen in years.

Lynn Ahrens and Stephen Flaherty's *Seussical*, based on the characters and stories of Dr. Seuss, should have been terrific. SFX Productions (formerly Clear Channel), Barry and Fran Weissler (whose *Chicago* was still going strong) and Universal Studios were all lead producers. Frank Galati had been hired to direct, but after a workshop in Toronto, under the coordination of Livent, and a tryout in Boston, he had separated from the production, leaving it with no official director. Another major problem was the role of the Cat in the Hat, the character who leads the audience through the musical. In workshops the role was played by Monty Python comedian, Eric Idle, and then by Andrea Martin. By the time the show arrived in New York the role was being played by David Shiner, a new-age clown and mime who was most comfortable being silent and least comfortable talking or singing. The production got terrible reviews, managed to eke out a run of 198 performances and lost its complete investment. However, its cast recording has inspired numerous productions by organizations that program material for young audiences or young performers.

The season also included a dreary musical version of *Jane Eyre* and a depressing musical about the life of lyricist Edward Kleban (who wrote the lyrics for *A Chorus Line*) using his own songs.

The Full Monty, a musical adaptation of the small quirky British film, opened in 2000. In the film a steel mill in Sheffield, England closes, putting their employees on the dole, causing six of the men to decide to do a one-night-only striptease to raise money. Adapting the show for Broadway, transferring the locale to Buffalo, NY, the musical lost absolutely none of the film's quirkiness and charm. *The Full Monty* introduced composer/lyricist David Yazbek to Broadway audiences.

Every show in the 2000–1 season was completely overshadowed, however, by Mel Brooks' stage musical version of his film, *The Producers*, which won twelve Tony Awards in 2001, more than any other musical. Just when America needed a comedy, the broadest kind of old-fashioned musical comedy showed up and felt, somehow, new again. *The Producers* ran for just over six years, spawned a network of national and international tours, and became a film (a second film, after the one it was based on). It was the biggest hit of the decade.

In a crazy idea, worthy of Max Bialystock (the fictional producer in the musical), Brooks and the producers of the show decided to offer a "premium" orchestra ticket for $480 per ticket. There was an uproar from the theatre community, but businessmen and corporate purchasers were willing to pay just shy of $1000 for a pair of theater tickets. Shortly other theaters began offering premium tickets. In some ways, the $480 theater ticket for *The Producers* was as clear a sign of the times as the success of the show.

The shifting economy of the Broadway musical at the end of the millennium

In 1993 the price of an orchestra ticket to *Cats* in the Winter Garden Theatre was $27.50; by 2001 an orchestra seat to *Mamma Mia!* in the Winter Garden had risen to over $110. Theater tickets increased 400 percent during this eight-year period; in contrast, the inflation rate in the economy overall was 35.4 percent.[14]

In 2001 producers proclaimed that Broadway was thriving. The amount of money being taken in at the box office was higher than it had ever been, but that statistic was greatly informed by the rise in ticket prices. And the astronomical rise in the expense of mounting a show and weekly operating expenses of running a show created market conditions under which only the biggest hits, the shows with the broadest possible appeal, had any chance on Broadway.

A study of the economics of Broadway was secretly conducted in the late 1990s by a coalition of theater professionals trying to find out why Broadway seemed to be in such decline, despite reports of Broadway's success. William Grimes of the *New York Times* obtained a copy of that report and wrote:

> Despite some signs of life, the New York theater industry is still in decline and beset by rising costs and lagging audiences, an unusually detailed industry-sponsored study has concluded. Bain & Company, a Boston-based consulting company that specializes in analyzing troubled businesses, has delivered a report that depicts the Broadway theater as performing at about half-capacity and losing market share to all other forms of entertainment. Runaway costs have made the economics of mounting and operating a show so forbidding, the report says, that producers have gravitated to the most risk-free productions, making Broadway a showcase for revivals and large-scale, long-running musicals rather than for innovative new work.[15]

The mega-musicals had become top-heavy to the point where they were no longer financially viable. Smaller shows were no longer viable on Broadway as people were less likely to pay hundreds of dollars for a show unless they were able to see their ticket dollar splashed across the stage. *The Producers* pointed the way to the future, offering a model for extraordinary success, but how many of those could Broadway sustain? The profits and the successes were limited to fewer and fewer shows, fewer artists and fewer producers. The monolithic hits continued to run. *Phantom of the Opera*, *Mamma Mia!*, *Chicago*, *The Lion King*, *Rent*, *Les Misérables* all continued to thrill and delight audiences into the next era. It was the extraordinary length of their runs combined with the network of national and international tours and productions that made them profitable. Only the mightiest, the most heavily marketed with the most companies dispersed around the world stood to earn a profit. Broadening the ticket-buying base and inspiring people around the world to buy tickets to the latest "event" musical, the one show of the year not to be missed is the only path to commercial success on Broadway.

Off-Broadway, and in regional productions, important and interesting new voices were singing new kinds of musicals and song cycles. Their concern was not the immediate recoupment of production costs, but a longer-term vision of the value of a property and of a particular artistic canon.

Chapter summary

- As the mega-musicals grow too financially top-heavy to show a profit, the corporate musical took their place. Corporations involved in producing musical theatre include: Disney Theatrical, Livent, PACE Theatrical, Clear Channel.

- The model of the corporate musical included multiple companies in cities around the world, and led to the use of national and international supervisors of dance, music, acting and production, creating a structure of middle management that had never existed in the theatre before.
- Michael John LaChiusa.
- Andrew Lippa.
- Adam Guettel.
- Jason Robert Brown.
- Jonathan Larson.
- Frank Wildhorn.
- With the dwindling number of writers, jukebox musicals became increasingly produced. Both revues and musicals with plots cobbled together around a catalog of songs were produced with growing frequency.
- The re-birth of musical comedy – *The Producers*.

Notes

1 David Richards, "Sunday View; Pinball Wizard Scores High on Visuals," *The New York Times*, May 2, 1993. Web, accessed March 23, 2013, http://www.nytimes.com/1993/05/02/theater/sunday-view-pinball-wizard-scores-high-on-visuals.html?pagewanted=all&src=pm

2 Alex Witchell, "Theatre; Is Disney the Newest Broadway Baby?" *The New York Times*, April 17, 1994. Web, accessed March 11, 2013, http://query.nytimes.com/gst/fullpage.html?res=9A03E0DF113EF934A25757C0A962958260

3 Boneau Bryan Brown, *News from Beauty and the Beast and Mamma Mia!*, July 11, 2007. Web, accessed March 11, 2013, http://bbb-blogger.blogspot.com/2007/07/news-from-beauty-and-beast-and-mamma.html

4 David Richards, "Stage View: On Stage, Survival of the Fizziest," *The New York Times*, June 12, 1994. Web, accessed March 11, 2013, http://www.nytimes.com/1994/06/12/theater/stage-view-on-stage-survival-of-the-fizziest.html?pagewanted=all&src=pm

5 Peter Marks, "The Outlook Is for More Money to Be Lavished on More Big Musicals," *The New York Times*, June 10, 1997. Web, accessed March 12, 2013, http://www.nytimes.com/1997/06/10/theater/the-outlook-is-for-more-money-to-be-lavished-on-more-big-musicals.html

6 Ben Brantley, "Theatre Review; The Promises of an Enchantress," *The New York Times*, December 3, 1999. Web, accessed March 16, 2013, http://www.nytimes.com/1999/12/03/movies/theater-review-the-promises-of-an-enchantress.html?pagewanted=all&src=pm

7 Ben Brantley, "'Giant,' With Brian D'Arcy James, at the Public Theatre," *The New York Times*, November 15, 2012. Web, accessed March 15, 2013, http://theater.nytimes.com/2012/11/16/theater/reviews/giant-with-brian-darcy-james-at-the-public-theater.html?pagewanted=all

8 Ben Brantley, "Theatre Review – '13' – Jason Robert Brown's New Musical – Teenage Stranger in a Strange Land," *New York Times*, October 6, 2008. Web, accessed March 15, 2013, http://theater.nytimes.com/2008/10/06/theater/reviews/06bran.html?_r=0

9 *Time Magazine*, March 10, 2008 issue, p. 66.

10 Gerald Bordman, *American Musical Theatre: A Chronicle (2nd Edition)*, New York: NY: Oxford University Press, 1992, p. 716.

11 Peter Marks, "Adding Drama to a Musical, Andrews Spurns the Tonys," *The New York Times*, May 9, 1996. Web, accessed March 23, 2013, http://www.nytimes.com/1996/05/09/theater/adding-drama-to-a-musical-andrews-spurns-the-tonys.html

12 Ben Brantley, "Ragtime – Review – Theatre," *The New York Times,* January 19,1998. Web, accessed March 16, 2013, http://theater.nytimes.com/mem/theater/treview.html?res=9d00e0dd1238f93aa25752c0a96e958260&_r=0

13 Patrick Healy, "Dream Big, Girl," *The New York Times,* March 24, 2013, Arts and Leisure, p. 1.

14 Calculations according to US Inflation Calculator.com. Web, accessed March 17, 2013, http://www.usinflationcalculator.com/

15 William Grimes, "Broadway Tries Analysis and Gets Shock Therapy," *The New York Times,* September 23, 1997. Web, accessed March 17, 2013, http://www.nytimes.com/1997/09/23/theater/broadway-tries-analysis-and-gets-shock-therapy.html?pagewanted=all&src=pm

Further reading

Corporate musicals

Each of the major corporations producing musicals on Broadway at this time has websites. Those websites offer a good starting point for research. Understand that they are one-sided in the material they present, and that magazine and newspaper articles on them and their shows offer a more balanced perspective.

Michael John LaChiusa, Andrew Lippa, Adam Guettel, Jason Robert Brown, Jonathan Larson and Frank Wildhorn

These writers are too young to have biographies or autobiographies. There are many interviews with them and articles about them online. Newspaper reviews of their works are available online, and copies of their shows are available in playscript, score and recorded forms.

Epilogue

14 The new millennium, 2001–14

The world shifts

In early fall, 2001, the 9/11 attacks caused the death of 2,996 people, threw the government into lockdown and a state of confusion, devastated the financial district in Lower Manhattan and wreaked havoc on New York City. The attack shut down the New York Stock Exchange for more than a week and shut down production in all Hollywood television and movie studios. All major league sports events were cancelled; the Emmy Awards Ceremony was postponed twice. Television programming was given over to twenty-four-hour coverage of the attacks for almost a week. New York and the country were devastated.

> It was matinee day on Broadway – shows in the afternoon and evening – but all the theaters were dark. Nothing at the Golden or the Imperial or the Shubert. Nothing at the Lunt-Fontanne or the Palace. Performances canceled "due to circumstances beyond our control." Two middle-aged women studied the notice on the door of the Lunt-Fontanne, where *Beauty and the Beast* usually plays, and one said, "No, no show today." Her friend said: "I didn't think so. How could there be a show? Who would show up? Who could perform?"[1]

The answer was, New Yorkers would come. Two days after the attacks, on Thursday evening, the Broadway theaters reopened. New Yorkers needed to gather together in groups and join in the communal act of seeing theatre. The New York tourist industry was devastated, and had to be slowly rebuilt. Fortunately, New Yorkers picked up some of the slack at the box office.

People were shaken; and going forward, people went to the theater to feel good. And so it was the "feel-good" musicals that had the most success in the following seasons. Two overriding trends predominated during these years: jukebox musicals and fairly literal adaptations of popular "feel-good" movies. Jukebox musicals, which had started becoming popular in the 1990s, became even more prevalent, and while musicals had previously been adapted from movies, in the 2000s this became more and more the norm.

Roughly twenty-seven musicals between 2001 and 2013 were produced using previously existing songs. Some have written a story around an existing catalog of songs, like *Jersey Boys* or *The Boy From Oz*, and others have transferred a movie musical to the stage with its original score relatively intact like *Chitty Chitty Bang Bang* or *The Little Mermaid*. Some have taken the revue form like *One Mo' Time*, and several have been full evenings of dance performed to pre-existing music like *Movin' Out*, *The Times They Are A Changin'* and *Come Fly Away*.

American musicals have historically been adapted from existing sources. In earlier periods those sources tended to be novels or plays. In the post-literate age of the twenty-first century, where more information is transmitted by visual images than by written narrative, it only made sense that the primary source of material would be visual. Many of the successful musicals of the 1990s had been adapted from movies – certainly *The Producers* (the biggest hit of the 2000–1 season), *Beauty and the Beast*, *Big*, *Kiss of the Spider Woman* and others. By the 2000s, popular movies had become the primary source material for musicals, for the fans they brought with them as much their compelling stories. Between 2001 and 2014 the majority of new musicals were based on successful movies; these include: *The Sweet Smell of Success*, *Thoroughly Modern Millie*, *Hairspray*, *Urban Cowboy*, *Dirty Rotten Scoundrels*, *Spamalot*, *Chitty Chitty Bang Bang*, *The Color Purple*, *The Wedding Singer*, *Tarzan*, *Grey Gardens*, *Mary Poppins*, *High Fidelity*, *Xanadu*, *Young Frankenstein*, *The Little Mermaid*, *Cry Baby*, *Billy Elliot: The Musical*, *Irving Berlin's White Christmas*, *Shrek*, *9 to 5*, *Women on the Verge of a Nervous Breakdown*, *Once*, *Newsies: The Musical*, *Ghost: The Musical*, *Leap of Faith*, *Bring It On*, *Elf*, *A Christmas Story: The Musical*, *Kinky Boots*, *Big Fish* and *Rocky, The Musical*.

2001–2 – timing is everything

As interesting as which Broadway musicals successfully ran in the 2001–2 season, is which failed. Of the six new musicals on Broadway, three succeeded and three failed. The failures were *Thou Shalt Not*, *By Jeeves* and *Sweet Smell of Success*.

A musical adaptation of Emile Zola's *Thérése Raquin*, by composer/lyricist Harry Connick, book writer David Thompson and director/choreographer Susan Stroman, *Thou Shalt Not* was dark and heavy-handed. The *New York Times* called it "limp and lugubrious," and commented about a morgue scene that had been cut in previews because audiences found it tasteless in light of the attacks. There might have been a place for such an unrelentingly dark musical a year earlier, but context is everything, and *Thou Shalt Not* closed after eighty-four performances.

An early Andrew Lloyd Webber musical with book and lyrics by Alan Ayckbourn based on P.G. Wodehouse's Jeeves and Wooster characters called *By Jeeves* premiered on Broadway in 2001, although it had played in London in 1975. New York critics commented that this kind of light entertainment was exactly what the Broadway stage needed, but unfortunately audiences disagreed and the show, which had originally run for thirty-eight performances in London in 1975, ran for only seventy-eight performances on Broadway in 2011.

Composer Marvin Hamlisch, lyricist Craig Carnelia and book writer John Guare contributed *Sweet Smell of Success* to the season, but it also never gelled. Critics complained that the piece tried so hard to find a dark "noir-ish" tone that it wound up mocking itself, and that the star, John Lithgow, never found the weight and threat that J.J. Hunsecker (played by Burt Lancaster in the movie) called for. Ultimately, the murky tone of the evening was not welcome in this season, and it closed after 109 performances.

Urinetown opened on September 20, nine days after the attacks, and made people laugh. It mocks the self-serious nature of didactic musical theatre by commenting directly on it. Several issues raised in *Urinetown* resonated with events of the past month; the death of innocents, the actions of those who suffer from and oppose the cruelty of capitalism and the wastefulness of lives of privilege. But what *Urinetown* was, mostly, was funny. It had been heralded at the 1999 New York International Fringe Festival, and in its off-Broadway run earlier in 2001. It lit a candle in the dark night, letting New Yorkers know that it was okay to laugh again.

Mamma Mia! provided a pleasant and innocuous story that required neither thought nor reflection. It gave people a chance to sing along with their favorite ABBA songs from the 1970s; singing along was encouraged during the show's "mega-mix" finale. The show's television commercial advertised that people couldn't stay in their seats and got up to dance in the aisles. Although *Mamma Mia!* had opened in London in 1999, the timing of the New York opening could not have been better. Ben Brantley opened his *New York Times* review by saying, "When the going gets tough, the tough want cupcakes. [...] As long as what's consumed is smooth, sticky and slightly synthetic-tasting, it should have the right calming effect, transporting the eater to a safe, happy yesterday that probably never existed. Those in need of such solace – and who doesn't that include in New York these days? – will be glad to learn that a giant singing Hostess cupcake opened at the Winter Garden Theatre last night."[2] There is no way to know if *Mamma Mia!* would have been successful before the attacks; but there is no question that New York was desperately in the mood for entertainment that offered comfort without digging at anything too deeply.

Thoroughly Modern Millie, with a score by Jeanine Tesori, lyrics by Dick Scanlan and book by Richard Morris and Scanlan, was about as old-fashioned as a musical could be. It harkened back to the Cinderella musicals of the 1920s, by way of the 1967 movie on which it is based. While George Roy Hill, director of the film, applied a self-conscious style to the film, including actors doing "takes" to the camera, silent movie titles and so forth, the musical chose a less arch approach to the material, making it warmer and fuzzier, and a little more perfect for the needs of audiences in the spring of 2002. *Millie* had been developed at the La Jolla Playhouse in San Diego; but like *Mamma Mia!* its appeal was enhanced by the audience's need for lighter, fluffier and more uplifting material.

The two big hits from the 2002–3 season were *Hairspray* and *Movin' Out*. *Hairspray*, based on the John Waters movie, tells the story of a plump teenage girl and her journey to acceptance, a central trope in the musicals of the 2000s, when substantial disposable income was in the hands of teen and pre-teen girls. The biggest hit of this period, *Wicked* (2003), tells the same story; plump or green girls should be accepted or their wrath might be terrible. *Hairspray* also asks its audience to support racial tolerance – not too big a stretch for the musical theatre audience in the 2000s, but it allowed audiences to feel good about themselves for being "progressive." The same "message" occurs in other musicals of this period, like *Memphis* (2009).

In *Movin' Out*, modern dance choreographer Twyla Tharp created an entirely danced story to the songs of Billy Joel. Tharp told the story of a group of American youths growing up on Long Island in the 1960s, and their experiences with the Viet Nam War. A live band performed the music, which was sung by the band's pianist, in faithful recreation of Joel's original versions.

The 2003–4 season saw more new musicals than any season for a long time. The fortunes of the Broadway musical seemed to be turning around, thanks in large part to the new markets opened up in this season. This season was the subject of a documentary, *The Road to Broadway*. Film-makers followed four musicals through their pre-Broadway trials and tribulations: the development of *Wicked*, *Taboo*, *Caroline or Change* and *Avenue Q* made fascinating viewing.

The biggest hit of the new millennium was Stephen Schwartz's *Wicked*. Schwartz had great success early in his career with *Godspell*, *Pippin* and *The Magic Show*, but his next several shows were failures. *Working*, which Schwartz directed and contributed several songs to, was savaged by the press and only lasted for twenty-four performances. *The Baker's Wife* closed on the road before reaching New York. And *Rags*, with music by Charles Strouse and a book by Joseph Stein, suffered when series of directors with different visions came and went while the show was out of town in 1986, leaving the show unfocused; it closed after four performances. After this Schwartz left Broadway to write songs for Disney films. *Wicked* marked a triumphant return to the musical theatre after seventeen years. Although it did not get good reviews, *Wicked* has a built-in audience that replenishes itself every year – there is not an adolescent girl in the world who has not worried about being an outcast with unrecognized inner powers, a green witch. *Wicked* lost the Tony Awards for Best Musical, Best Original Score, and Best Book of a Musical to *Avenue Q*.

Avenue Q set the coming-of-age angst of thirty-somethings who still haven't found themselves to the theatrical and musical style of *Sesame Street*, the entertainment equivalent of comfort food to actual thirty-somethings (the show's target audience) who were raised on *Sesame Street*. Playing the innocence of *Sesame Street* against foul language and adult subjects like pornography and sex in a production style that combined real-life actors and puppets was a winning combination, literally winning audiences and awards. After ending its lengthy and successful run on Broadway *Avenue Q* reopened off-Broadway in 2009.

The 2004–5 season offered three excellent musicals. *Spamalot*, based on the movie *Monty Python and the Holy Grail*, opened to rave reviews that it didn't need. Like *Wicked* before it, *Spamalot* had a built-in demographic. "*Spamalot*, Broadway's hottest show[…] has managed to tap into a rare, highly prized Broadway demographic: men; specifically, the kinds of teenagers and 20-somethings who find jokes about fish, flatulence and the French absolutely side-splitting and who normally wouldn't be headed to the theatre unless dragged by a girlfriend, school trip or court order. 'They are what movie preview experts call young males under 35,' said Mike Nichols, who directed *Spamalot*. 'And we have them.'"[3] Nichols had, indeed, tapped into a unique and profitable market. *Spamalot* ran for just under four years, with 1,575 performances on Broadway. In addition to the Broadway company, there were twenty-three companies mounted around the world including various tours and sit-down productions.

William Finn, who had had success with *March of the Falsettos, Falsettoland, A New Brain* and several other highly lauded off-Broadway musicals, had a hit on Broadway with *The 25th Annual Putnam County Spelling Bee*. Evolved from an improvisational play, *Spelling Bee* workshopped and premiered at the Barrington Stage Company. It moved to the Second Stage Theatre off-Broadway in 2005 and transferred to Broadway three months later. For many years the Broadway musical audience had been aging, but recently a whole new generation had discovered the musical theatre. The same people who kept *Avenue Q* running came to see *Spelling Bee*. The hip thirty-somethings proved a strong and lucrative market. *Spelling Bee* garnered great reviews and ran for two and a half years.

The artistic pinnacle of the season was *The Light in the Piazza*, which ran for 504 performances at Lincoln Center. Craig Lucas' book received positive critical reception, as did the direction, the design and performances by a cast that included Victoria Clark, Kelli O'Hara and Matthew Morrison; but the greatest accolades were given to Adam Guettel's score. *The Light in the Piazza* proved that a literate, beautifully crafted sensitive work of art could support a run of well over a year on Broadway. Despite poor reviews, David Yazbek's *Dirty Rotten Scoundrels* managed a successful run of 627 performances.

Other, less successful new musicals this season include: Stephen Sondheim's *The Frogs*, originally written in 1974 to be performed in the Yale University swimming pool, and Frank Wildhorn's *Dracula the Musical*. Inspired in tone by *Rent, Brooklyn Live* ran through the season, lasting 284 performances. Although critics agreed that *Little Women* failed to find the heart of the Louisa May Alcott book, it launched a successful national tour; the same demographic that kept *Wicked* running helped *Little Women*.

A successful West End stage production of the children's movie *Chitty Chitty Bang Bang* transferred from London to Broadway in 2005. *Chitty Chitty Bang*

Bang ran for over three years in London, earning more than £70 million; however, the Broadway production barely limped through eight months, losing most of its investment. Two jukebox musicals rounded out the season. *Good Vibrations* used the songs of the Beach Boys to help tell a slight tale of three high school friends; it only ran for ninety-four performances. *All Shook Up* did better, applying songs recorded by Elvis Presley to an adaptation of Shakespeare's *Twelfth Night* – it ran for 213 performances.

In the 2005–6 season, nine new musicals opened on Broadway. Three managed successful, profitable runs: *The Color Purple* (910 performances), *The Drowsy Chaperone* (674 performances) and *Jersey Boys* (more than 3,500 performances to date).

Originally workshopped at Atlanta's Alliance Theatre, media mogul turned producer Oprah Winfrey brought *The Color Purple* to Broadway. Based on the movie that had given Winfrey her start, critics complained that, in trying to cover so much material, the musical sped by everything without achieving any depth. However, with a terrific cast and Ms. Winfrey's imprimatur, the show found an audience and ran for well over two years.

Two less successful movie adaptations also opened in this season. Of *The Wedding Singer*, which somehow managed to lose the charm and heart of the Adam Sandler movie, the *New York Times* review began, "How quickly our dreary yesterdays become bright, cute and endlessly repackageable. ... 'The Wedding Singer,' the assembly-kit musical that opened last night ... might as well be called 'That 80's Show.' The transformation of a Hollywood movie into a Broadway musical, a trend that appears as irreversible as global warming, is an example of recycling, or second-hand nostalgia."[4]

The other movie adaptation was Disney's *Tarzan*, with a score by Phil Collins. *Tarzan* put more emphasis on tree swinging, flying and special effects to the point where the story got lost. "*Tarzan* feels as fidgety and attention-deficient as the toddlers who kept straying from their seats during the performance I saw."[5]

Jersey Boys is one of the most successful jukebox musicals. It followed *Mamma Mia!*'s formula in gathering the music that its audience grew up with into an attractive package. Des McAnuff, *Jersey Boys* director, workshopped the show at the La Jolla Playhouse. While it does not challenge its audiences, the 2000s audiences were not paying to be challenged at a Broadway musical.

There were other jukebox musicals in the season. *Lennon*, a sentimentalized version of John Lennon's life, confused audiences with a cast of nine actors, five of whom took turns playing John Lennon. It only lasted forty-nine performances. *Ring of Fire* was a revue of the songs of country singer Johnny Cash. Critics complained that the dark brooding soul of the singer known as "the Man in Black" was missing from *Ring of Fire*; the audience apparently agreed as the show only ran for fifty-seven performances.

The Drowsy Chaperone was originally written for the 1997 bachelor party of Canadian writer/actor/director Bob Martin. The loving satire of musicals of the 1920s took further shape and grew to full-length over the next nine years. The narrator character of Man in Chair did not exist in the original version, but

Martin played the role in Toronto, New York and London. Man in Chair describes to the audience his love of the musicals of the 1920s, which he knows only from their cast recordings, and the audience watches as they come alive in his head. Charming and light as a soufflé, *The Drowsy Chaperone* ran for 674 performances on Broadway and has been produced worldwide. As with the other successful musicals of this period, it is the comfort food of musicals.

The 2006–7 season also offered ten new musicals on Broadway, and keeping to the rule of 70 percent failure, three of these shows were successful, *Legally Blonde*, *Spring Awakening* and *Mary Poppins*. Four of the new musicals in this season were adapted from movies, and three used pre-existing music.

Mary Poppins only won one Tony Award, for best scenic design, but it ran three times as long as *Spring Awakening*, which swept the Tony Awards that year. Comfort and familiarity of the Disney film trumped the nineteenth-century German teenage angst in *Spring Awakening*. For alternative rock composer, Duncan Sheik, and book and lyrics by Steven Sater, *Spring Awakening* was their only Broadway musical. The press and the theatre community embraced the artistic bravery of Sheik and Sater's work, but in the end Disney's comfort won out.

In July 2007 NBC television began airing a reality show, *Grease: You're the One That I Want*. The familiar format, in which contestants are "voted off the island" every week until only one is left standing, led up to the grand prizes, which were the starring roles of Sandy Dumbrowski and Danny Zuko in the 2007–8, $10 million revival of *Grease* on Broadway. Andrew Lloyd Webber had successfully used this format in 2005 with a British reality show called *How Do You Solve A Problem Like Maria*, in casting his West End production of *The Sound of Music*. The NBC show casting *Grease* was not successful, but in 2008, when *Legally Blonde*'s ticket sales started flagging, the producers of that show created another reality show, *Legally Blonde – The Musical: The Search for Elle Woods*, to find Laura Bell Bundy's replacement. The replacement of Bundy with MTV reality show winner Bailey Hanks spiked ticket sales for about one week, after which they plummeted.

This disturbing trend signaled that, in a musical theatre designed to be reproduced in productions across the world, actors are mere interchangeable parts. If one wears out there are plenty others to replace him or her.

To critics and audiences alike, the hit of the 2007–8 season was *In The Heights*. Lin-Manuel Miranda's score was the heart of the musical, and won the Tony Award for Best Score. It also won Tonys for Best Musical, Orchestrations and Choreography. The story about the Latin-American community in Washington Heights was told in a score infused with rap, hip-hop and salsa. The characters' struggles to find their dreams while continuing to maintain the community was as universal as *Fiddler on the Roof*. *In the Heights* introduced a new niche audience, the Hispanic population, as well as crossover to the traditional musical theatre audience as well. Miranda had begun writing the show in 1999; many drafts, revisions, readings and workshops later it received a presentation at the O'Neill Theatre Center in 2005, an off-Broadway production in

2007, and moved to Broadway in early 2008. Ten months into the Broadway run, the producers announced that they had recouped its $10 million initial investment. The next two years of the run plus the national and international touring companies were pure profit.

The 2007–8 season also featured four musicals based on popular movies and two using previously existing music. Several new musicals that were expected to succeed did not. Lightning did not strike Mel Brooks twice; his stage musical version of *Young Frankenstein* managed to run just over a year, but lost a substantial amount of its investment. Disney's *The Little Mermaid* ran for a year and a half, but had nowhere near the staying power of *Beauty and the Beast* or *The Lion King*. It seemed as if Disney had found a formula for creating stage musicals, but once found, their stage musicals became fairly formulaic.

The 2008–09 season saw a return to the safety of the popular comedy movie adaptations. Country singer/songwriter Dolly Parton wrote a failed stage musical version of her movie *9 to 5*. *Shrek, the Musical* ran for a year and put out several touring companies, a West End production, an Asian tour and a few foreign companies independently mounted. But the initial investment for the Broadway production was $24 million, impossible to recoup on a run of one year. *Irving Berlin's White Christmas* was adapted from the 1954 movie. Put together primarily as a tour, the production made two stops on Broadway, in 2008 and 2009, as a means of enhancing the producers' ability to book the show on the road and enhance future royalties.

The hit of the 2008–9 season was the glam metal rock jukebox musical, *Rock of Ages*, which has just enough story to tie together everyone's favorite glam rock 1980s hits. With relatively low weekly expenses it has done consistently good business in the Broadway production as well as on its tours and international productions.

Elton John's *Billy Elliot: The Musical*, based on the movie *Billy Elliot*, was the second biggest hit of the season. *Billy Elliot* told the story of a boy whose love is dance, set during the 1984 miners' strike in Northern England. John's musical had taken London by storm in 2005, but there was concern that the social and political subject matter was too British for American audiences to care about. Those concerns were misplaced. *Billy Elliot* was a feel-good movie about a boy embracing and celebrating his differences, and so was the musical. The same sort of feel-good moral that *Hairspray* offered, *Billy Elliot: The Musical* offered. Audiences felt good cheering for Billy, and they did so for a little over three years.

Into the midst of all of these good feelings came *Next to Normal*, a serious rock musical about a mother who struggles with bipolar disorder. *Next to Normal* won rave reviews, awards, including the Pulitzer Prize, and a substantial run for a serious musical. After a series of workshops *Next to Normal* opened off-Broadway and then moved to Broadway in 2009. Like *Spring Awakening*, *Next to Normal* offered audiences an emotional life that was more genuine than much of the processed and manufactured musicals Broadway had seen lately.

Memphis opened on Broadway in 2009 with a score by David Bryan, the keyboard player of the rock band Bon Jovi. It had begun six years earlier with a regional production at the North Shore Music Theatre. In the intervening years the piece was rewritten, given more workshops and regional productions until it moved to Broadway. The reviews were mostly positive, although some complained about the formulaic nature of the show. The show presented a slick package of good music and good acting, but stretched no one in its audience with its moral that people of different races should get along. As with *Hairspray* and *Billy Elliot*, *Memphis* made audiences feel good for being on the right side of a fairly obvious issue. Nonetheless, *Memphis* was the hit of the season, running for 1,165 performances.

Four of the other five new musicals of the season used pre-existing music. One was based on a popular rock album, *American Idiot*, and one on a popular television/movie series, *The Addams Family*.

There were several interesting new musicals in the 2010–11 season, including *Bloody, Bloody Andrew Jackson*, which transferred to Broadway from the Public Theatre. It looked at Jackson, who founded the Democratic Party, as if he were an Emo rock star. *The Scottsboro Boys*, the final musical Kander and Ebb completed before Fred Ebb's death, told the story of nine young African-American men accused, convicted and imprisoned for raping a white woman on a train in the 1930s. The musical used the theatrical and staging conventions of a minstrel show to tell the story. Nominated for eleven Tony Awards, it won none. The only other shows nominated for eleven awards to win none were Kander and Ebb's *Steel Pier* in 1997 and the original production of *Chicago* in 1976. *The Scottsboro Boys* closed after forty-nine performances.

David Yazbek adapted Pedro Almodóvar's movie, *Women on the Verge of a Nervous Breakdown*. The cast included Sherie Rene Scott, Brian Stokes Mitchell and Patti LuPone. It had been workshopped at Lincoln Center. But audiences and critics agreed that it was a confused muddle and it closed after sixty-nine performances.

Catch Me If You Can was promising, coming from the creative team of *Hairspray*, except for book writer Terrence McNally. But the musical, based on the Steven Spielberg movie, failed to find inspiration and simply put the story onstage with songs. It ran for 166 performances.

Only two jukebox musicals appeared in the 2010–11 season: *Priscilla, Queen of the Desert*, based on the Australian movie about a group of drag queens crossing the outback, and *Baby It's You*, which told the story of The Shirelles, using their songs. Five of the nine new musicals on Broadway were adapted from popular movies.

The big hit of the 2010–11 season was *The Book of Mormon* by Robert Lopez, of *Avenue Q*, and Matt Stone and Trey Parker, of *South Park*. *The Book of Mormon* set a new record for number of Tony Awards nominations, with thirteen; it won nine of those (*The Producers* had been nominated in twelve categories). *The Book of Mormon* is funny and dirty and juvenile, appealing to the same audience that flocked to *Spamalot*. There is a vast audience for this kind of musical, and this show does this better than any other.

Spider-Man: Turn off the Dark was the most expensive musical ever mounted. A rock musical with a score by U2's Bono and The Edge, the production has been estimated to cost $75 million dollars and it has been reported that weekly operating expenses are well over $1 million. Because of the complex technical aspect of the show, in particular the flying battles, there were multiple cast injuries, some serious, that brought press coverage. In the spirit of David Merrick, no press is bad press, and audiences thronged to see the show despite the mediocre reviews for more than 1,000 performances.

The two big hits of the season were *Once* and *Newsies: The Musical*, both based on successful films. *Once* took a less traditional approach to putting the musical onstage, having the entire cast stay onstage throughout the show and accompany each other on various musical instruments, being the only orchestra. The story of the street busker and the girl he meets captivated audiences and swept the awards.

The other major screen to stage adaptation is the Disney musical *Newsies: The Musical*. The Disney offices, which had been marketing a stage adaptation of their television movie *High School Musical*, had received numerous requests for stage rights to another one of their filmed properties, *Newsies*. In an effort to satisfy those requests, they agreed to mount a stage production at the Paper Mill Playhouse. When the stage version appeared successful, they decided to move it to Broadway for a limited run. It turned out, though, that *Newsies: The Musical* was a big hit and was shifted to an open run.

The 2013–14 season has provided some crowd-pleasing musicals, while failing to deliver a single mega-hit. Several musicals came and went quickly, including *Soul Doctor*, the story of Shlomo Carlebach, the hippie Rabbi, and *First Date*, which depicts a blind date. Andrew Lippa's *Big Fish* came and went fairly unceremoniously. Many movies found themselves musicalized, such as *The Bridges of Madison County*, *Rocky: The Musical*, *Aladdin* and *Bullets Over Broadway*. And the requisite number of jukebox musicals (*Motown: The Musical* and *Beautiful: The Carole King Musical*) and revivals (*Violet*, *Hedwig and the Angry Inch* and *Cabaret*) gave theatergoers something to enjoy, without leaving any lasting impression.

Summing up the 2000s

Since the Golden Age, the percentage of the population interested in Broadway musicals has diminished. Despite this, there was an expansion to the twenty/thirty-somethings with disposable income with shows like *Avenue Q* and *The 25th Annual Putnam County Spelling Bee*. *Wicked*, *Hairspray* and others showed teen and pre-teen girls to be a very strong audience base on Broadway. Another niche market developed in the 2000s is the adolescent and post-adolescent male in comedies like *The Book of Mormon* and *Spamalot*. The nostalgic pull has also been strong in the 2000s, not only in jukebox musicals, but also in favorite childhood tales like *Mary Poppins*. Preaching to the choir has become very popular; having a leading character learn something that the audience already knew – like racism or bullying is bad – reaffirms an audience and makes it feel good about itself.

On the business side, almost all musicals now begin their lives in readings and workshops, followed by one or more regional productions. Frequently the next step is a production off-Broadway (or at one of the New York regional theaters) that may lead to a transfer to Broadway. There was a time when Broadway shows were produced on a larger scale and off-Broadway shows were smaller in scale; but nowadays off-Broadway is a springboard to a Broadway production, and sometimes, like *Avenue Q*, as a place for further New York life after Broadway.

Where to from here?

> The theatre is dying,
> The theatre is dying,
> The theatre is practic'ly dead.
> Someone everyday writes,
> We have no more playwrights,
> The theatre is sick in the head.[6]

The lyric above was proclaimed eight times a week from the stage of the Majestic Theatre in the early 1950s. Oscar Hammerstein wrote that lyric for "Intermission Talk" in *Me and Juliet*. Each generation feared that the musical theatre was dying, every generation has bemoaned the fact, and every generation has been wrong. The American musical may seem to be losing steam; but the lesson of this book is that this art form is in a constant state of change. Anyone who suggests that the Rodgers and Hammerstein musicals or the concept musicals or the mega-musicals were the pinnacle, and that it's all downhill from there, is wrong.

Among the things to celebrate in the musical theatre today is the fact that there are interesting articulate artists out there with something to say and the burning desire to say it through musical theatre. Certainly those artists and businesspersons examined in the last couple of chapters continue their trajectory in the musical theatre. Other writers like Ricky Ian Gordon, John Bucchino, Michael Koomon and Christopher Dimond, Joshua Salzman and Ryan Cunningham, Ryan Scott Oliver, Amanda Green, David Kirshenbaum, Laurence O'Keefe and many more are all pursuing production for their various projects in New York and around the world. During the 2000s more material is being presented in clubs and cabarets, or else recorded and disseminated through the internet.

There are more musical theatre training programs at colleges, universities and conservatories around the world than ever before. There are more training programs for musical theatre writers in graduate schools and professional organizations like BMI and ASCAP – more grants and fellowships and awards given to writers. There are more Arts Administration programs in colleges and universities, training the next generation of producers.

The future holds infinite possibility for the musical theatre. To know where we have been can help us imagine where we would like to go – the history of the American musical theatre holds the key to its future.

Notes

1 N.R. Kleinfield, "A City of Quiet – Nothing is Same One Day After," *The New York Times,* September 13, 2001. Web, accessed March 18, 2013, http://www.nytimes.com/2001/09/13/nyregion/13MOOD.html

2 Ben Brantley, "Theatre Review: Mom Had a Trio (and a Band, Too)," *The New York Times,* October 19, 2001. Web, accessed March 18, 2013, http://theater.nytimes.com/mem/theater/treview.html?res=9c0ce2d7153ef93aa25753c1a9679c8b63&_r=0

3 Jesse McKinley, "Theatre; 'Spamalot' Discovered The Straight White Way," *The New York Times,* April 10, 2005. Web, accessed March 18, 2013, http://www.nytimes.com/2005/04/10/theater/newsandfeatures/10mcki.html

4 Ben Brantley, "Something Borrowed, Something Renewed: The Return of the 80's in 'The Wedding Singer'," *The New York Times,* April 28, 2006. Web, accessed March 19, 2013, http://theater2.nytimes.com/2006/04/28/theater/reviews/28wedd.html?_r=0

5 Ben Brantley, "Tarzan Arrives on Broadway, Airborne," *The New York Times,* May 11, 2006. Web, accessed March 19, 2013, http://theater2.nytimes.com/2006/05/11/theater/reviews/11tarz.html

6 Oscar Hammerstein, "Intermission Talk," *Me and Juliet – Vocal Score,* London: Chappell Music, 1953.

Appendix

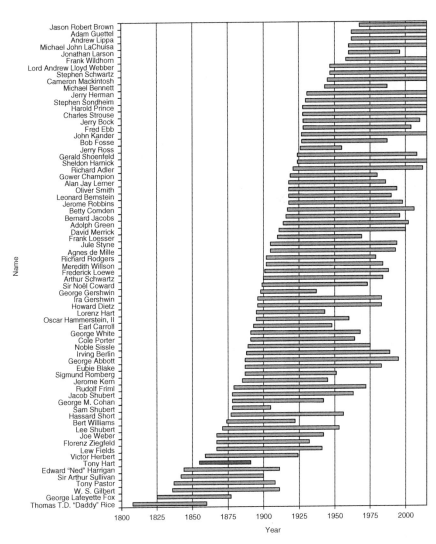

Figure A.1 Timeline of major figures who significantly affected the shape of American musical theatre

Bibliography

This selected bibliography is designed to help the reader begin to explore areas of interest further. It is in no way comprehensive.

Chapter 1: A very good place to start

Bareket, Donna, Anne Eisendrath, and Deborah Selig. *Student Projects – Beggar's Opera*. 2002. University of Michigan. April 14, 2013. http://www.umich.edu/~ece/student_projects/beggars_opera/

Best, Michael. *More Stage Designs by Inigo Jones*. February 1999. University of Victoria, Victoria, BC. September 1, 2010. http://internetshakespeare.uvic.ca/Library/SLT/stage/masques/cave.html

Brissenden, Alan. *Shakespeare and the Dance*. Princeton: Princeton Book Club, 2001.

Glixon, Beth and Jonathan Glixon. *Inventing the Business of Opera: The Impresario and His World in Seventeenth-Century Venice (AMS Studies in Music)*. New York: Oxford University Press, 2007.

Harris, John. *Medieval Theatre in Context: An Introduction*. London: Routledge, 1992.

Lindley, David. *Shakespeare and Music: Arden Critical Companions*. London: Arden, 2005.

MacDonald, Marianne and Michael Walton. *The Cambridge Companion to Greek and Roman Theatre*. Cambridge: Cambridge University Press, 2007.

Ravelhofer, Barbara. *The Early Stuart Masque: Dance, Costume, and Music*. New York: Oxford University Press, 2006.

Rosand, Ellen. *Opera in Seventeenth-Century Venice: The Creation of a Genre*. Berkeley: University of California Press, 2007.

Winton, Calhoun. *John Gay and the London Theatre*. Lexington: The University Press of Kentucky, 1993.

Chapter 2: 1735–1865

Allen, Robert C. *Horrible Prettiness: Burlesque and American Culture*. Chapel Hill: The University of North Carolina Press, 1991.

Anderson, Gillian B. "The Temple of Minerva and Francis Hopkinson: A Reappraisal of America's First Poet-Composer." *Proceedings of the American Philosophical Society*. Philadelphia: American Philosophical Society, 1976.

Cruikshank, George and Pierce Egan. *Tom and Jerry: Life in London; Or the Day and Night Scenes of Jerry Hawthorn and His Elegant Friend, Corinthian Tom*. Whitefish: Kessinger Publishing, 2010.

Dizikes, John. *Opera in America: A Cultural History*. New Haven: Yale University Press, 1995.

Fields, Armond. *Tony Pastor, Father of Vaudeville*. Jefferson: McFarland, 2012.

Henderson, Mary. *The City and the Theatre: The History of New York Playhouses: A 250 Year Journey from Bowling Green to Times Square*. New York: Back Stage Books, 2004.

Lhamon, W.T. *Jump Jim Crow: Lost Plays, Lyrics, and Street Prose of the First Atlantic Popular Culture*. New York: Harvard University Press, 2003.

Seilhamer, George O. *History of the American Theatre: Before the Revolution*. Vol. 1. New York: Haskell House Publishers Ltd, 1969.

Toll, Robert. *Blacking Up: The Minstrel Show in Nineteenth-Century America*. New York: Oxford University Press, 1977.

——. *On With The Show*. New York: Oxford University Press, 1976.

Victoria and Albert Museum. *Eighteenth Century Opera*. Victoria and Albert Museum, London, UK. 1 June 2011. http://www.vam.ac.uk/content/articles/0–9/18th-century-opera/

Chapter 3: 1866–1902

Ainger, Michael. *Gilbert and Sullivan: A Dual Biography*. Oxford: Oxford University Press, 2009.

Barde, Robert, Susan B. Carter and Richard Sutch, "Immigrants, by Country of Last Residence – Europe: 1820–1997," *Historical Statistics of the United States*, Millennial Edition, vol. 1, ed. Susan B. Carter et al., New York: Cambridge University Press, 2006.

Fields, Armond and L. Marc Fields. *From the Bowery to Broadway: Lew Fields and the Roots of American Popular Theatre*. New York, NY: Oxford University Press, 1993.

Hirsch, Foster. *The Boys From Syracuse: The Shuberts' Theatrical Empire*. Carbondale: Southern Illinois University Press, 1998.

Hornblow, Arthur. *A History of the Theatre in America from its Beginnings to the Present Time*. Vol. 1. Philadelphia: J.B. Lippincott Company, 1919.

Kahn, E.J., Jr. *The Merry Partners, The Age and Stage of Harrigan and Hart*. New York: Random House, 1955.

Kenrick, John. *1879–1890: The First Musical Comedies*. 1996. http://www.musicals.101.com/1879to99.htm

Leigh, Mike. *Topsy-Turvy*. Polygram, USA Video, 2000.

Prestige, Colin. "D'Oyly Carte and the Pirates: The Original New York Production of Gilbert and Sullivan." *Gilbert and Sullivan Papers Presented at the International Conference held at the University of Kansas*. Ed. James Helyar. Kansas City, KS: University of Kansas, 1971.

Senelick, Laurence. *The Age and Stage of George L. Fox, 1825–1877 (Studies in Theatre History and Culture)*. Ames: University of Iowa Press, 1999.

Williams, Carolyn. *Gilbert and Sullivan: Gender, Genre, Parody*. New York, NY: Columbia University Press, 2012.

Wren, Gayden. *A Most Ingenious Paradox: The Art of Gilbert and Sullivan*. Oxford: Oxford University Press, 2006.

Zellers, Parker. *Tony Pastor: Dean of the Vaudeville Stage*. Ypsilanti: Eastern Michigan University Press, 1971.

Chapter 4: 1900–07

Forbes, Camille F. *Introducing Bert Williams: Burnt Cork, Broadway and the Story of America's First Black Star*. New York: Basic Civitas Books, 2008.

Gould, Neil. *Victor Herbert: A Theatrical Life*. New York: Fordham University Press, 2008.

Hirsch, Foster. *Harold Prince and the American Musical Theatre*. New York: Applause Theatre and Cinema Books, 2005.

Lamb, Andrew. *Leslie Stuart: Composer of Floradora (Forgotten Stars of the Musical Theatre)*. London: Routledge, 2002.

McCabe, John. *George M. Cohan: The Man Who Owned Broadway*. Boston: Da Capo Press, 1980.

Moody, Richard, ed. *Dramas from the American Theatre 1762–1909*. Boston: Houghton Mifflin Company, 1966.

Traubner, Richard. *Operetta: A Theatrical History*. Garden City: Doubleday & Company, 1983.

Travis, Stewart, D. *No Applause, Just Throw Money: The Book That Made Vaudeville Famous*. New York: Faber and Faber, 2006.

Wertheim, Arthur Frank. *Vaudeville Wars: How Keith-Albee and Orpheum Circuits Controlled the Big-Time and its Performers*. New York: Palgrave, Macmillan, 2009.

Chapter 5: 1907–20

Banfield, Stephen. *Jerome Kern*. New Haven: Yale University Press, 2006.

Davis, Lee. *Bolton and Wodehouse and Kern: The Men Who Made Musical Comedy*. New York: James H. Heineman Publisher, Inc., 1993.

——. *Scandals and Follies: The Rise and Fall of the Great Broadway Revue*. New York: Limelight Editions, 2000.

Everett, William. *Rudolf Friml*. Urbana: University of Illinois Press, 2008.

——. *Sigmund Romberg*. New Haven: Yale University Press, 2007.

Farnsworth, Marjorie. *The Ziegfeld Follies*. New York: Bonanza Books, 1961.

Furia, Philip. *Irving Berlin: A Life in Song*. New York: Schirmer Trade Books, 1998.

Jablonski, Edward. *Irving Berlin: American Troubadour*. New York: Henry Holt & Co., 1999.

Kenrick, John. *History of the Musical Stage 1910–19 Part III*. 1996. July 20, 2011. http://www.musicals101.com/1910bway3.htm

Kimball, Robert and William Bolcom. *Reminiscing With Sissle and Blake*. New York: The Viking Press, 1973.

Krasner, David. *A Beautiful Pageant: African American Theatre, Drama and Performance in the Harlem Renaissance, 1910–1927*. New York: Palgrave, 2002.

Magee, Jeffrey. *Irving Berlin's American Musical Theatre*. New York: Oxford University Press, 2012.

Mordden, Ethan. *Ziegfeld: The Man Who Invented Show Business*. New York: St. Martin's Press, 2008.

Murray, Ken. *The Body Merchant: The Story of Earl Carroll*. Los Angeles: Ward Ritchie Press, 1976.

Chapter 6: 1920–29

Furia, Philip. *Ira Gershwin: The Art of the Lyricist*. New York: Oxford University Press, 1997.

Marmorstein, Gary. *A Ship Without a Sail: The Life of Lorenz Hart*. New York: Simon and Schuster, 2012.

Pollack, Howard. *George Gershwin: His Life and Work*. Berkeley: University of California Press, 2007.

Secrest, Meryle. *Somewhere for Me – A Biography of Richard Rodgers*. New York: Applause Books, 2002.

Chapter 7: 1929–39

Bell, J.X. *Cole Porter*. June 21, 2012. http://coleporter.org/bio.html

Citron, Stephen. *Noel and Cole: The Sophisticates*. Montclair: Hal Leonard, 2005.

Marx, Samuel. *Rodgers and Hart: Bewitched, Bothered and Bedeviled: an Anecdotal Account*. New York: G.P. Putnam and Sons, 1976.

McBrien, William. *Cole Porter*. New York: Vintage, 2000.

Chapter 8: 1939–45

Carter, Tim. *Oklahoma!: The Making of An American Musical*. New Haven: Yale University Press, 2007.

Easton, Carol. *No Intermissions: The Life of Agnes De Mille*. New York: Da Capo Press, 2000.

Marmorstein, Gary, *A Ship Without A Sail: The Life of Lorenz Hart*. New York, NY: Simon and Schuster, 2012.

Nolan, Frederick. *The Sound of Their Music: The Story of Rodgers and Hammerstein*. London: Everyman Ltd., 1978.

Chapter 9: 1945–64

Abbott, George. *Mister Abbott*. New York: Random House, 1963.

Adler, Richard, Lee Davis and George Abbott. *You Gotta Have Heart*. New York: Dutton, Adult, 1990.

Citron, Stephen. *Jerry Herman: Poet of the Showtune*. New Haven: Yale University Press, 2004.

Comden, Betty. *Off Stage*. Milwaukee: Limelight Editions, 2004.

Fordin, Hugh. *Getting to Know Him: A Biography of Oscar Hammerstein, II*. New York: Da Capo Press, 1995.

Gilvey, John Anthony. *Before the Parade Passes By: Gower Champion and the Glorious American Musical*. New York: St. Martin's Press, 2005.

Jablonski, Edward. *Alan Jay Lerner: A Biography*. New York: Henry Holt & Co., 1996.

Kissel, Howard. *David Merrick – The Abominable Showman: The Unauthorized Biography (Applause Books)*. New York: Applause Theatre & Cinema Books, 2000.

Lerner, Alan Jay. *The Street Where I Live*. New York: W.W. Norton and Company, 1978.

Mikotowicz, Thomas. *Oliver Smith: A Bio-Bibliography (Bio-Bibliographies in the Performing Arts)*. Santa Barbara: Greenwood, 1993.

Riis, Thomas L. *Frank Loesser (Yale Broadway Masters Series)*. New Haven: Yale University Press, 2008.

Robinson, Alice. *Betty Comden and Adolph Green: A Bio-Bibliography (Bio-Bibliographies in the Performing Arts)*. Santa Barbara: Greenwood, 1993.

Rodgers, Richard. *Musical Stages: An Autobiography*. New York: Random House, 1975.
Secrest, Meryle. *Leonard Bernstein: A Life*. New York: Knopf Publications, 1994.
——. *Somewhere for Me – A Biography of Richard Rodgers*. New York, NY: Applause Books, 2002.
Vaill, Amanda. *Somewhere: The Life of Jerome Robbins*. New York: Broadway, 2008.
Wilder, Alec. *American Popular Song: The Great Innovators 1900–1950*. New York: Oxford University Press, 1972.

Chapter 10: 1964–70

Bacharach, Burt. *Anyone Who Had a Heart: My Life and Music*. East Hampton: Harper, 2013.
Grode, Eric. *Hair: The Story of the Show That Defined a Generation*. Philadelphia: Running Press, 2010.
Hischak, Thomas S. *Off-Broadway Musicals Since 1919: From Greenwich Village Follies to the Toxic Avenger*. New York: Scarecrow Press, 2011.
Kander, John, Fred Ebb and Greg Lawrence. *Colored Lights: Forty Years of Words and Music, Show Biz, Collaboration and All That Jazz*. London: Faber and Faber Books, 2004.
Strouse, Charles. *Put on a Happy Face: A Broadway Memoir*. New York: Union Square Press, 2008.
Wasserman, Dale. *The Impossible Musical: The "Man of La Mancha" Story*. New York: Applause Theatre and Cinema Books, 2003.

Chapter 11: 1970–82

Banfield, Stephen. *Sondheim's Broadway Musicals*. Ann Arbor: The University of Michigan Press, 1995.
Gottfried, Martin. *All His Jazz: The Life and Death of Bob Fosse*. New York: Da Capo Press, 2003.
Hirsch, Foster, *Harold Prince and the American Musical Theatre*. New York, NY: Applause Theatre & Cinema Books, 2005.
Ilson, Carol. *Harold Prince: A Director's Journey*. New York, NY: Limelight Editions, 2004.
Mandelbaum, Ken. *A Chorus Line and the Musicals of Michael Bennett*. New York: St. Martin's Press, 1990.
Prince, Harold. *Contradictions: Notes on Twenty-six Years in the Theatre*. New York: Dodd Mead Co., 1974.
Schoenfeld, Gerald. *Mr Broadway: The Inside Story of the Shuberts, the Shows and the Stars*. New York: Applause, 2012.
Secrest, Meryle. *Stephen Sondheim: A Life*. New York: Vintage, 2011.
Wasson, Sam. *Fosse*. New York, NY: Eamon Dolan/Houghton Mifflin Harcourt, 2013.

Chapter 12: 1982–93

Lundskaer-Nielsen, Miranda. *Directors and the New Musical Drama: British and American Musical Theatre in the 1980s and 90s (Palgrave Studies in Theatre and Performance History)*. Hampshire, UK: Palgrave Macmillan, 2008.

Morley, Sheridan. *Hey Mr. Producer!: The Musical World of Cameron Mackintosh.* New York, NY: Back Stage Books, 1998.

Snelson, John. *Andrew Lloyd Webber (Yale Broadway Masters Series).* New Haven, CT: Yale University Press, 2004.

Sternfeld, Jessica. *The Mega Musical (Profiles in Popular Music).* Bloomington, IN: University of Indiana Press, 2006.

Traub, James. *The Devil's Playground: A Century of Pleasure and Profit in Times Square.* New York, NY: Random House Trade Paperbacks, 2004.

Chapter 13: 1993–2001

Isenberg, Barbara. *Making It Big: The Diary of a Broadway Musical.* New York, NY: Limelight Editions, 2004.

Prece, Paul and William A. Everett. "The Megamusical and Beyond: The Creation, Internationalization, and Impact of a Genre." *The Cambridge Companion to the Musical.* Cambridge, UK: Cambridge University Press, 2008.

Wollman, Elizabeth Lara. *The Theater Will Rock: A History of the Rock Musical from Hair to Hedwig.* Ann Arbor, MI: University of Michigan Press, 2006.

Chapter 14: 2001–14

As this period is quite recent, and the number of published books on this period quite limited, the books listed here are some of the many general resource texts available.

Bordman, Gerald. *American Musical Theatre: A Chronicle.* New York: Oxford University Press, 1978.

Brantley, Ben. *Broadway Musicals: From the Pages of the New York Times.* New York, NY: Harry N. Abrams, 2012.

Brockett, Oscar. *History of the Theatre.* Boston: Allyn & Vacon, 1968.

Burns, Ric and James Sanders. *New York: An Illustrated History.* New York: Alfred A. Knopf, 2003.

Flinn, Denny Martin. *Musical! A Grand Tour.* Belmont: Wadsworth Group/Thomson Learning, 1997.

Gordon, Lois and Alan Gordon. *American Chronicle: Year by Year Through the Twentieth Century.* New Haven: Yale University Press, 1999.

Jones, John Bush. *Our Musicals, Ourselves: A Social History of the American Musical Theatre.* Waltham: Brandeis University Press, 2003.

Knapp, Raymond. *The American Musical and the Formation of National Identity.* Princeton: Princeton University Press, 2006.

Mordden, Ethan. *Anything Goes: A History of American Musical Theatre.* New York, NY: Oxford University Press, 2013.

Smith, Cecil and Glenn Litton. *Musical Comedy in America.* London: Routledge, 1987.

Zinsser, William. *Easy to Remember: The Great American Songwriters and Their Songs.* Jeffrey, NH: David R. Godine Publisher, 2006.

Index